THE SPIRAL OF TIME SERIES

RAV DOVBER PINSON

THE MONTH of ADAR

vol **12**

TRANSFORMATION THROUGH
LAUGHTER & HOLY DOUBT

IYYUN PUBLISHING

Published by IYYUN Publishing
232 Bergen Street
Brooklyn, NY 11217

http:/www.iyyun.com

Iyyun Publishing books may be purchased for educational, business or sales promotional use. For information please contact: contact@IYYUN.com

Editor: Reb Matisyahu Brown

Developmental Editor: Reb Eden Pearlstein

Proofreading / Editing: Simcha Finkelstein

Cover and book design: RP Design and Development

Cover image: Max Budovitch "Adar" from the Misaviv Hebrew Circle Calendar (5776), used with publisher's permission as a gift to the Iyyun Center. See www.circlecalendar.com for more information.

pb ISBN 9781733813044

Pinson, DovBer 1971-
The Month of Adar: Transformation through Laughter and Holy Doubt
1.Judaism 2. Jewish Spirituality 3. General Spirituality

vol **12**

THE MONTH *of* ADAR

TRANSFORMATION THROUGH
LAUGHTER & HOLY DOUBT

IYYUN PUBLISHING

CONTENTS

༐

OPENING

*E*ACH MONTH OF THE YEAR RADIATES WITH A DISTINCT quality and provides unique opportunities for personal growth and spiritual illumination. Each month also has a slightly different climate and represents a particular stage in the 'story of the year' as expressed through the annual cycles of nature. The winter months call for practices and pursuits that are different than those of the summer months. Some months are filled with holidays and some have only one or none at all. Each month therefore has its own natural and spiritual signature.

According to the deeper levels of the Torah, each month's distinct qualities, opportunities and natural phenomena correspond to a certain set of data arranged within a twelve-part symbolic structure. The spiritual nature of each month is articulated according to its unique entries for each of these 12 points of light:

1) a permutation of G-d's Four-Letter Name 2) a verse from the Torah 3) a letter of the Aleph Beis 4) the name of the month itself 5) an experiential "sense" 6) a sign of the Zodiac 7) a tribe of Israel 8) a body part 9) an element 10) a unit of successive Torah portions that are read during the month 11) a season of the year 12) the holidays that occur during the month.

By reflecting on these twelve themes and categories, we reveal an ever-ascending spiral of insight, understanding and practical action. Learning to navigate and harness the nature of change by consciously engaging with the cycles of time, adds a deeper sense of purpose and heightened presence to our lives. The present volume will delve into the spiritual nature of the final month of the year, the month of Adar, according to these 12 categories.

☾

NOTE: *For a more comprehensive treatment of this twelve-part system and the over-arching dynamics of the "story of the year," an in-depth introduction has been provided in Volume One of this series, The Spiral of Time: Unraveling the Yearly Cycle.*

ʒ

The Month of Adar:

Transformation through Laughter & Holy Doubt

MOVING FROM HEAVINESS TO LIGHTNESS

OST CALENDARS THROUGHOUT THE WORLD follow one primary celestial cycle to keep track of time, that of either the sun or the moon. For instance, the Gregorian calendar is purely a solar count, making no concessions for the cycle of the moon. This means that the months of the year will always remain in the same season, but no attention or significance is given to the waxing and waning of the moon in the sky. On the other hand, other calendars are purely lunar, completely disregarding the annual circuit of the sun. Uniquely, our calendar integrates both the solar and lunar cycles in its creative conception and functional count of time.

From the solar cycle, we count the days of the year, ensuring that the holidays will always fall in their allotted season. From the lunar cycle we count the months, keeping us spiritually connected to the phases of the moon. The solar cycle begins in the fall with the first day of the year, Rosh Hashanah, making Elul the 'end' of the year. The lunar cycle, on the other hand, begins in the spring with the month of Nissan, making Adar the 'end' of the monthly cycle.

In addition to being the culmination of the *monthly* cycle of the year, Adar also concludes the *solar* phenomenon of winter. Therefore, towards the end of the month, in the Northern Hemisphere, we are transitioning on multiple levels, from the 'end' to the 'beginning' of the months and from winter to spring. This idea of coming out of winter and moving into spring is essential to the month of Adar, as we will now explore.

During the winter months people spend more time indoors, alone or with close friends and family. In general it is a time when people feel more insular and secure in their own space. There is a physical and metaphorical covering up of our external bodies as well as our inner selves. As we layer our bodies with more garments during the cold winter months, protecting ourselves from the elements, these 'garments' lead us inwardly toward a more introverted lifestyle and state of mind.

When spring begins to sprout and blossom, we begin, consciously or unconsciously, to think about resurfacing into the world. Simultaneously, there can emerge a sense of self-doubt and uncertainty. As people are about to embark on a more extroverted period of the year, they are leaving behind their shelter, the heavy garments and the energetic hibernation of winter, as it were; this can give rise to all types of insecurity and even anxiety.

Adar, being the final winter month, parallels Elul, the final month of summer and the end of the solar cycle. As Elul concludes the summer (which is naturally a period of heightened extroversion and interpersonal encounters) it is a good time to self-reflect, think about our past actions/interactions, and to perform a *Cheshbon* / accounting of our life. Similarly, as Adar wraps up the winter, it is an appropriate time to think about our essential identity, who we really are, including our certainties and uncertainties; what we believe in and stand for, before moving out to meet the world.

The entire month of Adar, and specifically how it relates to Purim, gives us the strength to uncover who we truly are, behind the 'masks' and 'garments' of our superficial appearance. (This is one reason why many people wear masks and costumes on Purim, as we will explore further.) Adar empowers us to reveal who we truly are and what we stand for. In this month we are given the *Ko'ach* / power to deal with doubts and uncertainties; to overcome and transform them into positive and productive forces for transformation in our lives and in the world beyond.

Another byproduct of the cold and dark winter months is a tangible sense of heaviness. Some experience physical weight gain, which can be the body's natural protection against the cold. Some experience a general sense of heaviness or lethargy, making it difficult to wake up in the morning with alacrity. These kinds of heaviness can have a psychological influence on one's sense of well-being and joy. As we are moving out of the winter into the spring during

Adar, this is another issue with which we may need to contend.

What's more, these physical feelings of heaviness and fatigue can even lead to depression, as there is a biopsychic feedback loop between our body and mind. This loop works both ways. Our mind not only affects our body, but our body can also affect our state of mind and emotions. Some people, when feeling tired or down, automatically think there is something wrong in their lives. They think to themselves, "Maybe I need more direction," or "Maybe my relationships are not working," or "Maybe I need a new job," when in truth all that is happening is that they are energetically depleted. Perhaps they are experiencing a physiological state such as low blood-sugar, or maybe they just ate a heavy meal, or didn't sleep well, and therefore they feel physically burdened. As mentioned, these types of feelings are exacerbated during the cold, dark winter months. As a result of these physical sensations, people often make the unfounded leap to a diagnosis of emotional or existential distress. This is not always the case. Sometimes you are just cold, underslept, underfed, or overslept and overfed. Often, taking care of your body first, before jumping to any drastic conclusions or 'meanings' behind your current experience, will reveal the root of your real issue. Simply knowing this can help.

To remedy these all-too-common seasonal sensations and feelings, the Torah reveals to us the *Ko'ach* / power of the month of Adar. This is a month of holy humor, lightness of being and unbounded joy. In accord with being the final month of winter, there is a certain sense of relief, a sense that one can loosen up and laugh again. Sometimes we need a little play and humor to break the built-up tension or to shake us out of the heaviness and drudgery of the winter, including everything that the colder and darker days represent for us. We thus need to learn how to utilize humor in a positive and productive way, Adar gives us the tools and guidance to do so.

Another behavior that counters states of heaviness is *Zerizus* / alacrity, swiftness, and doing things right away, without procrastination. This *Midah* / trait is also intimately connected with Adar. Again, on a biopsychic feedback level, when you are feeling down, heavy or depressed, the mere physical act of moving quickly — for example, running around the block or even moving your eyes rapidly from side-to-side — can help you feel lighter, more flexible, and perhaps even happier.

FROM HIBERNATION TO PROJECTION

Additionally, Adar is part of a greater progression of the yearly cycle, and as mentioned, occurs specifically at the end of the arc of fall and winter. In brief, the six months of fall-winter and their qualities are as follows. Tishrei, the first month of fall, has a celebratory quality in which we begin a new year and focus on new beginnings with joy. The month of Cheshvan gives us the wisdom of how to be alone with ourselves, and settle into a winter 'hibernation' without falling into *Yei'ush* / despondence. In Kislev, sometimes this aloneness became 'lonely' and we are compelled to get out of our home. With Chanukah, at the end of this month, there is a glimmer of light, hope and possibility to connect with the outside world. In Teves we began to seek interpersonal relationships with our closest loved ones. In Shevat we develop a more balanced relationship with our possessions and with food. When we learn to take in only what we need and to eat in holiness, we transform the harshness of the first half of the month of Shevat into compassion. We also realize how to be compassionate rather than judgmental in our intimate relationships.

Following Shevat comes the month of Adar, in which we move into our more personal self and become aware of how that self is going to be projected out into the world. Spring is about to begin and we are going to go 'outside' and reveal our true/inner selves. This awareness of impending revelation can bring up all types of self-doubt and uncertainty. Having been insulated in our cocoon of winter hibernation and now needing to leave the nest, so to speak, we may experience questions of identity: "*Who am I, not just within myself, but in relation to others?*" For some, the suffering of lower self-esteem can surface at such a time. During the month of Adar we are given the power to deal with these issues of doubt, uncertainty, identity and values. We are given permission to play with the masks we put on, hiding and revealing who we truly are.

When we create a proper *Tikun* / rectification and bettering of these areas in our psyches, we can then wholeheartedly participate in life with others; we can 'laugh' together and 'drink' together in an integrated and holy way. As we will see, both laughing and drinking are fundamentally connected with Adar and the *Yom Tov* / holiday of the month, Purim. The spiritual energy and context of this month allows us to engage in these precarious activities while remaining deeply rooted, stable, and grounded in our authentic identity and beliefs.

THE MONTH OF DRINKING

There are three months that make up the winter quarter of the year (Teves, Shevat and Adar) and they correspond to three basic needs of the body: intimacy, food and drink. There are other essential needs of the body, such as breathing and sleeping. Yet, these needs are fulfilled by the body automatically and passively. Even if you do not want to, you will eventually breathe and you will eventually (after three days at most) fall asleep (*Shavuos*, 25a). Procreating, eating and drinking, however, must be actively performed.

The strongest biological urge found throughout the animal and plant kingdoms is the drive to perpetuate one's species. Obtaining food and hydration provides living beings with the strength not only to survive, but to actively seek a mate and procreate.

Teves is connected with procreation, and thus *Chazal* / our sages refer to Teves as *Yerech sheNeheneh Guf min haGuf* / "a month in which one body takes pleasure from the (warmth of another) body" (*Megilah*, 13a). As Teves is the coldest, grayest month of the year, we naturally spend more time indoors with others. It is thus a time of reconnection, relationship and intimacy.

Food and eating are related to the second month of the winter, Shevat. This is the month of the new year for the fruit trees. It is thus a month that is conducive to making a *Tikun* / rectification of our eating habits and digestion. During the colder months, people tend to eat more and bulk up. Yet, paradoxically, at the coldest point of the winter (in the month of Teves), people often lose their appetite; it is simply too cold to eat. This is why Shevat is focused on the Tikun of eating — the intensity of the cold begins to weaken and as the climate begins to get slightly warmer, people start to focus on food again.

Finally, Adar is connected to the essential need of drinking. As we begin to eat more, we also naturally need to drink more; in many times and places this necessarily meant drinking more wine. In many regions of the ancient Jewish world, safe drinking water was unavailable, and therefore the beverage that accompanied meals was (diluted) wine, the drink of joy. Hence, with the seasonal increase in drinking, plus the joy of sensing the first hints of spring, Adar appropriately became a month of joy and holy laughter; punctuated by the Yom Tov of Purim, the day on which there is a Mitzvah to drink extra wine.

In Adar we are given the Ko'ach to learn how to drink in a healthy and truly joyful fashion, and to relate to what drinking evokes and represents in a holy manner. There is not, G-d forbid, a Mitzvah to imbibe alcohol only in order to become intoxicated. Holy drinking does not lead a person into the self-centered drive for drunkenness, irresponsibility, immoral behavior, or negative self-doubt. Adar, rather, explores the positive, healthy, enlightening connections between drink, laughter and happiness, offering a proactive Tikun for any residual self-doubt or tendency to substance addiction.

Again, Adar, as the last month of the lunar cycle, mirrors the month of Elul, the last month of the solar year. Elul precedes Tishrei, the days of awe and judgment, and thus the introspection in Elul is connected to *Yirah* / fear and awe, and thus a feeling of heaviness. Adar comes before the month of Nisan, the month of miracles and liberation, and thus the introspection of Adar is a Teshuvah of love, a recalibration fueled by lightness, openness and joy (*Yitav Lev*, Terumah. *Sefas Emes*, Likutim, Rosh Chodesh Adar). As the essence of Purim is the reacceptance of Torah through love (מאהבת הנס שנעשה להם Rashi, *Shabbos*, 88a), rather than fear, the whole month helps us aspire to connect with HaKadosh Baruch Hu through this expansive emotion. Now let us begin to explore the 12 points of the month.

ᏇᎧ

PERMUTATION OF HASHEM'S NAME

*T*HE FOUR-LETTER ESSENTIAL NAME, YUD-HEI-VAV-HEI (Hashem), is the Divine Source of all Reality. The last three letters of the Name, Hei-Vav-Hei, create the word *Hoveh* / is / the present. The root of this verb means "to bring into being." The first letter of the Name, Yud, serves as a prefix to the last three letters: Yud-*HoVeH*. In this way, the Yud modifies the verb *Hoveh* to represent a perpetual activity (Iyov, 1:5). In other words, the Divine Name can be understood to mean, "That Which is Continuously Bringing Being into Being."

For numerous reasons, this Essential Name cannot be spoken. Therefore a common practice is to rearrange its four letters into an alternative sequence that may be pronounced. This produces the word *HaVaYaH*, literally, Being-ness. This aspect of the Name refers to the Ultimate Being, the Source and Substance of All. The Ultimate Being does not depend on anything else to exist. It gives rise to all past, present and future manifestations, thereby bringing all things into existence ex nihilo, i.e., *Yesh meAyin* / something from nothing. Accordingly, the individual words for 'was' (*Hayah*), 'is' (*Hoveh*), and 'will be' (*Yihiyeh*) are all encoded within the Essential Name (*Shulchan Aruch Harav*, Orach Chayim, 5:1).

As the Source of all being and time, Hashem's Essential four-letter Name is intrinsically connected to and encoded within actual time and its subdivisions. For instance, each of the four seasons is connected to one of the four letters in the Name of Hashem, revealing something of its inner essence. Additionally, there are 12 unique months in the year; similarly, there are 12 different permutations of the Four-Letter Name. Each month is associated with a unique permutation of the four letters that comprise the Essential Name. The inner light of each month 'shines' through the 'prism' of its unique Divine signature, revealing the resident spiritual dynamics of that time.

The sequence of the four letters in Hashem's Name that corresponds to the month of Adar is Hei-Hei-Yud-Vav.* This is a type of reversal of the Name, as first there is the lower Hei and the upper

---

* The vowels in the sequence of Hashem's Name for the month of Adar are Chirik-Hei, Sh'va-Hei, Sh'va-Yud, Patach-Vav. Although, as we will see, the letters of this month's permutation of the Divine Name are derived from the last letters of the words in the verse of the month. The *Tikunei Zohar* (Hakdamah, 2b) explains that we should derive the vowels from the first letters of those words.

Hei, and then the Yud and the Vav — these last two letters would each precede a Hei in the original sequence (Yud-Hei-Vav-Hei). This reversal reminds us of how Haman's destructive decree was reversed in the Book of Esther: "For Haman... had plotted to destroy the Jews and had cast a Pur (lottery) to terrify and destroy them; but when she (Esther) appeared before the King, he commanded... that the evil scheme which he (Haman) had devised against the Jews should recoil upon his own head" (Megilas Esther, 9:24-25). Instead of Purim, whose date was decided by drawing lots (*Pur*), being the day on which the Jewish People were massacred, G-d forbid, a miracle occurred and it was transformed into a day and an entire month of joy and festivity. This 'reversal of fortunes' with its attendant energies, permeate and define the entire month of Adar.

Yud (graphically a point) and Vav (a line) are both considered masculine letters, representing the role of giver. The letter Hei, which is a more open, expansive letter, is receiver, a feminine letter. In the normal spelling (Yud-Hei-Vav-Hei), there is first a giver (Yud) and then a receiver (Hei); then another giver (Vav) and finally another receiver (Hei). In Adar's sequence, first come the receivers, the Hei and Hei, followed by the givers, the Yud and Vav. In Adar, the aspect of receiving, which is the responsibility and role of this world, and the power of the feminine are very dominant. This is expressed in the fact that in the case of Purim, salvation comes through the feminine character, Queen Esther; as well as the fact that Hashem, the Ultimate Giver, is not mentioned at all in the entire story. Hashem's hand is concealed beneath the 'mask' of history, as it were. The two Hei's being foregrounded in this month's permutation of the Divine Name represent both our own agency in life's events, as well as the doubly thick veil that conceals the presence of HaKadosh Baruch Hu in our world.

Cosmically, in terms of Creator and creation, Hashem is the masculine giver of life, while *Klal Yisrael* / the People of Israel and the creation 'below' are the feminine receivers of life. However, Adar in general, and the Yom Tov of Purim specifically, represents a creative transition from the 'masculine' paradigm of revelation from Above to the 'feminine' paradigm of innovation from below. As an illustration of this principle, the Bnei Yissaschar points out the difference between the *Gragger* / children's noisemaker of Purim, and the *Dreidel* / children's toy of Chanukah. The Dreidel is held and spun from above, and the Gragger is held and spun from below. Chanukah commemorates the revealed miraculous Divine influence on life from above, while Purim commemorates the concealed Divine influence from below, from within Klal Yisrael. Purim represents the aspect of the miraculous that is vested within the workings of nature.

Purim occurred after the destruction of the First *Beis haMikdash* / Temple, toward the end of the Prophetic era. It is thus the first holiday that was initiated by us, the people; it was therefore not technically instituted from Above through prophetic revelation. In this sense it could be called the first Rabbinical Yom Tov. And what's more, it was initiated by Queen Esther, embodying the feminine paradigm. It was Esther herself who suggested that the miracle of Purim be written as a scroll and celebrated each year: שלחה להם אסתר לחכמים קבעוני לדורות / "Esther sent to the Sages: 'Establish me for future generations'" (*Megilah*, 7a). It was Esther who specifically requested that the observance of Purim and the reading of the Megilah be instituted as an ordinance for all time. This was radical and innovative.

As mentioned, the miracle of Purim occurred at a crossroads in Jewish history. The Age of Prophecy was coming to a close, the last of the prophets and the memory of the glorious days of the Beis haMikdash were dwindling, and despite this, or in a way *because* of this, something quite marvelous was occurring. A new way of relating to HaKadosh Baruch Hu was percolating. The feminine, which had always been pictured as 'below' the masculine, was rising. This created a type of Divine connection whereby *light* is achieved through darkness, toil and exertion. This signaled the maturation of our relationship with Hashem. Revelation was no longer a monologue, but a dialogue that required the full presence and participation of both parties.

Prophecy is *direct*, a revelation of clear light. According to the Rambam, prophecy is similar to walking into a room and turning on the lights, everything becomes immediately illuminated (*Morah Nevuchim*, Hakdamah). It is a 'from above to below' paradigm. During the Age of Prophecy, Torah was revealed in the writing of the *Tanach* / Torah, Prophets and Writings. During the times of the First Beis haMikdash, miracles were revealed from above (*Yuma*, 21b. Note, *Avos*, 5:5). Once prophecy came to a full close, the era in which Hashem spoke to us and we simply listened and received, ended. Then began the era of the sages, the rabbis, and the revealing of the *Torah she-b'al-Peh* / the oral aspect of the Torah. This aspect of Torah is 'indirectly' revealed through human toil, mental exertion and innovation. It is a 'from below to above' dynamic, revealing Heavenly light from the earthly realm below.

As such, studying the Torah she-b'al-Peh engages a dialectic process; tension and resolution, doubt and certainty, question and answer. This is a form of discovering light, answers and redemption through the arduous labors of questioning, darkness and exile. Our sages tell us, במחשכים הושיבני כמתי עולם / "He placed me in darkness, like those long dead" (Eichah, 3:6); this refers to the Talmud of *Bavel* / Babylon (*Sanhedrin*, 24a). In fact, the sages of Bavel themselves are likened to 'darkness' (*Zevachim*, 60b. Ritvah, *Yuma*, 57a). This is understood on a deeper level to imply that they represent the revelation of a light that comes *from* the darkness. It is a type of learning where wisdom and clarity, light and resolution, are derived from the darkness of not-knowing and doubt, the dynamic tension of questioning and debate.

Regarding this, our sages teach (*Tanchuma*, Noach 3) that Torah she-b'al-Peh is, "difficult to learn and in the learning of it there is considerable anguish, comparable to darkness itself, as it is said, העם ההלכים בחשך ראו אור גדול / 'The people that walked in darkness have seen a great light' (Yeshayahu, 9:1). The people referred to in this verse are the masters of the Talmud, who beheld a great light when the Holy One, blessed be He, enlightened them as to what is prohibited and permitted, pure and impure."

Torah she-b'al-Peh is thus the completion of the full receiving of the Torah, when it truly becomes assimilated to the extent that the *below*, the feminine, can rise upwards and unite with the masculine above to reveal the light and truth of Torah.

Our sages tell us regarding Klal Yisrael at Mt. Sinai, "'And they stood under the Mount.' Rav Avdimi... said, This teaches that the

Holy One, blessed be He, overturned the mountain upon them like an [inverted] cask, and said to them, 'If you accept the Torah, good; if not, here shall be your burial.' Rav Acha... observed: 'This furnishes a strong protest against the Torah!' Said Rava, אַף עַל פִּי כֵן הֲדוּר קבלוה בימי אחשורוש / 'Yet even so, they re-accepted it in the days of Achashverosh... they consciously confirmed what they had already taken upon themselves through coercion at Sinai'" (*Shabbos*, 88a).

Purim is the culmination of the receiving of the Torah. Originally, at Mount Sinai, Klal Yisrael was 'forced' to accept the Torah. The mountain "suspended overhead" is a metaphor for an overwhelming encounter with the Divine that compelled them to simply surrender their free-choice and passively accept what was being given (as the Maharal explains, *Gur Aryeh*, Shemos, 19:17). During the events of Purim, however, we willingly accepted the Torah with love (Tosefos, *Shabbos*, ad loc), rather than out of fear. This completed and crowned the process that began at Sinai, for we could only fully and unanimously accept the Torah through our own free will, our own volition, and not under duress or external imposition from Above. In fact, we accepted the Torah so 'internally' that we even accepted our own experience as described in the Megilah as part of Torah, and therefore welcomed Purim as a Yom Tov. What was originally given from Above was now fully internalized below. Our own experience was thus Divinized.

What prompted Klal Yisrael to actively choose to accept the Torah which they had originally accepted only under pressure from Above? Writes the Ohr haChayim (Shemos, 19:5), this they did because "for the first time they realized that the actions of a Torah scholar such as Mordechai were responsible for their salvation from the decree of Haman." In other words, they recognized the Ko'ach of the Sages, the Ko'ach of Torah she-b'al-Peh, the full potential of humanity, and the ultimate role of creation *below*.

Purim is thus the beginning of the revealing of Torah she-b'al-Peh,* and it completes not only the process of Matan Torah, it completes, in a way, the *Torah she-b'Kesav* / the Written Teachings. The word תורה / Torah in numerical value is 611. The word בעל-פה / b'Al-Peh is numerically 187. The word בכתב / 'in writing' is numerically 424. Adding *b'Al-Peh* (187) to *b'Kesav* (424) produces a sum of 611 (*Torah*). This shows that the entirety of the Torah is only complete when there is a full revealing of the written dimension *and* the oral dimension of Torah, a marriage of Above with below, a dialogue between Heaven and earth.

Torah she-b'al-Peh begins to percolate during this transitional historical era, specifically outside of Eretz Yisrael. It is, perhaps, for this reason that Megilas Esther (8:17) tells us, ורבים מעמי הארץ מתיהדים / "...and many of the peoples of the land became Jews" (Rashi, ad loc). Torah she-b'al-Peh therefore has a special connection with *Gerim* / converts (*Pri Tzadik*, Yisro). Converts represent the *below*, that which is *outside* but through choice enters *inside*, one who experiences darkness, doubts and toil, yet rises through their own efforts to attach themselves to the *Above*. In this way, the first

---

* This is why Purim is particularly connected to Yehoshua, as the Mishnah (*Megilah*, 1:1) teaches, כרכין המוקפין חומה מימות יהושע בן נון / "Cities that have been surrounded by a wall since the days of Yehoshua bin Nun, read the Megilah on the fifteenth of Adar." Yehoshua, in comparison to Moshe, is Torah she-b'al-Peh. And Purim is all about Torah she-b'al-Peh.

translation of the Torah, a form of Torah she-b'al-Peh as it is an interpretative translation, was *created* by Unkolus the convert. Also, Rabbi Akiva, the embodiment of Torah she-b'al-Peh, was the child of converts (Rambam, *Hakdamah* L'Mishna Torah).

Within the written Torah itself there are elements of Torah she-b'al-Peh. For instance, the first revealing of Torah she-b'al-Peh is the *Parsha* / Torah-portion of Yisro, in which Moshe's father-in-law, a person outside of Klal Yisrael came, around the time of Matan Torah (either before or after, *Zevachim*, 116a. *Zohar* 2, 67b-68a), and with his own intuition and intellectual understanding suggested a system of courts to Moshe, which was accepted and become part of Torah. In fact, he is called Yisro (Rashi, Shemos, 18:1) because he *Yeser* / adds a Parsha to the Torah. (The core letters of Yisro's name are Reish, Vav, Tav, which are the same letters in the name of the other famous convert, Ruth. In numerical value Ruth equals 606, and with the addition of 7, for the 7 Noachide Laws, they equal 613, the number of Mitzvot in the Torah. 606 is also the value of the filling letters of Ado-noi. *Sha'ar HaPesukim*, Esther. The Concealing Name Ado-noi is connected to Purim, as explored, and connected to Torah she-b'al-Peh). Yisro too is a convert and thus intricately connected with Torah she-b'al-Peh.

The written part of Torah which is fixed and pre-defined, does not lend itself to human involvement. However, it was *given* to us, along with the task of expounding it and expanding upon its fixed principles. This is the oral aspect of Torah which is constantly being developed, creatively applied and made relevant anew by us, Klal Yisrael below. Using our intellectual abilities we are asked to be *Mechadesh* / one who unveils and initiates new insights of Torah in accordance with the principles of Torah pedagogy. Purim was therefore when we, the *below*, finally became a full partner and collaborator in the development and articulation of the Torah that was revealed to us from *Above*. In fact, Purim itself is one of the innovations that were meant to be initiated years after Matan Torah. (מצות העתידות להתחדש כגון מקרא מגילה / "Mitzvos that were to be initiated in the future, for example, the reading of the Megilah" *Shavuos*, 39a. ומה שהסופרים עתידין לחדש ומאי ניהו מקרא מגילה / "...and what the Scribes were destined to innovate in the future. And what is it? The reading of the Megilah" *Megilah*, 19b).

The initial *Ko'ach* / power for the 'below' to rise up and reveal the Divine Presence in the world was given at Sinai (as until Sinai the world existed merely because of the Chesed from Above, but now it rested upon our acceptance of the Torah. *Pesachim*, 118a). Similarly, it was at Mount Sinai that the Ko'ach for the 'below' to reveal the *Ein Sof* / infinite light of Hashem through Torah, was also given to Klal Yisrael (Alter Rebbe, *Torah Ohr*, Yisro, *Zechor Es Yom haShabbos*. See also *Yerushalmi*, Rosh Hashanah, 1:3. *Likutei Moharan*, Kama, 34. *Da'as Tevunos*, 158). Yet, the full assimilation and true rising up and participation of the 'below' was only fully manifest during the story of Purim.

"Even what a proficient pupil is destined to *Mechadesh* / innovate (*Megilah*, 19b) was already said to Moshe at Sinai" (Yerushalmi, *Pe'ah*, 2:4). This statement means that although there are *Chidushim* / innovations of applying and understanding Torah which are expressed in the Torah she-b'al-Peh and elucidated through the minds of our sages, the foundation of these is always the Torah revealed at Mount Sinai. "Hashem revealed to Moshe at Sinai the general principles" (*Medrash Rabbah*, Shemos, 41:6), and the sages throughout the generations extrapolated and unpacked the details and implications hidden in these principles. Our sages faithfully revealed how all the details of their teachings were ultimately given by the One Shepherd — by the One G-d through the one Moshe (*Chagigah*, 3b).

FROM MOSHE RABBEINU TO RABBI AKIVA

Rabbi Akiva, a child of converts, was one of the greatest teachers and transmitters of Torah of all time. It is recorded that he had 24,000 students in all, which were 12,000 'pairs' of students (*Medrash Rabbah*, Bereishis, 61:3. *Koheles Rabbah,* 11. *Yalkut Shimoni*, Koheles, 989). According to another source, there were actually 24,000 pairs of students, which were 48,000 students in total (*Nedarim*, 50a. The *Tanchuma* on Chayei Sarah 6, tells us that Rabbi Akiva had 300 students. Yet, we know that in *Chazal* / writings of the sages, the number 300 is not meant literally, rather it represents a large or exaggerated number. *Teshuvas Mahara m'Panu. Mei haShiloach* 1, Noach. See also Rashbam, *Pesachim,* 119a. Rashi, *Chulin,* 90b). And not only did he have a tremendous number of students, his teachings were also accepted as binding: "The ruling is always according to Rabbi Akiva" (*Sanhedrin,* 86a).

Our sages tell us (*Menachos,* 29b) that when Moshe ascended on high, he found the Creator attaching crowns to the letters of the Torah, and he asked, "Master of the world, why have You need for these?" Hashem said to him, "There will be a man some generations hence, whose name is Akiva the son of Yoseph, and he will expound mounds upon mounds of laws from each and every jot and tittle." Moshe said, "Master of the world, show him to me." Moshe was then projected forward in time and found himself sitting in the eighth row in the Yeshivah of Rabbi Akiva — the rows indicating the level of the students, the closer the row the higher the level. As Rabbi Akiva was teaching Torah, Moshe did not understand a word of what was being said, and on account of this his strength waned, until they reached one teaching, and R. Akiva's disciples said to him, "Master, from where do you know this?" To which R. Akiva answered, "It is the law given to Moshe at Sinai." Then Moshe's mind was put at ease.

Moshe's strength waned not because he did not understand, nor, of course, was his mind put to ease because he received a compliment when Rabbi Akiva attributed everything to Moshe. Rather, Moshe was uneasy because he thought perhaps the teachings of Rabbi Akiva had veered from the truth of the revelation at Mount Sinai, and that they were his own innovations and creativity, not part of the unfolding of the revelation of Hashem's Torah. Only when Rabbi Akiva cited his source, "Moshe at Sinai," had Moshe realized that his teachings were indeed valid expansions upon the Torah that was revealed at Sinai.

Rabbi Akiva lived at the end of the period of the Second Beis haMikdash, and flourished as the great *Tana* / teacher following the destruction of the Temple. Generally speaking, the period of the Second Beis haMikdash is when the Age of Prophecy came completely to a close and the era of the Sages officially began. There was overlap, however: the revealing of Torah she-b'al-Peh, the era of the Sages, began around the beginning of the Second Beis ha-Mikdash, and the builders of the Second Beis haMikdash were in fact the last of the Prophets. Purim thus stands at the threshold between these two eras, after the fall of the First Beis haMikdash, and right before the construction of the Second Beis haMikdash.

The First Beis haMikdash was a place of prophecy, daily miracles and revelations. Its destruction marked the beginning of a time of Divine withholding, a weaning of humanity from a certain childlike dependency, much like a parent weans a child. The tale of Purim, the Megilah, is a canonical text, and part of the Tanach; in this sense it is part of *Revelation from Above*. And yet, the Megilah is authored by human beings, it describes human experiences, and as mentioned, Hashem's name does not appear even once within it. Purim therefore contains competing elements and combines them in a complementary way, as all transitional stages do, it is from Above, and yet it is from below. It is a rabbinically inspired Yom Tov enacted at the request of Esther, yet it is a Mitzvah that is included in Tanach, Hashem's words.

ACHOR B'ACHOR / BACK TO BACK

A relationship that is top-down is also called *Achor b'Achor* / back-to-back. This is similar to parents' relationship with their small child. Parents love their children completely and give them whatever they need. Yet, this is not a mutual, two-way relationship. The child is attached to the parent; wherever the parent goes the child goes, automatically, without a significant degree of independence or choice. There is not yet a real dialogue between the two parties. Rather, the relationship is structured from the top-down. This is the manner in which Hashem related to us and to all creation during the Age of Prophecy. Hashem spoke through a prophet and we dutifully listened.

During the Age of Prophecy Hashem's *Panim* / face was clearly revealed in the world, e.g., the revealed miracles in the First Beis haMikdash. With the commencement of *Galus* / exile from *Eretz haKodesh* / the Holy Land and the Temple, the paradigm of *Hester Panim* / concealment of Hashem's 'face' comes into play. However, this lack of revelation, this concealment, also opens the space in which real *relationship* may develop.

According to this meta-historical process of spiritual development, Purim begins the process of *Panim-el-Panim* / the face-to-face phase of relationship between us and HaKadosh Baruch Hu, between the below and the Above. This phase of developing dialogue begins on Purim and reaches a fuller flowering with the building of the Second Beis haMikdash, which is an expression of 'receiving' from below.

Torah she-b'al-Peh is the paradigmatic expression of Panim-el-Panim. In a 'face-to-face' relationship we can always walk away, or talk back. As we experience ourselves as more independent and less attached, out of necessity, our relationship with the Giver of Torah no longer feels like a "mountain suspended above our heads." When we freely choose to be in a relationship with HaKadosh Baruch Hu it is more mature, real and meaningful.

This type of mature, face-to-face relationship is called a *Bris* / covenant. A Bris demands two partners with willing consent and free volition to choose to be with each other, as in a marriage. The *Bris haNesuin* / covenenat of marriage cannot be declared בעל כורחו / *B'al Korcho* / against one's will; there needs to be *Da'as* / awareness and consent for it to be binding (*Kidushin*, 2b). This is the reason why לא כרת הקב"ה ברית עם ישראל אלא בשביל דברים שבעל פה / The Holy

One, Blessed be He, made a *Bris* / covenant with the Jewish people only for the sake of the matters that were transmitted *b'al-Peh* / orally (*Gittin*, 60b). That is, the *Ikar* / main element of our Bris with Hashem is revealed *Davka* / especially with the revealing of Torah she-b'al-Peh, characterized by our active, freely-chosen, participation in it.

In the *Torah she-b'Kesav* / the written, revealed Torah, Hashem spoke *to* Moshe and the Prophets; in Torah she-b'al-Peh, Hashem speaks *through* the Sages. Similarly, in an Achor b'Achor relationship, Hashem reveals Himself to us from Above, and talks to us. In a Panim-el-Panim relationship, Hashem no longer merely talks 'to' us, rather 'through' and with us.

The events of the Purim story occurred during the time of the *Anshei Keneses haGedolah* / Men of the Great Assembly. This was an assemblage of 120 men composed of about 85 rabbinic sages and 35 prophets who lived following the destruction of the First Beis haMikdash until the early period of the Second Beis haMikdash. They were the bridge across the chasm of this transitional age, shuttling Klal Yisrael from the age of the Prophets (Hashem talking to us), to the Sages (Hashem talking through us), and guiding us forward into the future towards a new paradigm.

The Mishnah in *Avos* (1:1) that speaks of the transmission of Torah says, משה קיבל תורה מסיני ומסרה ליהושע, ויהושע לזקנים, וזקנים לנביאים, ונביאים מסרוה לאנשי כנסת הגדולה. / "Moshe received the Torah from Sinai and *transmitted* it to Yehoshua, Yehoshua to the Elders, the Elders to the Prophets, and the Prophets *transmitted* it to the Men of the Great Assembly." The first stage of transmission begins with

Moshe and ushers in the Age of the Prophets, continuing through Yehoshua and the elders until the *Nevi'im* / Prophets. This is the first mention of the word *u'Misara* / transmitted, above. The second use of the word comes in a new form: *m'Saruah*. It indicates a new kind of transmission, occurring between the Prophets and the Men of the Great Assembly. This is the shift from the written Torah, the Torah of the Prophets, to Torah she-b'al-Peh, the Torah of the Sages.

The question is asked: Why were they called the Men of the "Great" Assembly? The answer is given: Because they returned the crown of the Holy One, Blessed be He, to its former glory when they composed the Amidah, which says, "...*haKeil haGadol, haGibor, ve-haNora* / the Great, the Mighty, and the Awesome Divinity." For originally, Moshe came and implored Hashem in prayer, saying, "The Great, the Mighty, and the Awesome" (Devarim, 10:17). Later, the Prophet Yirmiyahu (Jeremiah) came and said, "The Gentiles, the minions of Nevuchadnetzar, are carousing in His sanctuary; where is His awesomeness?" Therefore, he did not say "awesome" in his prayer (Yirmiyahu, 32:18). Daniel came and said, "Gentiles are enslaving His children; where is His might?" Therefore he did not say "mighty" in his prayer (Daniel, 9:4). Finally, the members of the Great Assembly came and said, "On the contrary, this is the Might of Hashem, and the fullest expression of it: that Hashem conquers His inclination and exercises patience toward the wicked" (*Yuma,* 69b).

This profound statement by the Great Assembly means that throughout Galus, HaKadosh Baruch Hu shows Infinite might specifically through withdrawing, by stepping aside, hiding, and by no longer imposing a top-down, Achor b'Achor relationship upon us. This way, Hashem allows the world to be, to run its course, so to speak, as an apparently detached and independent entity. Hashem ceased talking to us in a revealed manner, and now allows *us* to do the talking. We are thereby allowed to hear the echo of Sinai within our own consciousness and voices as we think and speak. This concealment, paradoxically, is what 'allows' Hashem to speak *through* us, rather than merely *to* us.

Our sages (*Chullin*, 139b) say, "Where is a hint of the name and events of אסתר / Esther in the Torah? From the verse ואנכי הסתר אסתיר / *VeAnochi Haster Astir* / "And I will certainly hide (from Klal Yisrael)..." (Devarim, 31:18). The name *Esther* is alluded to in the word *Astir* / I will hide.

At Matan Torah we experienced the *Aleph* / the Oneness of אנכי / *Anochi* / the Divine 'I' openly through the revelation of the first of the *Eser Dibbros* / Ten Commandments, *Anochi Hashem* / "I am Hashem..." In the story of Purim, however, Hashem reveals the Divine 'I' through *Astir* / hiding — the *Anochi* is 'revealed' by means of deep concealment. We learn from the story of Esther and Purim that the Oneness of HaKadosh Baruch Hu is deeply hidden within the workings of nature and the flow of history.

Rebbe Tzadok writes that the revelation of the light of Purim is that "even in the concealment/darkness there is light" (*Resisei Layla*, 53). This means that there is light, even when the concealment remains a concealment; in other words, the very concealment is itself a kind of revelation. If the concealment were to evaporate when we saw Hashem's Presence within it, this would be a different paradigm than that of Purim. On Purim even in the *He'elem* / concealment there is *Ohr* / revealed light; even in *Galus* there is *Geulah*.

This is the idea of comfortable silence. With a deeply trusted friend, there is no need to fill up an extended silence with words; you know the person is with you even when they are not affirming their presence verbally. On Purim, when Hashem's name is absent from the text, we are celebrating our 'comfortable silence' with Hashem, knowing that HaKadosh Baruch Hu is with us — even when not 'speaking' to us. Purim opens the possibility of knowing Hashem even within the obstruction, darkness, duality, and seeming Divine absence within the world. In such a state, we have faith that Hashem is still speaking *through* us.

This represents a tremendous paradigm shift in our relationship with Hashem, and Hashem's relationship with the world. On the Pasuk (Tehilim, 102:19), "May this be written down for the coming generations, that a people yet to be created may praise Hashem," Chazal say, "'May this be written down for the coming generations' — this refers to the generation of Mordechai, which was leaning towards death. And 'A people yet created may praise Hashem' — this means that Hashem created a בריה חדשה / a new creation" (*Medrash Rabbah*, Vayikra, Emor, 30).

In other words, since the story of Purim there is a new world. A new reality was revealed through the experience of Klal Yisrael. A new relationship with HaKadosh Baruch Hu began to be articulated and expressed. This new reality has radical implications for all beings, as we will continue to explore.

It is important to understand how this quantum shift, in the way which the Creator reveals Himself to creation, sent ripple effects throughout the entire universe. What occurred within the realm of Torah and Klal Yisrael — within the *Penimiyus* / inner dimensions of the world — had an automatic effect on the *Chitzoniyus* / outer dimensions of the world. During this point in history, paradigm shifts of the same kind happened all around the world and across many cultures. This is known by some theorists as the Axial Age. They posit that in this historical transition old certainties were no longer seen as valid, in response humanity began asking deeper questions, and this launched a new era which continues still today. This is a Purim world.

FROM THE NAME HASHEM TO THE NAME ADO-NOI

The earlier *Yomim Tovim* / holidays, the ones recorded and commanded to us in the Five Books of Moshe, celebrate miraculous and extraordinary events such as our going out of Egypt, receiving the Torah at Mount Sinai, and being embraced by the Clouds of Glory journeying through our time in the desert. These events all speak of an open revelation of Hashem's Infinity, as it were. They are supernatural meta-events that occurred outside the *normal* limits of time/space, causality and nature. With the story of Purim, a paradigm shift occurred. Now Hashem speaks and reveals purpose and destiny through us, and through the limits and workings of time/space, causality and nature.

This shift in relationship is expressed in two principal Names of Hashem: the Name 'Hashem' (the Unspeakable Name: Yud-Hei-Vav-Hei), and the Name *Ado-noi* (the name of G-d that we audibly pronounce in place of the Unspeakable Name). Previously, Divine revelation was predominantly in the mode of the Name 'Hashem.' Since Purim and onward, Divine revelation has been in the mode of *Ado-noi*.

As mentioned earlier, Yud-Hei-Vav-Hei, when rearranged, can spell out the words *Hayah* (Hei-Yud-Hei) / was or past, *Hoveh* (Hei-Vav-Hei) / is or present, and — when you exchange the Vav for another Yud (because the Vav is, in a sense, an elongated Yud) — you create the word *Yihiyeh* (Yud-Hei-Yud-Hei) / will be or future. In this way, the Name 'Hashem' represents a totality of all past, present and future, and simultaneously a complete transcendence of time. Hashem is thus 'the Timeless, Infinite Being-ness' or 'the Eternal One.' However, the way the Name Hashem is actually indicated and pronounced today, in our post-Beis-haMikdash era of exile, is *Ado-noi*. The Name Ado-noi is the manner in which we get a grasp, as it were, of the Infinite / Ineffable One in this world of finite limitations. In this way, *Ado-noi* is the manifestation of the Infinity of 'Hashem' that is enclothed and concealed within finitude.

HaTeva / the (finite world of) nature, in numerical value, is 86. This is also the numerical value of the phrase *Kli Yud-Hei-Vav-Hei* / the vessel of the Name 'Hashem' (*Kli* is spelled Chaf/20, Lamed/30, Yud/10 = 60; the Name 'Hashem' is spelled Yud/10, Hei/5, Vav/6, Hei/5 = 26). Thus 'nature' is the vessel that 'contains' the revelation of Hashem's Infinite Light. This world is the hiding place of the Transcendent One.

The Mishnah says, "The Megilah is read on the 11th, the 12th, the 13th, the 14th, and the 15th (of the month of Adar); לא פחות

ולא יותר / no less and no more" (*Megilah,* 1:1). The words of the Mishnah, לא פחות ולא יותר / ...no *less* and no *more,* are a little peculiar. It seems the Mishnah should have said, "...not *before* and not *later.*" On closer inspection, however, the words "less" and "more" seem to hint at the idea of a number. What could be that number? The Arizal teaches that the days which the Megilah may be read — on the 11th, the 12th, the 13th, the 14th, and the 15th — are a spiritual equation: 11+12+13+14+15 equals 65, the numerical value of the Name Ado-noi. The days before and after the period when the Megilah may be read are the 10th and the 16th of the month — and 10+16 equal 26, the value of the name Hashem. In this way, the Mishnah can be interpreted as follows: 'The Megilah is read in (the consciousness of) the imminent Name Ado-noi; no less and no more – not in (the direct consciousness of) the transcendent Name Hashem.'

Ado-noi comes from the word *Adon* / Master. The Name *Ado-noi* can be written as *Ado-ni* / my Master, or *Ado-neinu* / our Master, whereas the Name Hashem is always *Hashem,* and does not change in spelling to fit the number of human subjects. This is because *Hashem* is beyond relationship, while *Ado-noi* means G-d is relatable to us as we are. The depth of the story of Purim lies in this new ability to relate to the Divine from within our own limitations. Hashem (the Transcendent) meets us within immanence, within our life-stories, within nature, within history, and within a hidden yet intimate relationship.

TRANSITIONING FROM ACHOR B'ACHOR
TO PANIM-EL-PANIM

Now, let's return to our earlier discussion of the two primary paradigms of relationship between Hashem and the world: Achor b'Achor and Panim-el-Panim. When one moves from one state to another, there is logically implied a third point between the two that serves as an intermediary, a transitional state. In our context, first comes the stage of *Achor b'Achor* / back to back. This is also called a *Zivug Temidi* / constant unity, such as in our example of a young nursing child and its mother who are virtually never separated, physically, emotionally or mentally. This was the kind of relationship Hashem had with us from when we were taken out of Egypt and brought to Matan Torah until the end of the First Beis haMikdash. (Although, within that period, during the times of the *Shoftim* / Judges, there was also a relative Divine withdrawal and concealment.) In the words of the *Navi* / Prophet Yirmiyahu, "Thus said Hashem, 'I counted in your favor the *Chesed* / devotion of your youth, your love as a bride, לכתך אחרי / *how you followed Me* in the wilderness, in a land not sown'" (Yirmiyahu, 2:2). This hints at the fact that we "followed" Hashem אחרי, on the level of *Achar* (אחר) / the back. This was a time of one-way relationship; like a child, we were 'behind' our Parent, as He guided through the wilderness. When we were obedient, we were protected from the unknown, when we misbehaved, we were punished like children.

This was the Age of Prophecy, as discussed. It was an imposed relationship, as it were (Maharal, *Hakdamah*, Ohr Chadash), in which we could only "devotedly" receive from Above. If we needed to know, for example, whether to go out to battle or not, we would simply ask the *Kohen Gadol* High Priest to request a prophetic insight via the *Urim v'Tumim* — the sacred Divine Name within the breastplate. Similarly, during our travels through the Desert we would move or stay put depending on the Divine Pillars of Cloud and Fire, if they moved we moved, if they stayed put we stayed put. Being always attached in this way to the Chesed of the Giver, we remained spiritually immature.

In order to achieve a more mature relationship with HaKadosh Baruch Hu, we required an experience of the *Gevurah* / severity of separation. Stage two, therefore, involved the destruction of the Beis haMikdash and the ensuing exile to Babylon and Persia. In order to progress from a 'back to back' relationship to a 'face to face' relationship there needed to first be a *Nesirah* / severing,* a pro-

---

* In more detail: Before the Nesirah, there was *Mochin* / intelligence only in ZA (the masculine, transcendent Sefiros), and ZA was *Mashpiah* / transmitting Mochin to Malchus (the feminine, receiver) — back to back. When ZA is aroused (with *Kishu* / arousal, *Kiviyachol* / as if), there is a live, animated Eiver, and it is unified with *Nukvah* / Malchus. This alters the dynamic between ZA and Malchus, changing it from a one-dimensional active giver – passive receiver relationship, to one more equal, dialogic and mature. It is thus a time that HaKadosh Baruch Hu, ZA, is unified with Malchus, which is Keneses Yisrael and the world in general. So first there is dependence of Malchus upon ZA (Back to Back), followed by a separation between ZA and Malchus (Nesirah), which leads to a higher level of unity between ZA and Malchus (Face to Face). In our current time period, the way people experience the *Yichud* / unity of ZA and Malchus is by sensing the *Mochin* / Divine Purpose and Intelligence hidden within *Teva* / nature. We see that Teva exists, but if we are spiritually mature we can sense within Teva the hidden Hand of Hashem guiding everything.
The time of the First Beis haMikdash was a time of *Nevuah* / prophecy and miracles; the 'hand' of Hashem openly revealed in nature. Then came the *Nesirah* / separation, the destruction and exile. The purpose of the Nesirah was so there could be a Panim-el-Panim relationship allowing for a revealing of Torah sheb'al-Peh. Yet, during the Nesirah there is a movement away, a sense that Hashem (Chas veShalom) has left us. We feel alone and rejected, like a divorced woman,

cess of separation. Imagine two people who are literally attached to each other back to back, what happens when they wish to en-

---

or an abandoned child. And that is what Klal Yisrael tells the prophet Yechezkel, that Hashem has divorced us. This is because now ZA and Malchus are no longer 'attached at the hip.' Of course, the purpose of the Nesirah is to eventually reach a deeper connection, but Malchus feels (meaning 'we' feel) abandoned, alone and divorced.

In such a state it seems as if *Elokim Yashen* / Hashem is sleeping. Haman says, "The G-d of Klal Yisrael is asleep" (*Medrash*, quoted by the Arizal in *Sha'ar haKavanos*, Purim). Indeed, during the period of the Purim story, there was a great danger and *Tzarah* / distress for Klal Yisrael. At such times, experientially, we feel as if nature has its own rules, as if Hashem weren't ruling it. There is an appearance of randomness, like the *Goral* / lottery of Haman. This is what many of Klal Yisrael originally thought when the decree of Haman became known: 'Hashem has left us, and now nature has taken over, and it is "might over right."'

Yet, during the Nesirah, Malchus is not left without Mochin altogether. Yes, ZA is separate from Malchus and is no longer pumping Mochin into Malchus, however, Malchus receives Mochin from *Av'ah* (Chochmah and Binah and even higher). This Mochin is not the 'Mochin of Creation' (as Mochin of ZA), since Av'ah is Higher than this world which is 'created by' ZA — the six Sefiros being the Six Days of Creation (like a six-sided cube of Creation with Shabbos / Malchus in the center) — rather it is a Mochin from beyond Creation. The separation then opens up the space for an even higher level of revelation to occur within the apparent concealment.

The Mochin within Malchus that is experienced (even during the Nesirah) is experienced as a sense that even though nature seems to function on its own, we have *Emunah* / higher Mochin that everything is going to work out for the best (even if we do not yet intellectually know how). When we experience this form of higher Mochin in Malchus, as during the time when the Purim narrative was unfolding, there is awoken within us (Malchus) a *Tenuah* / movement of total *Mesiras Nefesh* / self-sacrifice.

What is more, even after the Nesirah and the *Yichud* / reunification of ZA and Malchus in a mode of Panim-el-Panim, the Mochin from Av'ah remains enclothed within Malchus always. This is the *Chidush* / novelty of Purim, which, in this way, is beyond the level of Shabbos and Yom Tov. The mature reunification of Malchus and Za is thus on a higher level than the initial relationship of open revelation and childlike dependence.

counter each other face to face. To do so, they need to first detach and move away from each other so that they can then turn around to face each other. In other words, they need to create a temporary distance between themselves in order to bring their connection to a higher/deeper level.

Following our developmental paradigm that we have laid out to explain these relational dynamics, the period of Nesirah can be likened to the painful years of adolescence. In this stage, both the parents and their children are detaching and moving 'away' from each other. The child is no longer completely dependent upon the parents, and is staking out their own territory and sense of self. Although the parent wants the child to grow up and be independent, this can still be a painful and alienating stage for each of the family members. There is a separation from old habits of communication and connection. The unrestrained giving on the part of the parent may now be detrimental, and it may take strength to withhold their expressed love. But it is necessary now for each family member to evolve in order to enter into a genuine, mature, person-to-person relationship and dialogue.

It is interesting to note that *Achor b'Achor* and *Panim-el-Panim* are the terminology of the Arizal. The Alter Rebbe teaches (*Sefer haMa'amarim*, Tav-Kuf-Samach-Hei) that whatever the Arizal taught in esoteric language, the Baal Shem Tov was able to express as a *Mashal* / metaphor. The corresponding Mashal of the Baal Shem Tov (*Ohr HaTorah* [The Magid], Ekev) is that of a spiral staircase, what in Yiddish (German) is called *Shvindal-Trep* / spiral step. (Rashi in Melachim 1, 6:8 writes, "A *winding staircase*, and that is called in our language... the commonly used term, *Shvindel Steig*.") While walking up a spiral staircase we are moving constantly upwards, yet we are also constantly moving 'away' in order to come closer to our goal.

In the context of history, Hashem needed to 'separate' from us in order to give us the sense of independence and responsibility that it takes to establish a mature relationship. This included allowing us to begin developing the Torah she-b'al-Peh, and to establish lives of holiness and elevation, even without the Beis haMikdash.

In a 'pre-personal' stage of life, an infant senses no clear distinction between self and mother, nor between self and world. In their undeveloped mind, the external world is merely an extension of their own body. As the infant develops, he becomes increasingly aware of the dimensions and borders of his body, where it ends and external objects begin. Still, it lives under the impression that his parents and perhaps siblings are essentially parts of himself. And still, when he cries he gets fed, when he gets dirty he gets cleaned, when tired he gets rocked to sleep. It is only when his parents are willing to withhold his demands, and hold back for even a moment or two from immediately delivering what the child wants, that a healthy process of weaning can begin. Then, in numerous unfolding stages, the child builds more and more strength, until as a healthy adult, the child no longer needs to live in the protective home of the parent. The parent may even at some point 'exile' him and ask him to move out, for his own good.

Although the Presence of the Transcendent One is less palpable than it was during the time of prophecy and miracles, we have a new way of being connected, and a deeper level of intimacy with the Divine. This is the paradoxical nature of *Galus* / exile. There can be a 'face-to-face' relationship with HaKadosh Baruch Hu on the one hand, yet, with the severance from our dependent state we can also feel alone and alienated. While this is very painful, it brings out a deeper yearning within us. This yearning allows us to achieve, for the first time, a real conscious *acceptance of Torah*. We become deeply present in a way we hadn't been before, for now the relationship relies on our own active participation. In order to more fully understand this dynamic, we need to unpack the concept of Galus a bit more.

DIVINE SLUMBER

Galus is an experience of separation, and a burning sense of Hashem being asleep, so to speak, uninterested and distant from creation, as if the world has been left to its own devices. This is indeed very painful, but, like a stage of human development that is required to get to the next level of higher integration and capacity for genuine encounters, it is also necessary. It is like the spiral steps; the only way to get to the next rung is to move momentarily 'away' from the destination.

The events of Purim illustrate this dynamic. During the Persian Exile, in which there was no longer any revelation from Above, no open miracles nor prophecy, a poor, orphaned, exiled Jew named Esther suddenly rose to become the queen of Persia. Because of this, eventually permission was given to the Jewish people to complete the building of the Second Beis haMikdash, and this led to the flowering of the era of Chazal, our sages, the high time of revealing the Torah she-b'al-Peh.

This narrative occurred precisely during a time of national and cosmic sleep, as it were, at a peak of prejudice and subjugation. When Haman, the evil antagonist of the story, speaks to the king of the Persian Empire about the Jewish People, he said, "There is a certain people scattered abroad and dispersed…" (Megilas Esther, 3:8). The phrase "there is" in Hebrew is *Yeshnah*, which can also be read as *she sleeps*, as in *Yashen* / sleeping. Haman is alluding to the fact that exile is a form of sleep, and that not only was *she*, the Jewish People, asleep, but that the King of all Kings was also asleep, as it were (See *Medrash Rabbah*, Esther 10:1): "The G-d of these people *Yashen* / is asleep" (Medrash, as quoted by the Arizal in *Sha'ar haKavanos*).

As mentioned, the movement from 'back-to-back' to 'face-to-face' relationship with Hashem requires a painful stage of Divine separation, withholding. There is a sense of absence, of being ripped away from everything good in life. This is called *Hastara* / concealment. However, in addition to this occlusion there is the corresponding appearance of Divine slumber — resulting in a *double* concealment. And the world-transforming events of the Purim story are connected specifically with this double hiddenness, referred to above as, *Haster Astir* (Devarim, 31:18. *Chulin*, 139b).

Therefore, precisely because the separation and concealment of exile was so agonizing for both the Jewish People and for HaKadosh Baruch Hu, an anesthetic was necessary. When a young adult separating from the 'nest' does not yet have the keys to healthy self-comforting and self-reliance, they sadly can turn to substance abuse in order to numb their pain and anger. Rest and sleep are necessary for our bodies and minds to survive significant changes and traumas. And just as a patient needs to be put to sleep in certain surgeries, both humanity and Divinity needed a numbing of the pain of the first exile from the Beis haMikdash, an anesthetic of sorts that would allow for renewal and reconfiguration.

This meta-historical process described in the Purim story is parallel to the *Nesirah* / surgical separation and re-configuration of Adam and Chavah / Eve. How so? Originally, Adam and Chavah were created as a single body: "And G-d created Adam in His image... male and female He created them" (Bereishis, 1:27). That is, Adam and Chava were initially created as a single being, with two faces pointed in opposite directions, connected back-to-back (*Medrash Rabbah*, Bereishis, 8:1. *Eiruvin*, 18a); they were conjoined, but also paradoxically alone, without a real relationship with the *other*. Although they were merged as one, the Torah says, "It is not good for the man to be alone (back-to-back); I will make a helper *against* him (face-to-face)" (Bereishis, 2:18). Therefore, "Hashem caused a deep sleep to fall upon Adam... and He took one of his sides..." (Bereishis, 2:23), in order to separate them.

It was only in this state of *Durmita* / sleep, that a *Nesirah* / severing could occur without completely overwhelming Adam and Chavah. Only through this surgical operation could they begin to "know" each other, challenge each other, be "helpmates against" each other, and thus really help each other to grow.

SWEETER THAN WINE

We too can only truly benefit from a "helper" when that person is "against" us, standing face-to-face with us, seeing us and reflecting back to us fully. When two are facing each other by their own volition and desire, they can authentically choose to give and receive love and feedback. On the other hand, when a real relationship goes astray, they can choose to walk away from one another. Such a risk can bring true friends even closer; it stimulates an even deeper level of 'awakenness' and sensitivity within both parties.

Our relationship with HaKadosh Baruch Hu is of the same nature. In exile we can experience an even deeper relationship because it becomes something that we must both want and freely pursue. But we can also walk away, sadly. The stakes are therefore much higher. We are no longer attached to the 'back' of the Divine as it were, so our commitment must be fully chosen, making it all the more meaningful.

When we do choose to be in a conscious relationship with the Source of Life, our lives are so much more profound. This is the beauty and the sweetness of Torah she-b'al-Peh, which is even sweeter than the revealed Torah. "*Kneses Yisrael* / the congregation of Israel said before the Holy One, Blessed be He: 'Master of the Universe, the statements of Your beloved ones (the Sages) are more pleasant to me than the wine of the written Torah itself'" (*Avodah Zarah*, 35a). This sweetness comes from our wanting the relationship, wanting closeness and communication with Hashem. Torah she-b'al-Peh is not a forced connection, like a mountain suspended over our heads. It is Divine communication that comes from within, expressing our yearning to be together, and our active commitments to each other. This is the essence of Purim and, by extension, Adar.

The "pleasantness" and pleasures of such a mature relationship are experienced precisely because we are no longer engaged in an *Achor b'Achor* dynamic; it is not a *Zivug Temidi* / constant unity. If it were constant, it would not be sweet: תענוג תמידי אינו תענוג / "continuous pleasure is no (longer considered) pleasurable" (*Likutei Amarim* [the Maggid] 168, in the name of the Baal Shem Tov). The desire of separate entities to reunite, and the electrifying experience of real face-to-face connection, is what gives rise to such great pleasure in both the receiver and giver.

Hearing people talking about nonsense is not pleasurable, yet, hearing a parrot mimic a few nonsensical words evokes pleasure (*Keser Shem Tov*, 407). Pleasure comes from something novel or unusual. When we, in a state of separation, reach out to HaKadosh Baruch Hu to fully receive the Torah and are *Mechadesh Chidushim* / able to create novel insights in Torah, it causes a pleasure both for us and On High that is "more pleasant than wine." Precisely because of the absence of clear revelation from Above, a new, deeper level of revelation and relationship is able to flower and flourish.

At Purim we embraced the Torah with passion. This was in contrast to Matan Torah, at which point we were infatuated by it, yet so overwhelmed by Hashem's kindness that our acceptance was in a sense by force.

Purim, says the Arizal, is the revelation of the *Ohr* of *Yesod* of *Abba* / the light of the attribute of 'intimacy' within the Father. What does this mean? Yesod, says the Baal Shem Tov, is *Ta'anug*

/ pleasure. *Abba* is another term for the Sefirah of Chochmah, and experientially, this Sefirah is characterized by *Bitul* / selflessness and openness. Yesod of Abba is thus the *pleasure of selfless wisdom*. This is the Ta'anug of *Kabbalas haTorah* /acceptance of Torah, experienced on Purim, which is different than how we received it at Mount Sinai, under duress. What is different on Purim? Certainly, we received Torah through Bitul at Sinai, as we learn that our souls actually left our bodies upon hearing the Divine word. It is that on Purim we experience the Ta'anug of Bitul, we taste the pleasure of such selfless wisdom; primarily because we initiated the experience on our own, i.e., without the mountain being held over our heads, so to speak.

At Sinai, *Yirah* / awe was the dominant emotion experienced by Klal Yisrael, whereas at Purim *Ahavah* / love, and a conscious appreciation of our intimacy with Hashem, was most pronounced. Regarding Matan Torah, it says, "And all the people saw the voices and the torches, the sound of the shofar, and the smoking mountain, and the people saw and trembled, and they stood from afar" (Shemos, 20:5). This is the description of a completely overwhelming experience, where all one can conceivably do is stand back in awe. In the Purim story, however, Klal Yisrael drew close and made a commitment to Torah willfully and with heartfelt love: "They re-accepted it in the days of Achashverosh."

An allusion to this idea is hidden in the phrase *Har Sinai* / Mount Sinai, which is numerically 335 (*Har* is Hei/5, Reish/200; *Sinai* is Samach/60, Yud/10, Nun/50, Yud/10 = 335). The word *Purim* is 336 (Pei/80, Vav/6, Reish/200, Yud/10, Mem/40 = 336), so Purim is *Har Sinai* plus one. What is one, in Hebrew? It is *Echad*, which is *Ahavah*

— as both *Echad* and *Ahavah* have a numerical value of 13. There was one element missing at Sinai, and that was us — our love, our choice, our deepest desire.*

From Purim onwards we assumed a proactive role in our relationship with the Divine. We, the receivers and absorbers of Torah, became active partners in revelation. Thus we could innovate, in accordance with the principles received at Sinai, a new Yom Tov: Purim.

Purim represents the loving acceptance and re-affirmation of all Torah with all its commandments and mandated holidays. The five Hebrew letters that comprise the word *Purim* (Pei, Vav, Reish, Yud and Mem) can be understood as an acronym for all the Torah holidays of the year. Pei stands for Pesach, Vav for *v'Sukkos* / and Sukkos (as Sukkos also celebrates the journey in the Desert following the Exodus from Egypt, and is thus connected to Pesach). Reish stands for Rosh Hashanah, Yud for Yom Kippur, and Mem for Matan Torah, the holiday commemorating the giving of the Torah, which is Shavuos.

Purim is actually the central holiday of the year, since through Purim Klal Yisrael re-accepted all the other *Yomim Tovim* / holidays of the year. Therefore, Purim embodies qualities and elements of all the other Yomim Tovim. Purim is similar to Pesach in that it is a day of redemption (Although to a degree lesser than Pesach, as we remained 'servants' to the powers of the world. *Megilah*, 14a).

---

* On Purim we are asked to send מנות איש לרעהו / gifts one to another. The Mitzvos of Purim are meant to foster love and unity. The above words have the same numerical value as שמע ישראל ה' אלקינו ה' אחד / Shema Yisrael, Hashem Elokeinu, Hashem Echad (Komarna, *Kesem Ofir*, 10:19). To give to another with love is to truly express the reality of *Hashem Echad*.

It is like Shavuos in that there was a new acceptance of the To-rah. It is likened to Rosh Hashanah in that the books of the living and dead were opened and it was a 'trial' of the Jewish people. Pu-rim is connected to Yom Kippur in that it was a time of heightened spiritual awakening through Teshuvah. In fact the Torah calls Yom Kippur *Yom haKi-Purim* / the day like Purim. On some level Pu-rim is also like Sukkos, for just as Sukkos commemorates Hashem protecting the Jewish People with the clouds of glory, the same occurred during the time of Purim when Hashem protected and watched over us. Sukkos is *the time of our joy*, and Purim too is a day of great joy: ליהודים היתה אורה ושמחה וששן / *LaYehudim Haysa Orah veSimcha veSason* / "For the Jews there was light and joy and happiness..." (Megilas Esther, 8:16).

The entire month of Adar, as reflected in its unique permutation of the letters of Hashem's name, is a movement from the world below upwards to Hashem, through the double concealment of the two Heis back to the infinite point of the Yud and the connect-ing line of the Vav. Additionally, as explored in *The Spiral of Time*, the six months of the winter all embody this quality of arousal and movement from below to Above. The month of Adar, the final month and culmination of this process, shines with a particular brilliance of this energy of *arousal from below*, and Purim is the essential apex of this rising up in sweet yearning to achieve a true face-to-face relationship with the Beloved.

THE ULTIMATE END AND THE NEW BEGINNING

As mentioned, Adar is the conclusion of the lunar cycle of the months, as well as the end of the six months of winter-fall. Purim is thus the final Yom Tov of the lunar year, ending the cycle with a powerful awakening and resurgence from below.

As the final Yom Tov, Purim is also the ultimate Yom Tov, and the "end of all the holidays." It is the last Yom Tov to be recorded and canonized in the Torah. Similarly, it is the *final miracle*, or in the language of the Gemara, "the end of the miracles" (*Yuma*, 21a). From another perspective, Purim is not just an end and culmination, it is a 'new' receiving and dedication to Torah, and the birth of a new paradigm in Creation. In this way, Purim is also the 'first Yom Tov' of the future, the hidden beginning of all the holidays of the coming year, and macro-cosmically of the coming Era of Moshiach.

During the year that the miracle of Purim occurred, Queen Esther's three day fast in the month of Nisan pushed aside the celebration of Pesach (*Megilah*, 15a, Rashi). Therefore, part of the 'root' of Purim is 'pushing aside' Pesach, albeit only temporarily (Rambam, *Hilchos Mamrim*, 2:4). Pesach is the first Yom Tov which is commanded in the Torah, and is also the first Yom Tov according to the lunar cycle. What does it mean that the 'last' pushes aside the 'first'?

Recited in the name of many Tzadikim is the concept that in the future, the first Yom Tov of the year will be Purim. This is because in the future there will be a perfect unity between the fullness of the World Above (symbolized by Matan Torah), and the fullness of the world below (symbolized by Purim). However, in the future both of these fullnesses will be simultaneously revealed; Purim will be in the location of, or in place of, Pesach.

With Purim, the Hei-Hei of Hashem's Name (corresponding to the world below) stimulates a new revelation of the Yud-Vav from Above, illuminating ever-deeper dimensions of Torah.

To explain, the normal process of revelation is the revealing of the Above (Yud-Vav) to the below (Hei): Hashem reveals the Torah at Sinai to Klal Yisrael. Yet our sages tell us, "Even what a proficient pupil is destined to *Mechadesh* / innovate (*Megilah*, 19b) was already said to Moshe at Sinai" (*Yerushalmi*, Pe'ah, 2:4). This suggests a different process of revelation: a proficient pupil or Sage below (Hei) can 'create' Torah that is from Above (Yud-Vav).

The seeming dilemma is, if something was a Chidush then it was *not* already said to Moshe; and if it *was* said to Moshe it is not really a Chidush. In the process of the unfolding of finite time, there is indeed first the revelation of Matan Torah, and then later in history the sages unpack the general principles of Torah to reveal the specific details of Torah she-b'al-Peh. According to this view, theirs are not real Chidushim, rather, merely an unpacking of the seminal ideas given at Sinai. However, according to a higher perspective beyond linear time, they are real Chidushim and *simultaneously* they were already revealed at Sinai. How does this work? How can something be both new and simultaneously pre-existent? Ultimately, it all depends on our conception of time.

This simultaneity is possible because Torah and Yisrael both exist 'prior' to creation or 'beyond' the unfolding of historic and finite time, in eternity. Both are rooted in *Atzmus* / the Essence of the Creator. And furthermore, Yisrael is even higher or more *Kadmon* / primordial than Torah (*Tana d'Vei Eliyahu Rabba* 14. See also, *Medrash Rabbah*, Bereishis, 1:4. *Zohar* 2, 119b, the Rebbe, *Mayim Rabim*). So from this perspective, the Chidushim of the sages (the Hei), even if spoken thousands of years after the giving of the Torah, are rooted in Atzmus, within the Giver of Torah (the Yud) in eternity. And thus, when that which is beyond time is manifest within time, a new Chidush can be paradoxically both a real Chidush in historical time, and also one that was already revealed at Mount Sinai.

A prime example of the above is Purim. Purim is a Chidush, a 'new' Yom Tov, and yet, it was also originally revealed at Mount Sinai. In other words, the Hei (the Sages) rose up and stimulated the Yud (the Giver of the Torah) with the inspiration of Purim, and then the Yud revealed the concept of Purim to the Hei back in time, at Mount Sinai.

It is worth pointing out that Purim is not only about the Hei's rising or the basic pattern of 'arising from below' encoded in the winter months. Purim and Adar are unique in that their letter formation begins with both letter Hei's. As these are followed by the Yud, it is clear that the Hei's have the paradoxical power to stimulate the supernal Yud to give forth a new form of revelation by means of the next letter, Vav, which connects Heaven and earth. This cycles back to the beginning of the letter formation, as the new revelation is received by the lower Hei and then the higher Hei.

This, then, is the Chidush of the Yom Tov of Purim; a new Yom Tov and book of scripture originates from Esther's own initiative (lower Hei) which gave birth to her inspired understanding (upper Hei) and her request of the Sages to record and commemorate these events. This initiative and inspiration then rises to the timeless Giver of the Torah (Yud), and 'retroactively' becomes incorporated in the revelation (Vav) of Torah at Mount Sinai. The Book of Esther, seemingly authored by human beings, thus becomes part of Tanach, the *Kisvei haKodesh* / the sacred writings of Hashem's Torah.

This dynamic is also reflected in the paradigms of Achor b'Achor and Panim-el-Panim. The normal formation of Hashem's name, from Yud to Vav to Hei, is a path from the Giver Above to the receiver below, the pattern of prophecy and miracles. For the receiver, this is perceived as an Achor b'Achor relationship with the Giver, as there is no room for actual participation and response.

However, in Adar there is a reversal of this order in the structure of Hashem's name, in which the Hei's precede the Yud and the Vav. In this configuration, the receiver below becomes present and empowered, and the Hei rises as the feminine aspect of the Divine. First there must be a severing of the rigid and conventional top-down relationship between the Masculine attribute above and the Feminine below. Then the Feminine can turn around and arise to become a *Helper against Him*, Face-to-Divine Face. This refers to the revealing of Torah she-b'al-Peh, the paradigm of Hashem speaking not just to us but through us. Now we, the Feminine, are beginning to do the talking, and Hashem, the Masculine, is listening.

There will come a time, may it arrive speedily in our days, when this Panim-el-Panim relationship will reach complete manifestation; when the Feminine and Masculine are united in perfect peace, when there is perfect unity within the Name of Hashem. This quality of the Ultimate Redemption began its journey toward full revelation on Purim, the "first Yom Tov" of the future.

On the way to this completion there are four stages: 1) dissolving or deconstructing the immature Achor b'Achor relationship, 2) creating an immature manifestation of the Panim-el-Panim relationship, 3) accepting a mature Achor b'Achor relationship, and 4) finally establishing a mature Panim-el-Panim relationship.

DISSOLUTION OF THE IMMATURE
ACHOR B'ACHOR RELATIONSHIP

Our story begins with an immature Achor b'Achor paradigm, in which everything is about the Yud, Above. Hashem pulled us out of Egypt with an outstretched hand (Yad) from Above, like pulling a child from its mother's womb (*Yechezkel*, 16:4. Medrash *Shochar Tov*). Hashem carried us like a mother carries her young, or like an eagle that carries its offspring on its wings (*Shemos*, 19:4, Rashi). For the first phase of our history we were cradled by HaKadosh Baruch Hu, and 'attached to the hip' of Hashem. This top-down pattern started dissolving with the destruction of the first Beis haMikdash and the cessation of prophecy.

IMMATURE PANIM-EL-PANIM RELATIONSHIP

With the deterioration of this immature Achor b'Achor relationship there was an onset of Divine slumber; which allowed for deep disconnection from the old paradigm and opening for the potential of a Panim-el-Panim relationship. During the years leading up to the Purim narrative, the Jewish People were in just such a state of deep sleep.

A Nesirah or severing from Hashem's 'back' occurred within the double concealment of this sleep state. When Divinity Above stopped overwhelming the world below as a "mountain suspended overhead," a kind of cosmic helicopter parent so to speak, there was a space opened in which the building up and individuation of the person below could occur; giving rise to the formation of a healthy and separate ego, a *Panim*. Still, however there was no genuine encounter or mature Panim-el-Panim level of relationship. Like an adolescent with a newfound sense of freedom, we rebelled and we indulged ourselves in the non-Kosher feast of Achashverosh. Everything was about *us*. We drank to anesthetize our hidden pain, we became numb and we fell asleep.

MATURE ACHOR B'ACHOR RELATIONSHIP

At this point, certain key sages among our people realized that we were asleep and no longer conscious of HaKadosh Baruch Hu. Additionally, they also realized that HaKadosh Baruch Hu was, from a human perspective, asleep to our plight. We found ourselves in mortal danger, as the plot of Haman was to annihilate Klal Yisrael, Heaven forbid. Our leaders, like prophets, called upon us to wake up. We fasted and cried out to Hashem.

Our prayers were heard and everything began to turn around on the night when the king of Persia, who symbolically represents the King of Kings, was not able to sleep: "The sleep of the king was interrupted" (Megilas Esther, 6:1). "This means the sleep of Heaven was interrupted" (*Medrash Rabbah*, Esther 10:1). When we read in Megilas Esther the words, "On that night the sleep of the king was interrupted," there is a custom for the reader to raise their voice (*Darchei Moshe*, Orach Chayim, 690. *Magen Avraham*, ibid, 17), as this is the essence of the miracle (*Megilah*, 19a).

Whenever Megilas Esther says "the king" it is also making a subtle reference to the King of Kings (*Medrash Rabbah*, Esther 3:10. And from an even deeper perspective, it is a reference to both the earthy and the Heavenly King. *Resisei Layla*, 19).*

---

* In general, Rav Menachem Rikanti (a student of the Ramban) writes, that *Achashverosh* is an allusion to Hashem as the name is an acronym for *Acharis VeReishis Shelo* / the end and beginning are His (*Rikanti*, Parshas Vayetze). The Ramah, in his Sefer *Machir Yayin*, follows this interpretation throughout the text. (See also Rabbi Meir Papirush, *Meoros Nasan* (Meorei Ohr) Ma'areches Aleph, 182. *K'heles Yaakov*, Ma'areches Aleph.)

This idea can be understood in two ways, 1) the earthly king is rather superfluous in the story, and every time the name *Achashverosh* is read it really only means Hashem, the King, and that should be our *Kavanah* / intention during the reading. 2) There was an actual earthly king and his name was Achashverosh, yet Hashem is speaking through the world and through nature (as explained earlier), and so the earthly king is to be understood as Hashem's agent. Usually, it seems our choice is to focus solely on the spiritual or solely on the physical point of view in life. We may opt to close our eyes from the physical perspective, to see solely through the lens of the spiritual prism, and sense only Hashem's presence in the world. Or, conversely, we may understand the world of 'kings' and governments and people as having their own existence, volition and influence.

Yet, there is a third way that reconciles the spiritual/physical polarity; and Purim demands of us this deeper way of living and perceiving reality. As Adar is all about the unity of apparent opposites, we can view the world as a unity of spirituality and physicality. We can recognize Hashem's voice speaking through people and earthly phenomena, rather than overwhelming and canceling them out. We can keep our eyes open to both the physical and the spiritual realities simultaneously, knowing, for instance, that there is a real physical ruler, and yet

On that night, "the sleep of the King of the Universe, the Holy One, Blessed be He, was disturbed" (*Megilah*, 15b). This was *the waking up*, as it were, of the King (Tehilim, 121:4); for His people aroused Him and thereby stimulated a compassionate response. We needed to be rescued, in some ways like from Mitzrayim. Yet it was coming from a more mature place; rising up from below to re-claim and re-confirm our bond with the Infinite One. This initiative on our part opened the way for a mature reuniting with HaKadosh Baruch Hu in the manner of a 'face-to-Face' embrace.

MATURE PANIM-EL-PANIM RELATIONSHIP

In the Purim story there began the unfolding of a true and deep Panim-el-Panim relationship, in which the fullness of Hashem and the fullness of Humanity were both present. The culmination of this type of Panim-el-Panim will only be realized in the World of perfect *Yichud* / unity, with the arrival and revealing of Moshiach, but it has already begun with the minor redemption of Purim. For this reason, Purim (and Yom Kippur) will never be nullified, even in the times of Moshiach, although the other Yomim Tovim will be.*

---

it is Hashem who is really speaking and acting through that person.
This is the ultimate idea of *Yichud* / Oneness. It is not a cancellation of physicality, nor an idea that the world does not really exist but is mere illusion. Rather, *Yichud* means that existence itself is a non-separate expression and part of the *Achdus Hashem* / Oneness of Hashem, and that לית אתר פנוי מיניה / everything is Divinity.

* *Medrash Rabbah*, Mishlei 9:2. *Yalkut Shimoni*, Mishlei, 944. *Sefer Chassidim*, 369. *Torah Ohr*, Megilas Esther, 90d. See also, Rambam, *Hilchos Megilah v'Chanukah* 2:18, although it appears in the Rambam that only the Yomim Tovim that are recorded in *Megilas Ta'anis* will be nullified, not the Yomim

At such a time, Purim will be the first Yom Tov of the year, in the World to Come. "On that day Hashem (Above) will be One and His Name (below) will be One." We will see eye-to-eye, 'I' to 'I' Essence to Essence.

To summarize: In the original status of creation the only truly presence was the 'I' of Hashem. Klal Yisrael lived in the overwhelming Presence of the Absolute 'I' even in the Egyptian exile, until the destruction of the First Beis haMikdash. Although we were protected and nurtured, and our national identity was secured, we were not seen as a full person, a full *I*, although in terms of our identity we were secured.

Only with our dispersion from the Land of Israel and exile into the diaspora was our individual identity, our *I*, really challenged. No longer was our living as a people within the same national borders a source of identity; no longer did we have a physical spiritual center where we could automatically receive inspiration and revelation from HaKadosh Baruch Hu.

In order to rise to the occasion, to build and grow from this tragedy, we needed the *Durmita* / Divine and human slumber and a full *Nesirah* / severing from the old ways of living. Then, by being

Tovim of the Torah (as stated clearly in Sefer Chassidim and implied in the Medrash, as it includes Yom Kippur). In the words of the Rambam, ואע"פ שכל זכרון הצרות יבטל שנאמר כי נשכחו הצרות הראשונות וכי נסתרו מעיני, ימי הפורים לא יבטלו / "Although all memories of the difficulties endured by our people will be nullified, as Yeshayahu (65:16) states, 'For the former difficulties will be forgotten and they will be hidden from My eye,' the celebration of the days of Purim will not be nullified." This suggests that only the memories of the difficulties, and thus their corresponding 'holidays' will be nullified, and the Rambam is not talking about the Yomim Tovim in the Torah. (See also the Brisker Rav, *Reshimas haTalmidim*, Megilas Esther, 9:28.)

startled out of our sleep, opening our eyes and realizing that we were in imminent danger, were we able to arise and stand in our full personhood before HaKadosh Baruch Hu. For the first time in history, we were having a *choice* encounter rather than a *chance* encounter — relating to HaKadosh Baruch Hu out of our own volition (*Bechirah* / free choice arises because of the Nesirah. Ramchal, *Kelalim haRishonim*, Klal 28). This is still an immature 'i-to-I' dynamic, as it is still all about us and our needs. But the unfolding had begun.

When this unfolding process is complete, we will find ourselves in a *Geulah Sheleimah* / a complete state of Redemption. Then the fullness of Hashem's 'I' and the fullness of our 'I' will be revealed as they truly are, in a total embrace. This is the revelation, or 'un-masking' as it were, of the *Etzem* / Essence of HaKadosh Baruch Hu in oneness with our essence. May we merit to taste this experience of mature unity that does not dissolve the identity of its participants even now, and may it spread and completely heal our world quickly in our lifetimes.

☾

ॐ

TORAH VERSE

*T*HE FOUR-LETTER DIVINE NAME THAT SHINES DURING each month is rooted within a particular verse in the Torah (*Tikunei Zohar, Hakdamah* 9b. *Eitz Chayim, Sha'ar* 44:7). In other words, there is a 'verse of the month' comprised of a four-word sequence, in which each word either begins or ends with the letters of the *Tziruf* / name-formation for that month. In fact, the order of the Tziruf follows the corresponding verses (*Mishnas Chasidim*, Meseches Adar, 1:3). The meaning and context of the verse connected with each particular month is, of course, also part of the revelation of that month's guiding light.

The permutation of the Divine Name that we explored above, Hei-Hei then Yud-Vav, comes from the last letters of the verse: ...*IryoH V'lasoreikaH B'nI AsonO*... / "(He shall tie to the vine) his donkey, and to the vine branch his donkey's foal..." (Bereishis, 49:11). The last letter of each of these four words forms the Tziruf of the month, Hei-Hei-Yud-Vav.

The "donkey" in this verse refers to the body (the microcosmic Hei within oneself). The vine, according to Rashi, alludes to wine (Rashi, ibid), referring to the drinking of wine on Purim. "...Tying the body to the vine," means that we are nourished by our imbibing of wine in this month, as it becomes our portal to enter deeper levels of joy, lightness and laughter — qualities that permeate the entire month of Adar, as will be further explored. However, as the verse also implies, this drinking is to be done in a wholesome and anchored or grounded ("tied") way, as will be shortly explained in greater detail.

☾

LETTER

THERE ARE 22 LETTERS IN THE ALEPH BEIS. TORAH, THE blueprint of creation, is written in Hebrew, the *Lashon haKodesh* / holy tongue. IOur Sages teach that each of these 22 letters contain a host of metaphysical creative potentials. According to the Sefer Yetzirah, a profound book of early Kabbalah that pays particular attention to the inner dimensions of the Hebrew letters, the 22 letters of the Aleph-Beis are divided into three categories: three "Mother Letters," seven "Double Letters" and twelve "Simple Letters." Each month is connected to one of the 12 Simple Letters.*

---

* For a more in-depth analysis of all three categories of Hebrew letters and their relationship to the calendar, please see the introductory volume to this series: *The Spiral of Time: Unraveling the Yearly Cycle.*

Kuf (ק) is the letter associated with the month of Adar. Our sages teach that this letter represents **K**edusha / holiness (*Shabbos*, 104a). *Kedusha* is the attribute of an object, time period or person that is *Kadosh* / dedicated, set apart, removed from the normal mundane reality. A wedding is called *Kidushin*, because when a couple are being married the *Chasan* / groom declares, "You are *Mekudeshes Li* / holy to me." This means *Meyuchedes Li* / מיוחדת לי / dedicated as special to me (*Kidushin*, 2b). The woman thus becomes דאסר לה אכולי עלמא כהקדש / forbidden to anyone else like a consecrated item (Ibid); there is now a dedicated and exclusive relationship. We too are *Mekudeshes*, having entered a marriage with HaKadosh Baruch Hu (*Tanya*, 46). We became a *Goy Kadosh* / holy nation by entering into such a covenant, and we are in a monogamous relationship, dedicated to Hashem alone.

To experience 'holiness' is to find or dedicate what is מיוחדת / *Meyuchedes* / special within an object or time period — namely the point of *Yichud* / unity, wholeness or perfection within it. This point is a portal into an experience of infinity or transcendence within the tapestry of time and space. For example, the infinite point of 'unity' within time is Shabbos. When we sanctify Shabbos, dedicating it as special, it becomes a unifying factor in time for us. All of our other experiences revolve around this central point, and all are nourished by its transcendent quality. If you experience *Atzvus* / feelings of depression in your life, setting aside Shabbos allows you to transcend these feelings and unify with infinite light on a regular basis. Then, when this rhythm of rest and renewal is established within the weekly cycle, Kedushah and wholeness flow into your *Y'mei Chol* / non-Shabbos days as well, subtly coloring and nourishing all of your experiences.

As Kuf represents Kedusha it thus implies a sense of serious commitment. On the other hand, *Kuf* literally means *Kof* / a monkey, suggesting an element of play, lightness, mockery, or laughter (which is, as we will discuss, the 'sense' of the month). In similar but more negatively charged imagery, the Zohar says that the letter Kuf represents 'imitation' (*Zohar* 2, 148b), which is connected to *Sheker* / falsehood (*Zohar* 1, 2.2, see also *Shabbos*, 104a, regarding the letters of the word *Sheker*), *Gehenom* / hell (*Zohar* 2, 155a), and 'the other side' (*Zohar* 3, 180b). These are all actually images of the opposite of Kedusha; that which is not sacred, 'special' or original, and on the contrary, something that is false, fake or fabricated.

Kuf imitates or 'mocks' the letter Hei (ה) — the only other letter that has two separate lines in its graphic design, as all other letters are created from a single *Golam* / substance.*

---

* כל אות צריכה להיות גולם אחד... / Every letter needs to be of one substance... besides the letters Hei and Kuf. ...And if the left leg of a Hei or Kuf touch the roof (top horizontal line of the letter), the (entire) Sefer Torah is *Pasul* / void (Tur and Mechaber, *Shulchan Aruch*, Orach Chayim, 36. Rosh, *Sefer Torah*, 12). The *Beis Yosef* (on the Tur) writes that this is the ruling of the Rosh, based on the Gemara in *Shabbos*, 104a (ומאי טעמא כרעיה דקוף תלויה), and this is also the opinion of the Rashba (*Teshuvos haRashba*, and the Ramban and the Ran writing on the Gemara in Shabbos). Yet, the Rivash rules that בדיעבד / after-the-fact if the left leg of the Kuf touches the roof (top line), the Sefer Torah is Kosher, as suggested from *Menachos*, 29b. (*Teshuvos haRivash*, Teshuvah 120). The Tashbetz also rules that בדיעבד it is Kosher (*Teshuvos haTashbetz*, Part 1:50-51). In fact, he brings an interesting story from the Ran: עוד שמעתי כי הרב ר' נסים גרונדי ז"ל שהי' בברצלו"נא והיה רבם של רבותי ז"ל שכתב ס"ת לעצמו והיו רגלי הקו"ף דבוקות לגגם. ואנוידל סופר שהי' ש"ץ במיורק"ה שאל אותו על זה כמדומה לו שהוא פסול ושתק הרב ז"ל ולא ענהו / "I heard that the Ran, when he was in Barcelona (and was the teacher of our teachers), that he himself wrote a Sefer Torah and the left leg of the Kuf was actually touching the roof (of the letter). And the Sofer who was the Sheliach Tzibur in Mallorca once asked the Ran about this, and the Ran just remained silent and did not answer." (Regarding this Sefer Torah, see also, the Rebbe, *Igros Kodesh* 15, p. 189.) This is a very interesting story, as

Indeed, Kuf looks very similar to Hei, the letter through which the world was created (*Menachos*, 29b). As a 'fake' Hei, it is the 'other side' of Hei. The first time the Torah mentions the idea of imitating another person's behavior is in the story of **Kayin (Kuf)** and **Hevel (Hei)** (Bereishis, 4:4). Structurally, Hei and Kuf are dissimilar only in that the left line of Kuf extends below the baseline (ק), while the Hei remains above the baseline (ה). Kuf thus seems to be anchored more deeply into the ground, with a solidifying peg pushed beneath the surface.

Let us now try to understand how Kuf can mean both 'Kedusha' and 'mockery,' the side of truth as well as the 'other side.' And what does it mean, in relation to Adar and Purim, that Kuf is similar to the letter Hei, except that its left leg extends lower, as if anchored within the ground?

Our sages tell us that if someone sees the letter Tes in his dream it is a *Siman Yafah* / beautiful sign (*Baba Kama*, 55a). Although there are many words in Torah that begin with the letter *Tes* (some signifying good and some not), it is still considered to be a good sign because the first time *Tes* appears in the Torah is at the beginning of the word *Tov* / good (Bereishis, 1:4). Similarly, the first time any letter appears as the beginning of a word in the Torah, signifies the underlying spiritual quality of that particular letter (*Toldos Yitzchak* by a Talmid of Rav Yitzchak Chaver, p. 39b. See also *Bnei Yissaschar*, Iyyar, Ma'amar 3).

the Ran himself rules (*Shabbos*, 104a (*Ritvah*), and in his commentary on the *Rif*) that the left leg must not touch the roof, and yet, he himself wrote such a Torah with the left leg of the Kuf touching the roof. Perhaps, there is a difference regarding other people — outside of Spain writing such a Torah (where the Mesorah is not to attach the left line to the roof), and within Spain, where the Mesorah was to write the Kuf with the leg touching the roof.

The first time the letter Kuf appears in the Torah as a first letter of a word is in the name *Kayin* / Cain (Bereishis, 4:1). Kayin is an inverted reflection of his brother, *Hevel* / Abel. *Hevel* begins with the letter Hei. Kuf is connected to Kayin and Hei to Hevel, on deeper levels as well (*Sha'ar haPesukim*, Bereishis, "Vayehi Mikeitz").

These archetypal brothers, the first brothers to be mentioned in the Torah, are photo-negatives of each other. For example, Kayin is a farmer, a person rooted in the land; Hevel is a shepherd, a detached and nomadic person. The word *Kayin* alludes to *Kinyan* / acquisition or establishment — a practical, earthy or settled quality. The word *Hevel* means breath, wind, or emptiness — a light and ethereal quality (Rav Avraham Abulafia, *Sisrei Torah*, Orach Chayim, p. 24). For this reason Kayin worked the land, whereas Hevel was a shepherd, roaming the countryside like the wind, like air.

Kayin and Hevel were not just children of Adam and Chava, they are the primary types of souls. All souls are rooted within the great *Adam Kadmon* / primordial human including and embodying both Adam and Chavah as a singular whole being. From Adam Kadmon, souls flow downward through the prism of Kayin or Hevel. Some souls become rooted within either one or the other energy pattern. There are people whose soul is from the *Shoresh* / root of Kayin and those whose Shoresh is in Hevel.

People who are rooted within Kayin are physically stronger, more physical and tactile than people who are rooted in Hevel. Kayin souls are earthier and more grounded, like farmers. They may fear fluidity and even bodies of water, whereas people rooted in Hevel are more ethereal, cerebral, subtle and spiritual. Hevel souls can be artistic people, and they are usually comfortable with or enjoy water (*Sha'ar haGilgulim*, Hakdamah, 36, 38). Incidentally, people who are sourced in Kayin need to be more scrupulous with their actions, being people of action, whereas people from Hevel need to be very careful with the words they use, as their words have a greater effect on others.

Kuf's leg extending below the baseline represents the deeper rootedness and earthliness of Kayin souls. The ethereal, intangible breath sound of Hei corresponds to the personality of Hevel souls.

As mentioned, Kuf is also *Kof* / monkey, suggesting images of mockery, play, lightness and laughter (which is the 'sense' of the month). The positive, productive element of laughter associated with Adar is connected with a quality of Kayin. On the surface laughter may look like the kind of lightheaded, air-like, and almost frivolous characteristic one would more readily expect from an 'ungrounded' Hevel. However, there is a laughter of Hevel and there is a laughter of Kayin. It is true that when our laughter is 'of Hevel,' it is empty, detached, not rooted in the sacredness of life, and thus not transformative, rather it leads ultimately to cynicism and depression. When our laughter is 'of Kayin,' on the other hand, it comes from deep within a rooted, grounded state. This laughter can release us from conventional form, helping us break free from our fixed definitions of reality, our rigid identities and rote patterns of mindless living. Kayin's is a laughter of paradox — simultaneously rooted and free, expressing both certainty and doubt, both 'Kedushah' and 'Kof,' monkeying around.

The negative, flip side of Kayin is self-centered *Ga'avah* / arrogance: 'I am the master of my life — I, I, I...'* People who are self-possessed are always jealous of others, and indeed in the narrative we find Kayin extremely jealous of Hevel.

In counter-balance to the arrogance of Kayin, the positive aspect of Hevel is making light of all things brutish, physical and mundane. Engaging in this 'mockery of the mundane' can get a person unstuck and expand their perception of what is possible. However, there is a negative side to this as well, if not monitored consciously. When one identifies strongly with spirituality, intellectualism, and the ethereal or artistic aspects of life, one may come to sense the ultimate emptiness and shallowness of the 'mundane world,' too much of this 'medicine' can lead one to a hopeless state of *Yei'ush* / 'giving up' on the world (*Sheim miShemuel*, Korach).

An exaggerated sense of spirituality can even lead to a cynical resignation of one's drive to live. The Torah hints at this when it reveals that Hevel was an 'imitator': "And Hevel *also* brought from the firstborn of his sheep" (Bereishis, 4:4). When Hevel saw his brother had brought an offering, גם־הוא / "also he" brought one. This 'mimicry' shows that he had lost his creativity, authenticity, and zest

---

* Hevel is also connected to *Ta'avah* / desire (Maharal, *Derech Chayim*, Avos, 4:21). Ga'avah and Ta'avah are the two dominant types of Yetzer haRa, as the Gra explains. The archetypes of the 'other side' of Kedusha are Yishmael and Eisav. Yishmael, the son of Avraham, is Ta'avah; Eisav, the son of Yitzchak, is Ga'avah. There are three grand sins in the Torah: idol worship, murder and adultery. Idol worship is a denial of the Oneness of Hashem. Murder is connected to Ga'avah and aggressively protecting one's space, a negative expression of the Gevurah of Yitzchak. This is Eisav. Adultery, is connected to Ta'avah, the over-expansion of self into other people's space, a negative offshoot of Chesed, Avraham.

for life, he was just copying others.

In a sense, he was killed because he had already 'died' within; he had given up his unique claim and perspective on the world and on himself. (The Arizal teaches that Hevel sinned in the *Mochin* / mind of Ima (the higher 'Mother,' Binah), which is connected to the Name Ehe'yeh (*Sefer HaLikutim*, Shoftim, 19). Perhaps, since the name *Ehe'yeh* / "I Am Now, and Will Be in the Future" is connected to the world of 'becoming,' sinning against this Name means becoming stuck in Yei'ush, and 'giving up' on one's powers of original creativity or passion.)

Such cynicism, in which nothing is considered important or sacred, 'dedicated' or special, is the root of negative, empty laughter. Much contemporary humor is based within this mindset, and it thus leads to nihilistic malaise and self-defeating depression.

'Kayin laughter' is the more rooted laughter we are aspiring for, especially in Adar; a healthy, holy laughter of Kedusha. Like the letter Kuf, it is grounded, stabilized, contextualized laughter. Thus, as an allusion, the letters of the word שחוק / laughter spell the phrase חוש-ק / a sense of *Kuf*, a sense of correct, rooted, balanced, holy laughter.

Clearly, 'rooted laughter' is not a laughter of cynical mockery or meaningless silliness in which nothing is sacred. Rooted laughter thus strikes a balance between the groundedness of Kayin, and the ethereal, wind-like quality of Hevel. We are anchored, yet not so stuck in our narrative that everything is about 'I, I, I.' This is the deeper work of Adar: the paradoxical fusion of laughter, humor and drinking, with grounded Kedusha, dedication, meaning and discernment.

HIDING REVEALS MORE DEEPLY

Here are two additional points about the letter Kuf and Adar that will be more fully understood later on. On a personal level, Kuf represents a *Kof* / monkey, and the corresponding qualities of trickery, playfulness and hiding. On the 'playful' day of Purim, it was once customary to light a bonfire inside a pit, and children would amuse themselves by leaping over the bonfire (Rashi, *Sanhedrin*, 64b). Today, this playfulness is expressed in the custom of dressing up in costumes, as mentioned by the Ramah in *Shulchan Aruch*. Obscuring your identity or playfully imitating others represents hiding your superficial identity with the intention of revealing your true self. Paradoxically, the veiling of one layer of self allows for the unveiling of a deeper layer that lies beyond appearances and externality. When the conditions are right, to conceal is to reveal.

Additionally, Kuf represents earthly kingship, whereas Hei represents *Malchus* / Divine Kingship. It may seem that the earthly plane is ruled by randomness, chaos, mockery, and the obscuration of Hashem's Malchus. However, Purim teaches us that despite these appearances, Hashem actually reveals Divine Malchus at all times. Purim shows us a way to see the miraculous within nature and mundane history, to see that everything in this world imitates and mimics what is present and occuring in the World Above. Ultimately, Purim demonstrates that the hiding of Hashem's Infinite Light, and the concealing of miracles and prophecy, actually allows for an even deeper revelation — a revelation (*Kiviyachol* / so to speak) of the *Etzem* / Essence of Hashem, beyond His attributes.

NAME OF THE MONTH

ORDS AND NAMES ARE VERY POWERFUL (*Yumah*, 83b. *Tanchuma*, Hazinu. *Berachos*, 7b), as their letters and letter-combinations represent and shape the attributes of that which is named (*Tanya*, Sha'ar haYichud ve-haEmunah, 1). Our personal names, for instance, unlock and reveal hidden potentials present within our own spiritual makeup. Similarly, names of places and periods of time provide subtle hints as to their deep purpose or poetic significance. Additionally, changing your name is akin to a kind of rebirth; some might even say that a change of name initiates a change of Mazal (Rashi, *Bereishis*, 15:5. *Rosh Hashanah*, 16b. *Yerushalmi, Shabbos*, 6:39. Ramah, *Yoreh Deah*, 335:10).

Each of the twelve months of the year has a distinct name with layers of meaning. According to our Sages, the current names we have for the months were imported to our tradition upon our return to Israel from the Babylonian Exile. (They can in fact be traced to ancient Babylonian or Akkadian names. See *Yerushalmi, Rosh Hashanah*, 1:2. *Medrash Rabbah*, Bereishis, 48:9. Tosefos, *Rosh Hashanah* 7a. Even Ezra, *Chezkuni*, Shemos, 12:2.) In the times before the Babylonian Exile, the months were mostly known by their number in the sequence of the year. For example, the month of Av was called, "the Fifth Month," and Cheshvan was known as "the Eighth Month."

As mentioned in the *Megilah* / Scroll of Esther (Megilas Esther, 3:7), Adar is one of the months' names appearing in the post-Babylonian Exile writings of Tanach — along with Nisan (Ibid, 8:9) and Teves (Ibid, 2:16. Elul and Kislev are mentioned in *Nechemiya*, 6:5 and 1:1). While the origin of the name Adar may be an Akkadian root, as in *Adaru*, which means *cutting grain*, in Hebrew the name *Adar* comes from the word *Adir* meaning *strong*, solid, firm, noble or certain, as in the verse, *Adir baMarom Hashem* / "Mighty on high is the Creator" (Tehillim, 93:4). Perhaps in ancient Akkadian culture 'cutting grain' would have been considered an act of strength and power.

Chazal / our sages have a custom of teasing out Hebrew meanings from words of other languages (Rav Yaakov Emden, *Lechem Nikudim*, Avos, 2:14). Even though the names of the months are Babylonian or Akkadian in origin, our sages interpreted and explained these names according to similar Hebrew words. For example, the name Nisan alludes to the *Nisim* / miracles which were revealed during that month (*Pesiktah Zutresah*, Bo, 12:2. *Medrash Lekach Tov*, Shemos 12:2).

In the words of Rashi (*Berachos*, 56a), שע"י נסים נקרא ניסן / "Nisan is called Nisan because of the miracles."

Adar / *Adir*, our sages say, has בריא מזליה / *Bari Mazal* / strong Mazal, meaning that it can bring good fortune. Therefore, if you have litigation, you should arrange for it to occur in the month of Adar (*Ta'anis*, 29b. *Aruch HaShulchan*, Orach Chayim, 686:6). Elsewhere, Chazal tell us, "He who desires his property to be preserved should plant therein an Adar (read as *Eder*) tree" (*Beitzah*, 15b. Rabbeinu Chananel writes that this means giving charity). Planting and taking root are generally connected to the entire month of Adar, as the letter of the month, Kuf, is associated with Kayin, rootedness, the archetypal farmer. It even appears that there is special value in planting on Purim itself (*Megilah*, 5a). "Just as when the month of Av enters we decrease in joy (as it is the time of the destruction of the first *and* the second Beis haMikdash), so when Adar enters we increase in joy" (*Ta'anis*, 29a). From the phrasing of "just as... so," it is clear that Adar is the antidote to Av. In Av we decrease in joy because it is a time of cosmic, national, and personal destruction. In Adar we rejoice because it is a time to 'build' and plant, especially "plantings of joy."

From one perspective, Adar is connected with a quality of strength and rootedness, and yet, from another perspective it is a month of the seemingly opposite quality: laughter, drinking and playfulness. However, as mentioned earlier, Adar is a month when lightness and fluidity are paradoxically rooted, strong, and solid. This paradox reflects a deeper reality that tolerates and maintains the coexistence of opposites: the *Etzem* / essence of Creator and creation. This idea will be further developed later on.

A LEAP YEAR WITH TWO ADARS

Before going further, it should be mentioned that during a leap year, which occurs about every third year, there are two consecutive months of Adar.

As explained, our calendar follows both the cycles of the moon as well as the seasons of the sun. That is, our months follow the lunar cycle, while our years follow the fixed solar cycle. The challenge of the calendar is therefore to align the lunar and solar cycles, as a lunar year consists of approximately 354 days, whereas the solar cycle is about 365 days. This roughly eleven day difference must be addressed, for the Yomim Tovim of the year must be on specific days of the month, and also aligned with particular moments in the seasons and agricultural cycles. For example, Pesach falls on the 15th day of the month, the full moon of Nisan, but the Torah directs us to observe it in the beginning of the spring. Without an adjustment for the eleven day discrepancy, within three years the full moon would migrate ahead more than 30 days in the solar cycle. Within nine years, the full moon of Nisan would occur in the winter season. Torah says that Pesach is called the *Chag haAviv* / Spring Festival, thus it is imperative to ensure that the 'lunar day' of the 15th of Nisan remains within the 'solar season' of spring. To accomplish this, an extra month is occasionally added at the end of the monthly cycle — seven times in a 19-year cycle, to be exact. Adar is defined as the last, 12th month of the lunar year, so another Adar is added after it to make up the time.

Parenthetically, the reason why the added month is Adar and not any other month is because Tanach calls many months by a number. For example, Nisan is called *the First Month*, Av is *the fifth month*, and in the Megilah, Adar is called *the twelfth month*. As such, if there would be an added month of Nisan for example, then Av would be counted as the sixth month instead of the fifth, and Adar as the thirteenth month, not the twelfth. The only month that could be added without tampering with or confusing the numbers of the other months is the final month of the year, Adar (*Tosefos haRosh*, Sanhedrin, 12b).

Speaking of the two months of Adar in a 'leap year,' the Mishnah says, "There is no difference between the first Adar and the second Adar except the reading of the Megilah and the giving of gifts to the poor" (*Megilah*, 1:4). In other words, Purim is to be celebrated in the second month of Adar, the one closer to the month of Nisan. However, there are elements of the joy of Purim present within the first Adar, "When Adar enters we increase in joy." (*Ta'anis*, 29a. From Rashi, ימי ניסים היו לישראל, פורים ופסח / "days of miracles for Jews, Purim and Peach," it appears that this principle only applies to the second Adar, not the first, as the first is distant from Pesach, see also, Shu't *Chasam Sofer*, Siman 163.) Thus, we are forbidden to fast on the 14th and 15th days of both months, and the 14th to 15th of the first Adar is called *Purim Katan* / Small Purim and the 16th of the first Adar is called Shushan Purim Katan (Rambam, *Hilchos Megilah v'Chanukah* 2:13. S'mak, Esai, 148). In fact, we should perhaps even make a festive meal on Purim Katan (S'mak, ibid. Ramah quotes two opinions, *Orach Chayim*, 697). Furthermore, some opinions suggest that we might need to give *Mishloach Manos* / gifted portions of food to friends on Purim Katan (*Kesav Sofer*, Torah, Tetzaveh), although this is not a common custom. (Although the Ran on the Mishnah writes clearly that we do not need to send Mishloach Manos on Purim Katan, as Mishloach Manos is like "gifts to the poor" and just as we are exempt to give gifts to the poor on Purim Katan, we are also exempt from Mish-loach Manos. Perhaps, the Kesav Sofer holds that Mishloach Manos is to increase joy and friendship, and thus if joy is applicable on Purim Katan so is Mishloach Manos, whereas the Ran would hold that Mishloach Manos is part of ensuring that even the poor have food to feast on Purim, and if there is no obligation of gifts to the poor, thus no obligation for Mishloach Manos).

From the simple words of the Mishnah, "There is no difference between the first Adar and the second Adar except the reading of the Megilah and the giving of gifts to the poor," it is clear that with regards to everything else besides reading the Megilah and giving gifts, the two Adars are the same and we should therefore increase in joy even during Adar One as well (See Shu't, *Sheivet haLevi*, Vol. 10, 105. This is especially true according to the *Yerushalmi* whose position is that the story of Purim occurred in the first Adar. *Yerushalmi, Megilah,* 1:5, *Korban haEida,* ad loc. Although, see *Shu't Chasam Sofer,* Siman 163). In fact, we need to in-crease in joy the moment the first day of Rosh Chodesh Adar One begins. Regarding despair, all Rebbes agree — it is never too late. Regarding joy, we can say with confidence — *it is never too soon!*

However, Adar Two is the 'main' month of Adar. For example, when someone born on the 10th of Adar in a regular year (i.e. with only one Adar) celebrates his birthday and Bar Mitzvah in a leap year, he will celebrate it in the second Adar.* In a sense, during the

---

* Regarding a Bar Mitzvah celebration in the second Adar, see Ramah, *Orach Chayim,* 55:10. *Teshuvas Mahari Mintz,* Siman 9. The sages (*Megilah,* 6b) ask, when is Purim in a leap year: in the first Adar or in the second Adar? What is the Halacha, and which is more preferable? Do we observe the principle of אין מעבירין על המצות / we do not forgo a Mitzvah, and thus celebrate Purim in the first Adar? Or do we follow the principle of מסמך גאולה לגאולה / we juxtapose one redemption (Purim) with another redemption (Pesach), and thus celebrate Purim in Adar Two? There is an additional debate: which Adar is the 'regular'

first Adar we are 'warming up' for the second Adar, the full manifestation of holy joy. The second Adar also becomes the last month
of the year, proximal to the month of Nisan, with which it shares
a special relationship: ימי ניסים היו לישראל, פורים ופסח / Purim and Pesach were days of miracles for Klal Israel. Both being months of
miraculous redemptions, the two belong together (although, there is
also an opinion that we celebrate Purim in the first Adar, which is next to the
month of Shevat, following the natural progression of the year. *Megilah*, ibid).

Adar and which one is the added one? For example, if someone is dating a
document during the month of Adar One, does he write "Adar One," or simply
"Adar"? In Adar Two, does he write "Adar Two" or simply "Adar"? Rabbi Meir
holds that in Adar One, a person writes "Adar One," and in Adar Two he writes
simply "Adar," as the *Stam* / regular Adar is Adar Two. Rabbi Yehuda says the
reverse: in Adar One, he writes simply "Adar," and in Adar Two he writes "Adar
Two" (*Nedarim*, 63a). The Mishnah (*ibid*) states regarding vows, that if someone
takes a vow until the beginning of Adar in a leap year, this means until Adar
One. This follows the opinion of Rabbi Yehuda, and such is the Halacha, writes
the Rosh (ibid), and the *Shulchan Aruch* rules the same (*Yoreh Deah*, 220:8). In
general, when there is an argument between Rabbi Meir and Rabbi Yehudah
the Halacha follows Rabbi Yehudah (*Eiruvin*, 46b). Regarding documents,
the Tur (Orach Chayim, 427) and Ramah (ibid) rule that in Adar One, we date a
document simply "Adar" and in Adar Two, we date the document "Adar Two."
The Rosh, as well, seems to argue that the real twelfth month is Adar One,
and Adar Two is the added month (See *Tosefos HaRosh*, Sanhedrin, 12b). The Ramban
seems to rule like Rabbi Meir, with regards to vows, and Adar Two is therefore the regular Adar (*Hilchos Nedarim*, 10:6). This opinion is also brought down
in *Yoreh Deah* (ibid. See also: Shu't, *Sheilas Ya'avetz*, 1:117) regarding the 7th of Adar
and Yahrtzeits in general. It could also be argued that the opinions which hold
that Yahrtzeits are commemorated in the first Adar (Ramah, *Shulchan Aruch*, Orach
Chayim, 568:7, although the *Mechaber* holds that Yarhtzeits are commemorated in the second
Adar) are not based on the ruling that it is the main Adar. Rather, it may be
because of the issue of a mourner needing to recite Kaddish for eleven months
and not for twelve months on a leap year. Additionally, we do not want to make
distinctions between the Yahrtzeit of the first year (if that was a leap year) and
subsequent normal years.

When Purim is celebrated in the second Adar during a leap year, we are to increase in joy throughout the entire first month of Adar until we reach Purim, and even beyond, to the end of the second month. Thus, we rejoice for 60 days (the 30 days of the first Adar include the 29 days of the month proper, plus the first day of "Rosh Chodesh Adar One," which is actually the 30th day of the prior month of Shevat).

The (Lubavitcher) Rebbe זצוק"ל / may the remembrance of a holy Tzadik bring blessing, would declare during leap years that these 60 days allude to *Bitul* / nullification, and thus complete transformation from one status to another. This idea comes from the Halachah regarding a piece of non-Kosher food which has unintentionally fallen into a pot of Kosher food. In most cases, if the non-Kosher food is less than 1/60th of the volume of the Kosher food, and if that non-Kosher food becomes completely assimilated and lost within the Kosher food, then that non-Kosher food has become *Bitul* / nullified and is now considered completely Kosher. A Jewish person can therefore recite a *Berachah* / blessing and eat any morsel of food from that pot. This is similar to the power of 60 days of holy joy. If some 'non-Kosher' *Atzvus* / depression, dejection, or *S'feikus* / paralyzing doubt 'falls' into our experience during these 60 days, it can be nullified and transformed into holy joy and blessing.

BEYOND MAZAL

Sixty days of Adar contain the power to nullify and transform our spiritual status. All of our negativity, sadness and seeming 'bad Mazal' can be converted into positivity, joyful empowerment and good fortune. In fact, these two Adars together have a power that is even beyond the world of Mazal.

To explain, in a leap year, the first month of Adar is considered to have a בריא מזליה / strong Mazal (namely the Mazal of *Dagim* / fish, as will be explained), while the second month of Adar has "no Mazal." It is therefore a month that is above Mazal, stronger than *strong*, bringing fortune that is beyond *good fortune*. This indicates a reality beyond 'goodness' which is the collective 'Mazal' of Klal Yisrael, as will be explained later on.

Having "no Mazal" means there is no possibility of being influenced by negative sources because one is inhabiting a status beyond all external influences (*Chizkuni*, Shemos 17:9. *Rabbeinu Ephrayim,* ad loc. *Yearos Devash,* 1, Derush 3. *Devash L'phi,* 20; 16). Others write the opposite, that the second Adar has the strong Mazal (of Dagim) and the first Adar has "no Mazal" (*Levush*, Orach Chayim, 685). If so, the first Adar is beyond Mazal. Either way, the point is that during these 60 days of Adar there are tremendous positive energies available, both 'strong Mazal' and 'beyond Mazal.' When a person is tapping into these energies, he or she can abolish their negative doubt, crippling uncertainty or melancholy, and attain a genuine status of true joy.

ADAR IS AN ACRONYM FOR "REISHA D'LO IS'YADA"

As explained, *Adar* means *Adir* / strong. It also can be derived from the Hebrew root words *Dar* / to dwell (in space), or *Dor* / generation (in time). Each of these interpretive etymologies suggest powerful permanence and a sense of rootedness and continuity. However, Adar also paradoxically communicates a sense of transience and fluidity. The word *Adar* is connected to the (Aramaic / Talmudic) word *Idra* (אידרה) / fish bone (*Shabbos*, 67b), and as will be explained further on, the astrological sign of the month is fish, which also represent fluidity and easy frictionless movement.

As this month includes the opposite qualities of rooted strength and fluid transience, openness and lightness, it is clear that Adar is connected to a reality that is beyond both. Indeed, this reality is even beyond definition and knowability.

This is represented by the fact that *Adar* is an acronym for ***Reisha D'lo Is'yada*** / 'the Unknowable Head' or 'the head that does not know,' usually called by its acronym, *Radla*. This refers to the deepest level within the Divine Self, so to speak — the highest of the three levels within *Keser*, the metaphorical crown that sits above Hashem's Head. Although inexpressible, for our purposes, Radla can be thought of as *Divine doubt*, a place where all is possible, for nothing is yet defined.

'Below' Radla there is a level called *Galgalta* / skull, which is the meta-source of all defined masculine qualities. Below that, in turn, there is *Mochin Stima* / hidden 'brains' or mind, which is the meta-source of all defined feminine qualities. The level of Radla is so transcendent, it cannot be known by any living being or angel, nor even by itself, so-to-speak. In Radla it is as if the Everpresence is hiding from Itself.*

---

* There is a phrase found in Chassidus, quoted in the name of the Arizal: פנימיות עתיק הוא פנימיות אבא / the inner essence of Chochmah is the inner essence of Atik, the level of Keser (See *Kuntres Limud haChassidus*, p. 6, the Haga'ah of the Rebbe, for the source of this 'idea' in the writings of the Arizal). Rav

This is the paradox of paradoxes, the ultimate reality, *Etzem /* Essence.

Here is a metaphorical image to help us resonate with Radla: the human body has divergent parts, a right side and a left side. The right side represents *Chesed /* giving and outward movement in general. The left side embodies the quality of *Gevurah /* restrictive strength and inwardness. The head, by nature of its being centered above the body, transcends, includes and unifies all of the body and its qualities. The 'crown' rests above the head, transcending and unifying even the different regions of the brain and skull, as well as their corresponding levels of consciousness. Keser thus represents a dynamic that transcends and includes all dimensions; it is the all-unifying meta-level that embraces fundamental paradoxes, maintaining the harmonious functioning of opposites, including all dimensions of reality. Because Keser is beyond all forms and definitions, it can contain impossibilities and paradoxes without needing to resolve them. Keser is the root and source of all possibilities.

Keser is simply not knowable, because to be a knower means you are not that which is being known. Knowing implies a subtle separation between the knower and the known, and Keser contains everything, including you, the knower, as well as the known. Keser is the knower, the known and the knowing itself all in one indivisible, simple unity. Therefore, Keser does not know itself, as it were,

Chayim Vital writes concerning what this means, and why it is this way, ולא ידעתי הטעם / "I do not know the reason." Regarding these words, לא ידעתי הטעם, the Alter Rebbe teaches: it is not that he does not know the reason, rather, it is rooted in Atik, which is a place beyond reason, that of *not knowing* (*Pelach haRimon*, Bereishis, Toldos, p. 156. Tzemach Tzedek, *Ohr Torah*, Bamidbar 2, p. 699).

because even self-knowing or self-awareness would suggest a measure of inner separation, the Self somehow removing itself from itself to look back upon itself. However, on the deepest level, the Self *is* itself. And in fact, within Keser all 'parts,' all *Kochos* / potentials, all modes of knowing, senses and points of view are seamlessly unified within itself.

There is no 'this or that' in Keser, rather only 'this *and* that' even when it seems to contradict our rational way of thinking. For example, there is no up *versus* down or past *versus* future. Rather, all potentials are simultaneous; up *and* down, past *and* future, all swirling inseparably within a dynamic state of infinite oneness.

Because in the realm of Keser nothing is yet defined, and everything is a possibility, meaning that the impossible is always possible, Haman sought to draw power from Keser in order to accomplish an impossible task: to uproot and annihilate the Jewish people, Chas v'Shalom. Our sages (*Chulin*, 139b) ask, המן מן התורה מנין? המן העץ / "From where in the Torah can one find an allusion to Haman? From the verse (following Adam eating from the Tree of Knowledge (of opposites), when Hashem asks Adam): '(Have you eaten) *HaMin haEitz* / from the Tree?'" (Bereishis, 3:11). The word *HaMiN* has a similar sound and the same spelling as *Haman*.

In this way, Haman's name means, "Have you...?" His name is a question, suggesting an uncertainty, a doubt, something undefined. The question may even imply a wish that it not be answered and defined. On this level, it is as if the Creator, the Knower Itself, does not know. Similarly, Haman attempts to instill doubt and cause us to live in a state of perpetual questioning and second-guessing ourselves. If he can ensnare us in a place of crippling doubt, he hopes to cool down our longing or drive for deeper answers, which is driven by a certainty that there are in fact such deeper answers worth striving for.

When Haman wished to dedicate a date in the calendar to the annihilation of Klal Yisrael, he cast a lot (a Pur) and let the dice choose. "In the first month... a Pur (which means lot), was cast before Haman concerning every day and every month (until it fell on) the twelfth month, that is, the month of Adar" (Megilas Esther, 3:7). He chose to employ a tool of randomness and unpredictability — the power of Keser, the possibility of all possibilities — to establish his plan, as the lottery could fall on any date within any month.

Using a lottery is as if to say, 'I surrender my free choice in thinking that I know what is the best possible outcome, and enter into a place of uncertainty and doubt, in order to let the random (although nothing is actually random) movement of the dice dictate an outcome; I am hereby asking for 'chance' to take over.'

The Hebrew word for lot is *Goral*, which has a numerical value of 239 (Gimel/3, Vav/6, Reish/200, Lamed/30). With the *Kollel* / the addition of 1 for the word itself, the number comes to 240. This is the same value as the word *Safek* / doubt, uncertainty. A Goral is a *Makom haSafek* / a place and realm of doubt. Haman (whether consciously or subconsciously) wished to connect to this Divine space of 'doubt' and 'unknown' in order to activate the Kelipah or 'dark side' of Keser, and from there draw down havoc and destruction.

THE SOURCE OF BECHIRAH / FREE CHOICE

We all have *Bechirah* / free choice to manifest good or perpetu-ate evil: רשות לכל אדם נתונה / "Permission is given to each person." If he desires to bend himself toward the good path and be a Tzadik it is within the power of his hand to reach out for it, and if he desires to bend himself to a bad path and be a Rasha it is within the power of his hand to reach out for it (Rambam, *Hilchos Teshuvah*, 5:1).

The question is, as Hashem is the sole Creator, Sustainer and Giver of Life, and also the Source of Goodness, what is the me-ta-root of evil and negative actions? From where does a person who chooses to turn away from the Source of Life and become a Rasha draw any *Chayus* / life and vitality? Surely it is not from the Source of Life. We are not discussing the question of Hashem's knowing and providence versus our free choice; rather it is a question of the source of our Bechirah.

A complex issue, this actually deserves more than a few passing words, but the simple answer is that the root of evil is in the Divine act of *Tzimtzum* / contraction and (apparent) Self-withdrawal or 'Self-separation' of Hashem in the process of Creation. Hashem creates life, and gently guides history forward, yet, Hashem does not overwhelm creation, He allows it independence; Hashem stands back, so-to-speak, and allows creatures to 'doubt' the fact that they are actually subsumed in Oneness. This is the reason why we can, on a practical level, have free-choice.

In the language of the Arizal (and the Ramchal), the *Sod* / secret of Bechirah is linked to the idea of *Durmita of ZA* / the supernal slumber of the Light of Hashem that normally flows into Creation, and to the process of *Nesirah* / separation. In other words, there is a Self-concealment, a vacuum, a *Chalal* / empty space and an apparent absence of Hashem's 'Infinite' expression — and this allows human beings to experience choice. Yet, this paradigm merely answers the *possibility* of choosing evil. It does not answer regarding from where we could derive the life-force and power to actually choose to do evil. What gives us the Chayus to choose? An 'absence' is, of course, not a source of Chayus.

Once again, the question is this, what aspect of HaKadosh Baruch Hu's interaction and sustenance, what dimension of Hashem's giving of Chayus to this world, empowers humans to freely choose? What allows a person, if he or she so wills, to choose and cause their own destruction or the destruction of others? Everything is created, delineated, appropriated and sustained by *HaRachaman* / the Compassionate One, the All-Beneficial Light of Hashem.

Hashem's Light is revealed in two manners. There is a light that transcends and *surrounds all worlds*, the *Ohr haSovev Kol Almim*, which is like a *Keser* / crown in relation to the world below. And at the same time there is also a light that *fills all worlds*, the *Ohr Memaleh Kol Almin*, an immanent all-pervasive Ko'ach, a light that fills the universe, permeating all phenomena. The world of law and order, of direct cause and effect, is a world dominated by the Divine expression of Ohr Memaleh, whereas in the world of Sovev everything exists as a oneness and pure potential. The power and process of Creation is initiated and sustained by Sovev, whereas the particular forms of creation are articulated and sustained by Memaleh.

Related to this there is a Chassidic Yiddish saying, "There, where refinement cannot grasp, איז גראבקייט אויך נישט קיין סתירה / "coarseness is also not a contradiction." In the world of Memaleh, of cause and effect, righteousness breeds goodness and negativity generates destruction. There is strict law and order here; like seeks like, so to speak. Only in the world of Keser or Sovev is coarseness "not a contradiction," and everything receives Chayus equally. שממית בידים תתפש והיא בהיכלי מלך / "Spiders — they are easy to catch, but they are found even in kings' palaces" (Mishlei, 30:28). This symbolically means that because it is the King's Palace, the infinitely open space of Keser, even spiders (representing the powers of Kelipah) have a place there and receive Chayus. Anywhere else less transcendent leaves no room for spiders, and seeks to drive them off.

Haman, the archetype of evil, understood (on some level) that to truly go through with his diabolical scheme not only did he need physical prowess to bribe the king in order to wipe out, G-d forbid, Klal Yisrael, but he needed meta-physical prowess as well. He intuited that he needed to evoke and harness the power of Keser, beyond distinctions, beyond form, and tap into a Divine space of pure potential where, אם־חטאת מה־תפעל־בו ורבו פשעיך מה־תעשה־לו אם־ צדקת מה־תתן־לו או מה־מידך יקח / "If you sin, what do you do to Him? If your transgressions are many, how do you affect Him? If you are righteous, what do you give Him; what does He receive from your hand?" (Iyov, 35:6-7).

Throwing a lottery is reaching for Sovev, where merit or the opposite does not play a role in the outcome. In Sovev every outcome is equally possible. In a lottery all pieces are the same, otherwise why use a lottery and not make a conscious decision? The mechanism of a lottery transcends predictability and rationality, thereby breaking down all equations. We cannot suppose that one person is more fit or meritorious to win the lottery than any other.

Not only does Haman throw a lottery, which is surrendering his volition and choice, but the way the Megilah phrases the throwing of this lottery is very peculiar, and indicative of a total surrendering of involvement. The Megilah says "They cast a Pur, that is, a lot" (Megilas Esther, 3:7). It does not say that 'Haman *chose* to cast a Pur and he threw a lot,' rather, a mysterious "they" cast a Pur for Haman. This wording stresses the point that Haman surrendered and transcended his power of choice, and allowed it to simply happen. It is as if he even had others throw the lot for him — a 'concealment within a concealment' of his ability to choose. By using a random throw of dice to determine his day of destruction, Haman was hoping to tap into the place of Keser, a place that is 'above good and evil' and above volition and causality; and from that place draw down evil upon a people who 'deserved' good.

HAMAN REACHING FOR 50/ TRANSCENDENCE

In a place 'beyond good and evil' where "if you sin, what do you do to Him," there can paradoxically be an eclipse of goodness. The power unleashed through transcending or fusing opposites can be used to wipe out the lines between life-giving acts and life-destroying acts, and then to inflict vast harm.

Haman wishes to commit arguably the greatest evil, killing innocent men, women and children. Yet when he speaks to the king he deliberately blurs the lines, "If it is *good* for the king, he should write to *kill...*" and the king agrees, "Do what is *good* in your eyes" (Megilas Esther, 3:9-11). The word "good" is used here in the most perverse manner, as if there is something good, or even profitable, in committing mass murder of innocent people.

Fascinatingly, in the first part of the Megilah, the part that speaks of the evil decree to annihilate (*Chalilah* / G-d forbid) Klal Yisrael, the word "good" appears 16 times, but not once does the word *Ra* / bad or evil appear. In the system of Gematria called *Mispar Katan Mispari*, the digits of the number 16 are added together to equal 7. Seven is the number for Creation of our world, the world of good and bad, as in the Six Days of Creation plus their culmination in Shabbos, the Seventh Day.

In his nefarious imagination, Haman wished to hang Mordechai, his archenemy, and so he erected a "tree," a gallows of 50 *Amos* / cubits. This is the number that symbolizes transcendence of the world of seven, beyond good and bad. The fullness of seven is 7 x7 (49), and to take a step beyond 49 is to enter into the realm of 50, a realm beyond Creation. Rav Eliezer of Worms (c.1176-1238), known by the name of the book he authored, *Rokeach*, writes that the letters of the name Haman in numerical value are 95, and with the *Kollel* / addition of 1 for the name itself, *Haman* equals 96. This is the same numerical value of the words *Nun Amah* / fifty cubits (*Sefer Rokeach*, Hilchos Purim).

As part of his diabolical plan Haman takes this 50-Amos plank of wood from the Kodesh haKodashim / Holy of Holies (*Pirkei D'Rebbe Eliezer*, 50. *Medrash Talpiyos*, Achashverosh). This means that Haman is aiming for the highest place of Transcendence, the Divine level of Keser. (The *Yalkut* writes that he gets the plank from the Ark of Noach. *Sefer Rokeach*, Hilchos Purim.)

The name Haman can be broken down into two words, *Ha Mann* / This is manna. The amazing quality of the Mann was that it contained the possibility of all tastes (*Yuma*, 75a), this is because the Mann originates in the 50th level; *Mann* (מן) spells *meNun* / from *Nun* / from 50, and thus it contains all possibilities. Haman desired to tap into the place that contains all possibilities, where nothing is yet defined or distinguished; for it was only from such a place that a decree could be issued which overturned the causal mechanics of Creation below Keser.

According to ur Sages, Haman is similar to the primordial *Nachash* / Snake (*Medrash Rabbah*, Bamidbar, 14:12. *Nachash* begins with the letter Nun. The other letters in *Nachash* spell *Chush* / sense, the snake has a sense, a *Chush*, for 50). The Snake, too, represents the blurring of good and evil. Hashem tells Adam and Eve that the day you eat from the Tree of Knowledge you will die (Bereishis, 3:1), and the snake agues, that if you eat from that tree, "your eyes will open, and you will be G-d-like" — in fact, it will actually be 'good' for you. Haman as well says, "If it is *good* for the king, he should write to *kill*..." in a similar blurring of good and evil.

משרש נחש יצא צפע / "From the source of the snake sprouts an asp" (Yeshayahu, 14:29). The word צפע / asp in numerical value is 240, which is the same value as the word *Safek*. Safek is sourced in the Snake; the Snake functions in a world of uncertainty, a blurring of what is good and what is evil. The Snake wants Adam and Chavah to eat from the Tree of Knowledge and enter into its world of uncertainty, doubt and distortion of moral clarity. In fact, for this reason, many later Chassidic Rebbes (Ishbitz / Radzin) call the Tree of Knowledge אילנא דספיקא / "the Tree of Doubt." Haman embodies crippling doubt, and like a spiritual asp, aspires to harness the Divine source of doubt, the source of the Snake, which is the Tree of Doubt.

And so, to access this place of Transcendence, Haman threw a lottery. When the lottery fell on a date in the month of Adar, Haman was glad because he knew that Adar was the month when Moshe died, and he took this as an omen of death and demise for Klal Yisrael. What Haman did not know, say our Sages, was that Moshe was also born in Adar (*Megilah*, 13b). What does this mean? And how does the birth of Moshe 'undo' the potential for negativity in the Ko'ach of Sovev, as it were?

Haman was indeed able to rise beyond causality and empower himself with Keser (Sovev), where everything is possible. He thus acquired the power to choose and attempt to bring death and annihilation to a righteous people — a people who, according to causality, did not 'deserve' death.

What Haman did not realize was that Sovev is not Hakadosh Baruch Hu, but just an expression of HaKadosh Baruch Hu. Hashem transcends transcendence! There is a finite expression of Hashem's light, the Ohr Memaleh, and there is an infinite, transcendent expression of Hashem, the Ohr of Sovev. But there is also the Manifester of Light Itself, the *Etzem* / Essence, from which the finite and infinite emerge, and in which they converge. Klal Yisrael is rooted (*Kiviyachol* / so-to-speak) in this Etzem of HaKadosh

Baruch Hu. Our existence is therefore rooted in the Essence *beyond transcendence*.

Haman failed to understand that the deepest reality is beyond even the infinite. The Keser of Keser, the highest level of Keser, is beyond transcendence. And there, HaKadosh Baruch Hu always chooses "the spirit of the righteous" (*Medrash Rabbah*, Bereishis, 8:7. *Medrash Rabbah*, Rus, 2:3). Beyond the space of no-choice, where good and evil are equal, Hashem still inherently chooses goodness, righteousness. Haman's ploy was thus existentially preempted by Hashem's inalterable choice of goodness.

The Primal Cause that is free of bias and unaffected by any influence, always chooses life and the goodness/righteousness of Klal Yisrael. This is a choice that is rooted in the Essence of HaKadosh Baruch Hu, so to speak. No actions below can impede this position nor force a different reaction from Above.

This means that we are each chosen for life and for eternity. We are rooted in the Keser of the Keser and in that Essential space we were, and are, chosen. This choosing is not *caused*; our manifest level of righteousness does not impinge on or impact the Infinite One's choice. Rather, HaKadosh Baruch Hu chooses, simply because He 'desires' to choose, in such a way.

When the king asks Haman what should be done to a person who finds favor in the king's eyes, Haman says, "Let royal garb which the king has worn be brought, as well as a horse on which the king has ridden, and on whose head a royal diadem has been set. And let the attire and the horse be put in the charge of one of the king's noble courtiers. And let the man whom the king desires to honor be attired and paraded on the horse through the city square, while they proclaim before him, ככה יעשה לאיש / "Such shall be done for the man whom the king desires to honor!" (Megilas Esther, 6:8-9). The word ככה says the Baal Shem Tov is an acronym, for *Keser Kol HeKesarim* / the Keser of all Kesers, Higher than High, deeper than deep.

There is a realm 'beyond' distinctions, beyond Da'as and *Havdalah* / separation. There is also a Divine space that is beyond being defined as *beyond*, a reality that transcends transcendence. Being beyond distinctions, yet paradoxically choosing distinctions, HaKadosh Baruch Hu chooses "the spirit of the righteous." Why? ככה / just because, as the word means in Modern Hebrew. Hashem chooses the souls of the righteous — ככה — because that is what Hashem wants, *Kiviyachol* / so-to-speak, beyond the reaches of 'reason' or duality.

There is Da'as, the place of Havdalah and distinction, a place of choice and discernment, and then there is a place beyond Da'as, beyond knowing, beyond comprehension and beyond distinction — this is Keser. And then there is a reality beyond all of this, as explained earlier, called *Radla* / Absolute Unknowability in which Infinity does not even know Itself, *Kiviyachol*. This is the Keser of Keser. Here, in utter innocence, the way of righteousness and goodness, life and affirmation of life, are spontaneously chosen. And that is the Essential reality wherein our souls are rooted.

As a microcosmic reflection of Radla, in a glimpse of unknowability, we celebrate Purim. On Purim there is a Mitzvah to drink until we reach a state of *Lo Yada* / not-knowing. Because our not-knowing is rooted in Hashem's own not-knowing (as if), and we are spiritually strengthened during this month, rather than weakened. Moshe, who represents our higher spiritual Da'as, passed away during this month, and thus we too pass beyond knowing. But Moshe was also born, or 'sourced' in this month of Divine not-knowing, so our knowing is intimately connected to our not-knowing.

As mentioned, Adar is an *Adir* / strong and powerful month to plant and be grounded. Paradoxically, our not-knowing does not leave us in nihilistic despair, dis-attachment or disinterest in life, nor are we drawn to death, evil or destruction. Rather the opposite, it leads to an ever-deeper re-acceptance of Torah, greater responsibility, fantastic achievement, and pure joy.

Normally when a person drinks a little too much they enter a place of forgetfulness, and sadly, they 'forget' their inner goodness and make bad choices. On Purim, we drink and tap into the Keser of all Kesarim and 'forget' the bad; we forget Haman and the world of curses, and enter into the world of total goodness, above and beyond reason. On Purim we drink and reveal our deepest sense of compulsion within, beyond the world of strict reason, which is the holy compulsion to serve Hashem and choose goodness always.

The Above reflects the below; as we forget the bad, in Heaven there is also a cosmic forgetfulness of the bad. Purim in this way is akin to the day of atonement, Yom Kippur (*Tikunei Zohar*, Tikun 21). Yet, whereas on Yom Kippur we ask forgiveness, on Purim there is not even any 'bad' to be forgiven.

TRUE FREEDOM IS TO CHOOSE & THE CHOICE IS ALWAYS FOR LIFE & GOODNESS

"I have set before you life and death, the blessing and the curse. You shall choose life" (Devarim, 30:19). This is a very puzzling statement. The *Reisha* / first part of the statement clearly says you have options, you can choose life or death, blessing or curse, and the *Seifa* / last part of the statement says, "You shall choose life." What does this mean? Is the Torah giving a command or a prediction? Either way, the second clause contradicts the first clause and seems to deny us any free choice.

Beyond this question, why does the Torah need to even suggest that we choose life? Would anyone *freely* choose death and curse over life and blessing?

On another level, the whole idea of true free-choice is problematic. In the world of cause and effect, action and reaction, every choice we make is apparently based on a previous choice, an ingrained pattern or an 'innate' tendency. For example, say you have two foods in front of you, one spicy and the other one sweet, and in general both are equally tasty to you. If you choose the spicy one because you are currently 'in the mood' for spicy, then it's not purely a free choice, rather, it is driven by fluctuating feelings, instincts or body chemistry. Some elements in the scenario conspired to *force*, or at least guide you, to choose the spicy food. If you would instead say, "I would rather overcome my current preference for spicy and exercise my free choice to choose sweet," then that too would be an imposed choice, as you rationally assessed that you wished to overcome your tendency, based on prior experience or expected rewards.

Every choice we make is apparently predicated on a previous choice, a belief, or on social, physical, psychological or emotional conditioning; in other words, on nature or nurture. Also, true choice can only exist when the options are exactly equally attractive or beneficial to you, and that is rarely the case. If it were the case, for example, that two identical cups of water were in front of you, both were equally distant from your hand and there was no prior conditioning at play regarding your selection, including left or right placement — if you then chose one cup over the other, it would simply be a random choice, which again is not a true choice.

It follows that the only one who is truly free of conditioning and can make truly free choices is the Creator. Everything and everyone within the domain of Creation is by definition part of a chain of cause and effect. When one effect leads to the next, there is no absolute freedom. The only way we could ever be free from the chain of causality and make authentically free choices is to be at one with the Creator, the Uncaused Cause of All Causes.

Another way of saying this is that free choice can only exist within the realm of absolute objectivity, which can only belong to the Creator. The state of created reality is subjectivity, where perception and behavior are always being affected by other experiences, and every seeming choice is necessarily shaped by a precedent.

Understanding that free choice is rooted in the perfect objectivity of the Creator helps us unpack the Torah's statement which we are examining: "I have set before you life and death, the blessing and the curse. You shall choose life." In essence, the Torah is saying, 'Yes, you have free choice; you can choose a life that is openly connected with the Creator of life, goodness and blessings — and you can choose to *not* choose that, but you can never choose curses and death.'

If you choose not to choose, not to live at one with the Creator and within the Creator's objectivity, then you are functioning like everything else in Creation, encompassed in a world of subjectivity and causality, and thereby living as the 'effect' of life. Basically, you can choose to choose or opt not to choose. But any real, objective choice, by definition, is choosing life and blessings, for that is the eternal 'choice' of the Blessed One, the Life of All.

Any choice 'to choose' is therefore a choice to choose life. Choosing not to choose is living in subjective and mindless reactivity, which by definition leads to curse and death, for it is a life that is not dedicated to perpetuating the Creator's 'desire' to give life and blessing. Since humanity ate from the Tree of Knowledge, subjectivity is always mixed with negativity, as it is existentially severed from the objectivity of the Creator of life and blessings, at least from our persepctive.

The only objective choice is to live in the world of choice. However, once you have chosen 'choice' there are no longer any such 'vertical' choices, only 'lateral' decisions regarding the *content* of the life that you have chosen.

In other words, *Bechirah* / free choice comes from the deepest place within HaKadosh Baruch Hu (as it were), the level of Radla (or Etzem), the Keser of all Kesarim. This is a place of total freedom, unhindered and unimpeded, uncolored and unbiased, unconditioned and unaffected. When we choose to *choose*, inevitably our choice is to live committed to Torah and Mitzvos, positivity, and life-affirming righteousness and goodness, "And you shall choose… life."

To choose life is the positive side of the not-knowing and freedom associated with Radla. Holy not-knowing thus leads one to be more engaged with life, more knowing, more connected to others and oneself, with ever-renewed excitement and passion for Torah and Mitzvos, charity, goodness and the vital path of righteousness.

"Every day Mordechai would walk in front of the court yard, the house of the women, *laDa'as / to know* how Esther was doing (*Shalom Esther*, 2:11). Says the Komarna (on this Pasuk, *Kesem Ofir*), "to draw down a spark of Da'as from the place of Radla." The Da'as of Kedusha is rooted in the openness of not knowing, knowing you don't know, yet wanting to know.

AMALEK: THE ANTITHESIS OF KLAL YISRAEL

However, not-knowing also contains a negative flip side, which leads to crippling doubt, uncertainty, cynicism, nihilism and cooling down of any passions for growth or anything good. This is the paralyzing negativity of Amalek. Haman was a descendant and embodiment of this archetype of all the 'enemies' of Israel and its mission.

As the People of Israel left Egypt and were journeying to the Promised Land, the ראשית גוים / *Reishis Goyim* / first of the nations (Bamidbar, 24:20) to attack and wage war upon them, was Amalek. Amalek went to war not as an act to protect their own land, nor out of fear of being overwhelmed in their own land (as the Egyptians feared); rather, just to 'cool down' the passion and create doubt in Klal Yisrael regarding the omnipotence of Hashem and in the nature and importance of their mission.

There are two types of enemies: an *Oyev* / enemy and a *Soneh* / foe. The Pasuk says, ויפצו איביך וינסו משנאיך / "May Your enemies (*Oyvecha*) be scattered and may Your foes (*Sanecha*) flee before You" (Bamidbar, 10:35). What is the difference between an Oyev and a Soneh? And why is the blessing that our 'enemies' be scattered and our 'foes' flee?

Rashi tells us that your 'enemies' are those who are massed for battle, whereas 'foes' are those enemies who pursue you. In other words, an enemy sits in its own land and amasses an army for battle, as a result, if it is invaded it can attack. An 'enemy' may feel frightened, whether by a real or assumed threat, and there is some type of justification for their armament and readiness for battle. A 'foe' pursues another; they are aggressive warriors who often simply wish to expand their own territory or destroy someone they despise. They are not protecting their homeland, nor do they specifically feel the threat of being conquered or overwhelmed. A Soneh simply hates for hate's sake, beyond reason.

There are those who have felt (or feel) threatened by a powerful Klal Yisrael; whether Klal Yisrael is perceived as an external threat or as a 'fifth column' or even saboteur from within. This is an *Oyev*. And there were and are others who are simply irritated by the existence of Klal Yisrael, and feel impelled to chase them around the world or annihilate them once and for all, Chas veShalom. This is a *Soneh*.

Some nations practice expulsion, throwing Jews out of their lands. Then there are nations for whom that is not enough, even if they have tried expulsion, they still feel they must hunt them down, may Hashem have mercy on us. This type of Soneh is called "Amalek."

Amalek, as an abstract force that emerges repeatedly throughout history as different cultures of cruelty, sees Klal Yisrael as an existential threat to their *Metziyus* / existence. They live in a purely 'us or them' world.* In fact, Amalek is considered both an Oyev and a Soneh, of the greatest degree, as the Rambam writes, שאסור לשכח איבתו ושנאתו / "for it is forbidden to forget their enmity (Oyev) and hatred (Soneh)" (Rambam, *Hilchos Melachim*, 5:5). Accordingly, Amalek wages war against everything that Hashem and the Torah represent, including there being a purpose in Creation, a historical evolution towards a world of perfect goodness, and the insight that every person is born with a Tzelem Elokim and therefore each individual's dignity should be honored. Amalek cannot stand the existence of hope, charity and righteousness. This is the mortal enemy

---

* The "Seven Nations" that we needed to conquer (spiritually) as we entered Eretz Yisrael represent the seven lower Sefiros, in their negative form (*Likutei Torah*, Arizal, Devarim. In *Agra d'Kalah*, Lech Lecha, the Dinover explains how every nation corresponds to their corresponding Sefirah). The Seven Nations embodied the forces that seem to stand in the way of the purpose and goal of Klal Yisrael. We needed to settle in our Holy Land in order to fulfil our spiritual purpose, and these seven nations stood up against both our settling there and our purpose. They are the enemies of the goals of Klal Yisrael. Similarly, the Four Kingdoms that inflicted harm and caused the Four Exiles, the Babylonian, Persian, Greek and Roman Empires, represent spiritual enemies of the spirit (*Nefesh*), body (*Guf*), mind (*Seichel*), and the 'everything' (*HaKol*) of Klal Yisrael. Yet, Amalek is unique among all of these, as the sworn archenemy of the very *Metziyus* / existence of Klal Yisrael.

and foe not only of Klal Yisrael, but by extension of all humanity and all living beings.

Amalek does battle not simply with the existence of Klal Yisrael, but more deeply, with the existence of Hashem, as it were, and thus, "Hashem's Name is not complete until Amalek is eradicated completely." The Rambam writes in *Igeres Teiman* / Letter to the Yemenite Jewish Community, who were suffering terrible persecutions, that the enemies of Klal Yisrael really wish to wage war with HaKadosh Baruch Hu but they direct their fight towards Klal Yisrael instead. Amalek in particular wars against everything that Hashem, Hashem's Torah and Klal Yisrael stand for. This archetypal enemy is existentially opposed to all commitment, goodness and righteousness.

AMALEK WISHES TO COOL DOWN SPIRITUAL EXCITEMENT

On the literal level, Amalek wants to annihilate Klal Yisrael, but symbolically Amalek wants to kill off anyone's excitement and passionate commitment to a world of goodness and kindness, *Kedushah* / holiness and *Teharah* / purity. This force wants to distort or destroy any commitment to Torah and Mitzvos, any effort to bring the world towards Moshiach and Redemption. The whole lifestyle of striving for a higher purpose, with a powerful optimism that the world will soon reach its Tikun, is a thorn under the skin of Amalek. The fact that we are not passive in the process of Tikun, rather, actively ensuring it comes as soon as possible, is an unbearable insult to Amalek. Progress, hope, intentionality and love, all sicken them. Thus, Amalek wages war on the whole concept of

Klal Yisrael, the representatives of Hashem's Goodness, and desperately attempts to instill in us dark cynicism, pessimism, sarcasm, negative doubt, a lack of enthusiasm and love, and a general sense of purposelessness.

There are two ways for a 'foe' to fight the truth. The first is to assert an imaginary impostor 'truth.' If one seeming truth can be pitted against another, the result is unpredictable. The other way, Amalek's way, is not to fight truth with an alternative view, rather, to simply cast doubt on the real truth, and thereby cool down any excitement for it.

For example, let's say you feel passionate about giving Tzedakah and Chesed to others, or you have great passion for *Davenen /* prayer and you meditate in your service with fervor and excitement. The force of Amalek comes along and says, 'What you are doing is very important, but don't you think there are other things besides this that you should be doing; wouldn't it be 'better' to spend less time Davening, or less time giving Tzedakah, and to study more Torah? You're so into extending the Amidah prayer, but did you even finish studying the Parsha this week? Who do you think you are?' This is not a direct challenge to what you are doing, rather, it is 'innocently' planting a kernel of doubt, and trying to deflate your enthusiasm in the name of realism, responsibility or even righteousness.

ראשית גוים עמלק / "Amalek was the first of the nations…" (Bamidbar, 24:20). The first letters of these three words spell the word רגע / *Rega /* moment. In conversational Modern Hebrew, the word *Rega* means 'Wait a moment.' Amalek says, 'Wait a minute, cool it, why are you getting so excited and passionate right now? Hold your horses, slow down, get real.'

The historical attack of the people called Amalek, say our sages, is similar to a situation where there is a tub of scalding water which no one dares to enter, until someone comes along and jumps into the tub. Although he is burned in the process, he cools the water for the others, and now others may also jump in (*Medrash Tanchumah*, Ki Tetze, 9). When Klal Yisrael left Egypt and went through the Splitting of the Sea, they completely believed in Hashem and in themselves; they passionately believed that they were worthy to be the conduits of the revelation of Hashem's Presence in the world. They were certain about where they came from, where they needed to go and what they needed to do in this world. They had confidence in who they were and what their mission was. They had a fiery commitment to be ambassadors of Hashem's Light in this world.

Then Amalek came along, physically attacked them and created doubt in their hearts. In terms of our analogy above, Amalek jumped into the hot bath, removing some of the heat from the passions of Klal Yisrael. Intellectually they would still 'know' their higher purpose and conceptually believe in their mission, but their passion, their heart and enthusiasm was to be tampered and cooled. This invasive intervention caused a severing between the (cool) minds and (fiery) hearts of Klal Yisrael.*

---

* The root letters of Amalek are מלק, which are also the root letters of מליקה, a type of offering performed in the Beis haMikdash in which the head of a bird was detached from its body by the nail of the Kohen's thumb. Similarly, Amalek severs the 'head,' the intellect, from the rest of the body, and does this through his hands. When Amalek saw that רפו ידיהם / their 'hands' became weak in the

AMALEK & PARALYZING DOUBT

Amalek is *Makom haSafek* / the place of doubt. This is reflected in the fact that Amalek and Safek both have the same numerical value (240). (The Mishnah says, "The fittest of butchers is a partner of Amalek" *Kidushin* 82a. Rashi comments: ...ספיקי טריפות באות לידו / "Doubts regarding unkosher foods come into his hand..." Thus there is a connection between Amalek and Safek. The *Kelev* / wild dog is also connected to Safek: there is a debate ('doubt') in the Mishnah as to what type of animal a Kelev is — כלב, מין חיה? רבי מאיר אומר, מין בהמה (Mishnah, *Kelayim*, 8:6). Similarly, a Kelev is never satiated (והכלבים עזי-נפש לא ידעו שבעה, Yeshayahu, 56:11), as they are never certain if they ate already or not. Amalek is likened to a *Kelev*, as negative doubt is never satisfied: כך היה לוהט עמלק אחר ישראל ככלב *Tanchuma*, Ki Teitzei, 9. "Amalek is like a Kelev" *Megaleh Amukos*, VaEschanan, 140.)

Moshe tells Yehoshua, "Pick some men for us, and go do battle with Amalek — tomorrow — I will station myself on top of the hill" (Shemos, 17:9). Our sages say, the word "tomorrow" is one of the five words in the Torah on which there is a Safek regarding where the word should be placed (*Yuma*, 52b). In other words, there is a

---

fulfillment of the law and the commandments (*Tanchumah*, Yisro, 3:3), meaning when there was already some level of disconnect between their minds and their actions, Amalek saw the opportunity and attacked. (When one's 'hands' are not connected to Da'as, then the principle is ידיים עסקניות הן / one's hands are busy, and they tend to come into contact with dirt or impure objects. *Shabbos*, 14a. Rashi, ad loc. This weakens them.) As such, Moshe needed to create a Tikun for Klal Yisrael's weakness and wage battle with Amalek through his hands. Thus, והיה כאשר ירים משה ידו וגבר ישראל / "And it was, whenever Moshe held up his **hands**, Israel prevailed" (Shemos, 17:11). Moshe lifted his hands upwards, near his head, the place of Da'as, and beyond, connecting the lower world of action to the heart and head above. When Klal Yisrael were lifted into this state of unity, Amalek could not prevail.

doubt whether the verse should read, 'Pick some men for us, and go do battle with Amalek *tomorrow*. I will station myself on top of the hill,' or, 'Pick some men for us, and go do battle with Amalek. *Tomorrow*, I will station myself on top of the hill.' The whole battle with Amalek is marred in the Makom haSafek. Not only does *Amalek* equal *Safek*, but the battle itself, and what Moshe wants from Yehoshua, is steeped in ambiguity, doubt and uncertainty. (Parenthetically, Moshe needs ידי / his hands to be אמונה / *Emunah* / steadfast, resolute in belief, so he can be a force of ודאי / certainty, to counter the uncertainty of Amalek. Thus the word ידיו / his hand, plus the Aleph of *Emunah*, creates the word ודאי / certain.)

Amalek, the *Reishis Goyim* / 'head' of all the nations, is the head or *Keser* / crown of all the enemies of Klal Yisrael. In this way, Amalek symbolizes and embodies the destructive and negative side of holy 'doubt' and 'not-knowing' of Keser, the shadow of Radla. When this negative force of Amalek attacks us, it attempts to create pessimism in the place of optimism, cynicism in the place of enthusiasm, and sarcasm and indifference in the place of commitment and passion.

Amalek battles truth with relativism. The not-knowing of relativism hinders resolute action. When we cannot muster the moral strength to act when action is needed, we can fall into pessimism, cynicism, sarcasm, passivity and indifference. If everything is relative, then nothing really matters and ultimately life itself does not matter, G-d forbid.

This Kelipah of Amalek sadly resonates deeply with our generation, in these moments before the coming of Moshiach. The challenge to the contemporary committed Jew is not that there are seemingly competing 'truths' with a capital 'T'. The challenge is the relativity of *all* ideas. If everything is relative, then everything is true. If everything is true, ultimately nothing is true, and nothing (no one) appears worthy of deep commitment.

Haman, who embodies the quality of Amalek, is a manifestation of the *Kelipah* / negative side of *Da'as* / knowing, connectivity. (Arizal, *Likutei Torah*: 'Balak (Amalek and Bilam) are Da'as of Kelipah. Da'as that is *Balah* / swallowed up. *Eitz Chayim*, Sha'ar 8:4. Bilam (Balah) draws power from the letters קר, *Megaleh Amukos*, Ki Tisa, Derush 3:3, and *Kar* / cold is the quality of Amalek, as discussed.) On one level, 'Da'as of Kelipah' implies the idea of waging war on Da'as itself, an attack on *knowing* and by extension on the All Knowing One (*Derech Mitzvosecha*, Mitzvas Zechiras uMechiyas Amalek, 1). Amalek argues that there is nothing worth knowing, and ultimately, nothing at all to know. Everything is in the *Bechina* / aspect of *Safek* / doubt; everything is relative, and in itself devoid of any meaning.

This is one level of the Kelipah of Da'as. On a deeper level, since Kelipah implies negativity, *Da'as of Kelipah* can be translated as *negative knowing; knowing of not-knowing.* It is in effect a (small-minded) 'knowing' or certainty and conviction regarding the uncertainty of existence. It could also be called *Da'as of Safek* / a knowing of doubt, such as a tenacious clinging to a mindset that says, 'I don't know, and can never know, as there is nothing that can really be known.' There is an attachment to the notion of 'not knowing.' Ending with that. A place of perpetual doubt and questions, with no desire to seek answers, wherein relativism is the *absolute.* It is a place of absolute nihilism.

Amalek (and Amalek's later personification and embodiment as Haman) is connected to the Nachash, the primordial Snake in the Garden of Eden, who cast doubt in the mind of Chavah regarding what was good and what was the opposite.

Our sages tell us that the *Nachash* / snake is connected to *Zehuma* / זהומה / spiritual filth (*Shabbos*, 146a. Zehumah is *Tumah* in the language of Gemara. *Resisei Layla*, 19). The word זהומה can be read as a Hebrew word, and further broken down into the words זו מה היא / This, what is it? (*Pirush HaSulam, Zohar* 1:17). Amalek, like a snake, tries to inject the *Tumah* / impurity of doubt in people, 'Ok, you *Davened* / prayed with focus and intent, but 'what is it' worth, really? Yes, you are such a good person — you just helped a needy person — but really, 'what is it?' In the greater scheme of things it probably means nothing.'

The not-knowing of Kedusha, on the other hand, is freeing, opening us up to ever-deeper knowing and deeper probing as well. The *Tehara* / purity of 'holy doubt' leads to a life filled with infinitely renewable purpose and commitment to meaning. We engage in more acts of goodness and kindness than when we had a static, fixed 'knowing.' Not-knowing of Kedushah can involve, for example, an intellectual or existential question that leads to answers, which in turn leads to even deeper questions, and then even deeper answers and finally to more impactful actions.

In the world of holy intellect, our not-knowing is rooted in a place that is actually beyond not-knowing, the Keser of Keser. This is the same place, so-to-speak, where HaKadosh Baruch Hu freely chooses *the spirit of the righteous*. When we exercise free choice, our choice too is only to be optimistic, enthusiastic, and passionate for Mitzvos, as a direct result of the fact that HaKadosh Baruch Hu chooses goodness, purpose and meaning, in that 'place.'

Torah and Mitzvos, Tzedakah and Chesed, all transcend the normal categories of certainty (Da'as) and uncertainty (beyond Da'as). And when we tap into this deep transcendence, we tap into who we really are in our Source. Thus we harness the forces of *Radla*, Divine 'uncertainty,' to open our minds and hearts to radical new possibilities in life. This life-giving kind of doubt frees us to perceive and pursue unexplored possibilities and answers, and to plunge into unknown levels of optimism. We do not become more indifferent, rather more passionately engaged, instead of more passive, we become more proactive and dynamic. This is all in the aspect of 'Moshe Rabbeinu was born in Adar.' It is a month of becoming alive, beginning to truly exist, of humbling oneself and surrendering to ever-higher visions of what is possible.

One life-affirming choice gives us the freedom to make more life-affirming choices, with ever-expanding confidence and belief in Hashem and in Hashem's Creation. Here is the reason: Safek in the form of an 'openness to possibility' brings us to a deeper commitment to a new *P'sak* / ruling or certainty (ספק / *Safek* and פסק / *P'sak* have the same letters). When a P'sak, which we confirm, is rooted in the freshness and openness of Safek (in Radla) that P'sak remains fluid, vibrant, healthy and truly beneficial. (Rav Chayim Vital writes of the various *Sefeikos* / doubts regarding levels within Keser, how they function, what they reveal and draw down, from where they draw their source, and so forth. The deeper reason for these Sefeikos is that sometimes they are revealed one way, and other times another way, depending on the situation (*K'lach Pischei Chochmah*, 86), and depending on the level of the generation and the people who are tapping into these levels, as the Magid of Koznitz writes).

Da'as of Kelipah is the small-minded stubbornness of what you think you know, and what you think can or cannot be known. A person can get stuck in a false perception that they know everything they need to know, and there is nothing beyond that to know. This is a form of death.

Mordechai tries to convince Esther to go to the king and ask him to annul the decree against the Jewish People: ומי יודע אם־לעת כזאת הגעת למלכות / "And who knows, perhaps you have attained a royal position for the sake of a crisis such as this" (Megilas Esther, 4:14). Why does he say, ומי יודע / "And who knows"? Why does he not speak with conviction? Perhaps he should tell Esther, "It is clear to me that the whole reason you are queen is to help save the Jewish People." Because the whole idea of Purim is *Lo Yada*, letting go of what you know or think you know, and not getting stuck in Kelipah of Da'as.

In our Avodas Hashem in general we need to free ourselves from being stuck in certain set patterns of behavior, even those that seem positive and have worked up until this point. We need to refrain from holding on to ideas or methods of service that are not working any longer. It is said in the name of the wise Rebbe, Reb Bunim of Peshischa: "The principle is, in Avodas Hashem there are no principles...and even *this* principle does not exist" In Yiddish: דער כלל איז, אז לגבי עבודת ה' איז נישט דא קיין כללים, און אפי' די כלל איז אויך נישט דא!

"You shall *not do so* to Hashem, your G-d" / לא תעשון כן לה' אלקיכם
(Devarim 12:4). The phrase "not do so" means not to perform the
idolatrous actions the Torah had described just prior to this verse
(Rashi, ad loc). Yet, the early Chassidic Rebbes re-read the verse to
mean, "You shall not do 'like this' to Hashem your G-d." Meaning,
we should never think we must 'do the exact same thing' repeatedly
in our service of Hashem — *that is like idol worship.* We should
therefore not make our Avodas Hashem into a particular *Kein* /
'this is the way we do things,' and not ever try any other ways (The
Chozeh of Lublin, *Hagadah Shel Pesach, Ma'areh Yechezkel*, p. 25).

Even with regards to positive *Hanhagos* / practices, we need to
subtly sense what is working for us, what is expanding us and making us more connected to HaKadosh Baruch Hu — and also what
is not working for us or becoming mere routine. The Chozeh of
Lublin, after writing about the various positive customs he had
taken upon himself, adds, "All of the above practices have many, infinite branches and details. And yet, ולפעמים צריך להתנהג להפך / sometimes a person has to act exactly the opposite" (*Zos Zicharon*, p. 4).

This is true throughout the year, but the 'headquarters' of this
idea is Purim. Purim is all about the reality that 'you never know,'
or 'Who knows.' By opening ourselves up beyond what we know,
we can open to greater possibilities and to an ever-deeper Avodas
Hashem.

AMALEK SAYS THERE IS NO TOMORROW

Amalek is negative doubt, from the Kelipah side of Keser. This force devastates people with stifling uncertainty and even moral paralysis, because it convinces them that 'you cannot do anything, because there is really nothing to do.' In the pessimistic worldview of Amalek there is no tomorrow, as it were, and thus no responsibility, as everything is in perpetual existential *Safek* / doubt. Sometimes, even imperceptibly, a person can gradually begin to believe that there has never been and never will be real progress, hope, future or redemption for history and civilization — and by extension, for oneself.

With regards to Amalek the Torah says, "Go and wage battle with Amalek *tomorrow*" (Shemos, 17:9). We need to fight enthusiastically and with great passion against the devastating Kelipah of Amalek, and its notion that there is no tomorrow. We must engage in this battle.

It is not enough to rid the world of evil people who raise a banner of destruction and wish upon us genocide, *Chalilah* / Heaven forbid. We must wage war with מחשבת המן / *Haman's thoughts* (Megilas Esther, 8:5); the very mindset, intellectual paradigm and thought process of Haman and Amalek. This includes the idea that everything is random and without progress, and that tomorrow is really nothing but an extension of today and yesterday.

Sefer Bnei Yissaschar (Adar, Ma'amar 4:10, p 114) says that the 30 days from mid-Adar to mid-Nisan (Pesach) are about overcoming Amalek. There are 720 hours in these 30 days. The numerical value of Amalek is 240. Three times 240 is 720. Therefore, there are three levels of Amalek with which we must struggle and overcome during this period; doubt in thought, speech and action.

AMALEK REPRESENTS INEVITABILITY & ABSENCE OF HOPE

The inner Amalek says, 'there is no need to take action, because no action can substantially change anything.' It sells us the idea that we have sunk so low into negative or addictive patterns, that that negativity is now our life. It creates the false appearance that the negative condition of life is a מחוייב המציאות / necessary existence, there is no alternative. It is absolute — and absolutely hopeless (Chas veShalom).

But *is* there in fact a level of negativity in which the individuals connected to that level have sunk to such a low place that there is no longer any hope or possibility to change their ways? Is there a place where impurity is a מחוייב המציאות / necessary existence? Is there a place where there is no alternative and possibility for goodness, in which change can never occur?

The dimensions of this world are connected to the number seven, as in the seven days of Creation, and the fullest measurement of this world is 49, seven sublevels within each of the seven dimensions. In fact, the word *Midah* / measurement has the numerical value of 49 (*Sefer Rokeach*, Hilchos Pesach, 294. *Megaleh Amukos*, Parshas Behar). For this reason, as the light of Torah 'descends' into creation, it refracts into 49 possible ways of *Isur* / prohibition and 49 possible ways of *Heter* / allowance (*Medrash Tehilim*, 12); 49 ways of purity and

49 ways of impurity (Yerushalmi, *Sanhedrin*, 4:2. See also, *Eiruvin*, 13b; *Ritva*, ad loc).

This 'world of 49' is the world of opposites and therefore of choice. The more highly one is functioning on the 49-rung ladder of Kedushah, the more he or she is connected to the world of purity and transparency with the Divine. The lower one is functioning on the 49-rung ladder of impurity, the more one is connected to the world of negativity, stuckness and impurity.

When a person lives on any of these 98 levels there is always the possibility of choosing to move in the opposite direction. Thus, any level of goodness within the 49 levels of purity is called a אפשרי המציאות / possible existence. It is possible to function in purity at a given moment, but it is also possible to fall from that rung and begin to choose the opposite.

On both scales there is a 50th level. In the world of Kedusha, the 50th level is termed *Yovel* / Jubilee; which is absolute freedom from the *Yetzer haRa* / negative inclination and from death itself (*Medrash Rabbah*, Shemos, 41). This is goodness without an opposite; it has no relation to the paradigm of impurity or the prohibited. Purity is, at this point, a מחויב המציאות / necessary existence. There is no alternative and there is no falling. Purity, on this level, is endless and everlasting. The question remains, however, whether or not the 50th level of *Ra* / evil, negativity and impurity is absolute and endless as well.

Many sources (although not the regular Zohar, nor in the teachings of the Arizal) speak about a 50th level of *Tumah* / impurity, on which negativity seems absolute. As such, just as one can become endlessly free on the 50th level of Kedushah, it seems one can become so removed from the *Yetzer Tov* / positive inclination that there is no longer even a possibility of doing good (*Shaloh haKodesh*. Alshich, *Siddur Reb Shabtai*, Hagadah. *Chayei Adam* (in their respective Hagados, on "Matzah Zu") *Chesed l'Avraham*, 2:56. The Ramdu, *Eis LeCheninah*. *Ohr haChayim*, Shemos, 3:8. The *Beis haLevi*, Derush 2, and many places in Chassidus). Yet, other sources write that there is in fact no 50th level of Tumah (Gra, Mishlei, 16:4), no place where negativity is absolute.

As explored earlier, Haman erected a wooden plank of 50 *Amos* / cubits, and upon that structure he wished to hang the righteous Mordechai. It seems as though by doing this, Haman wanted to connect to a place where negativity is absolute and endless. According to this, it appears that there is indeed a 50th level of evil.

To resolve this question and reconcile the above argument, it could be said that there is truly *no* real 50th level of Tumah. In actuality there is no such thing as sinking so low that there is no longer a possibility of rising up and changing one's ways. As we learn elsewhere, nothing stands in the path of *Teshuvah* / inner transformation (*Zohar* 2, 106a. Yerushalmi, *Pe'ah*, 1:1), and "There is no misdeed that cannot be mended through Teshuvah" (*Tanya*, Igeres haTeshuvah, 4 and 11. *Ohr Hashem*, Ma'amar 3, Klal 2:2. Meiri, *Chibur haTeshuvah*, Meishiv Nefesh, Ma'amar 1:3. "The doors of Teshuva are forever open." *Psikta deRebbe Kahana*, 45:8). It is only that Amalek wants you to believe that all hope is lost and that there is a 50th level of absolute negativity.

Haman therefore says, 'I am going to erect a gallows 50 feet high to indicate that there is a place where negativity is a מחוייב המציאות / necessary existence, and that is where you and Klal Yisrael as a whole are functioning. You are so lost, so misdirected, so steeped in Tumah, that you are hopeless and your demise is inevitable. You have sunk so low, there is no getting up. Tomorrow is merely nothing but an extension of today and yesterday, there is no movement or progress, and so you are permanently doomed.'

AMALEK & THE DESCENDANTS OF RACHEL

"Moshe said to Yehoshua, 'Pick men for us, and go out to do battle with Amalek'" (Shemos, 17:9). Moshe specifically chooses Yehoshua, who is a descendant of the matriarch Rachel, to wage battle against Amalek because, "Amalek can only be destroyed through the descendants of Rachel" (Medrash, *Pesikta Rabbah*, 13, as Yehoshua and Mordechai). Later on, in Shoftim, the book of Judges, the verse says, מני אפרים שרשם בעמלק / "Out of Ephrayim, came they whose roots are in Amalek" (Shoftim, 5:14). Ephrayim is a grandson of Rachel, and it is out of Ephrayim that Amalek will be destroyed (this is an allusion to Yehoshua specifically, as Rashi writes, and a general allusion to the tribe of Ephrayim. מן אפרים יצא שורש יהושע בן נון, לרדות בעמלק לחלש אותו לפי חרב). What is the power of the descendents of Rachel to destroy Amalek?

Amalek says there is no tomorrow and no better reality to yearn for. The word *Amalek* is numerically 240, similar to the Hebrew word פעמים /*Pa'amayim* / twice, repetition. Amalek's sole power is in creating the illusion that nothing will ever change, everything is but a repetition of what came before — yearning is useless and irrelevant. The descendents of Rachel possess a great spiritual weapon that targets exactly this issue.

Yaakov had two main wives, Leah and Rachel. After being married to both of them for many years, only Leah merited to have many children with Yaakov. Rachel was at this point not able to have children, and her yearning for children was tremendous. She had an unbridled *Tzimayon* / thirst to have children. She lived with such an infinite longing to build a family, that she tells Yaakov, "Give me children, and if not, I am dead" (Bereishis, 30:1).

Rachel's very existence is tied to always yearning for more. When she finally does have a child she names him Yoseph, saying, "May Hashem grant me yet another son" (30:24). This quality of yearning for more is transmitted to Yoseph, as indicated in his name, and also to her other son Binyanim, whose tribe longed to house Hashem's Presence (*Zevachim*, 53b. *Megilah*, 26a).

When Klal Yisrael is exiled from Eretz Yisrael following the destruction of the Beis haMikdash, it is our mother Rachel who weeps for her children and "refuses to be comforted for her children, who are gone." Hashem responds to her, "Restrain your voice from weeping, and your eyes from shedding tears; for there is a reward for your labor... and there is תקוה / hope לאחריתך / for your future" (Yirmiyahu, 31:16-18).

Rachel yearns and longs for Redemption, and is told that there *is* hope for the future. Her longing pays off and there is reward for her labor. Amalek's attempt to exterminate yearning and hope is powerfully countered by Rachel and her descendants in their embodiment of spiritual desire, passionate yearning, constant hoping for a better world, and unshakable faith that they can achieve it against all odds (*Resisei Layla*, 52).

All of Klal Yisrael lives with the knowledge that, ויש־תקוה לאחריתך / "There is hope for your future..." (Yirmiyahu 31:17). And there will certainly be an *Acharis* / אחרית / end, a culmination of history, a healing of all wounds, a dazzling perfection of righteousness; and for this we yearn with our *haKol* / very existence.

Amalek also has an *Acharis* / אחרית / end, but not one that is filled with healing and hope, quite the opposite. ראשית גוים עמלק ואחריתו עדי אבד / "Amalek was the first of the nations, and his fate shall be *everlasting destruction*" (Bamidbar, 24:20). Since Amalek rejects all hope and yearning for progress and Redemption as futile, and since Amalek in effect worships destruction, the end of Amalek is destruction. Amalek simply ends, forever. Thus Hashem has קץ שם לחושך / "placed an 'end' to darkness" (Iyov, 28:3, as interpreted by the Frierdiker Rebbe in *Reishis Goyim Amalek*). As such, there is *no absolute/ endless* negativity. All injustice comes to an end.

When we live deeply in the present, yet with a strong longing and movement toward the times of Moshiach, no negativity can entrap us. The schemes of Amalek and Haman ultimately come upon their own heads in a self-fulfilling prophecy of ruination.

MOVING TOWARDS A TOMORROW

There are *RaMaCH* / 248 positive Mitzvos in the Torah (Reish/200, Mem/40, Ches/8), and the letters *RaMaCH* are the same as the letters of the word *Machar* / tomorrow (Mem-Ches-Reish). Torah and Mitzvos are all about *haYom* / today and our presence in the moment, coupled with a strong awareness of how the present impacts the future — how every thought, word and action today contributes incrementally to a brighter tomorrow. With even one good deed or good word, any of us can "tip the scales for himself and the whole world to the side of virtue, and bring about his own and the whole world's salvation" (Rambam, *Hilchos Teshuvah*, 3:4).

In the paradigm of Kedushah, characterized by a revealed connectivity to the *Ohr Ein Sof* / Infinite light of Hashem, as well as holy doubt, everything is possible and meaningful. The future Divine salvation is so close that it resonates in the present. In the paradigm of Amalek, nothing seems possible or meaningful; there is instead a flat denial of the very existence of the Creator and the intentionality of Creation/Salvation.

Say our sages, "Hashem's Name will not be complete until Amalek is completely eradicated" (*Tanchuma*, Ki Tetze. Rashi, Shemos, 17:16). Amalek's war against hope, progress and meaning is actually a battle against Hashem Himself, the Creator of hope, progress and meaning. The whole notion of a Creator implies that the world has been created for a purpose, that life has direction and meaning, and that we are moving towards redemption. Because Klal Yisrael are witnesses and ambassadors of this idea here on earth, Amalek targets Klal Yisrael exclusively.

As explained earlier, Amalek, "the *Reishis* / Head of all the nations," is rooted in the head or Keser of Kelipah, which manifests negative, crippling doubt. Klal Yisrael, however, is rooted in an even higher power: *Radla* / the Unknowable Head, which manifests liberating, empowering, holy doubt.

Negative doubt paralyzes us. We become ruled by doubt and it leaves us feeling powerless. Negative doubt cripples us and leaves us thinking that no meaning or purpose can be found in our actions. Nothing can be done, and there is nothing to do. Positive doubt, on the other hand, liberates us and gives us a new and fresh platform upon which we can freely choose new life.

The Yom Tov of Purim, which affirms the victory of Klal Yisrael over Haman and Amalek, is named after the *Pur* / lottery, alluding to a notion of randomness and doubt. It would have made sense to name the *Yom Tov* / holiday after something connected to their salvation, maybe 'the Day of Esther' or 'the Day of Shushan' (the location of the event). Why did they name the Yom Tov after the very instrument of randomness which Haman used to dictate the date upon which to annihilate Klal Yisrael? Why name it something connected to the negative decree rather than something connected to the salvation? It is because Adar and Purim are intricately connected to Radla, the deepest level of seeming 'randomness' and not-knowing; from which all knowing, mindful, and meaningful choices flow.

HAMAN-AMALEK: NO MEMORY & NO HISTORY

Doubt, cynicism, and uncertainty are part of a consciousness and worldview in which everything is mere happenstance, nothing is purposeful or intentional as there is simply no purpose — to anything. Thus, it proclaims, there is no destiny, no tomorrow, and no possibility for Redemption. Life is simply cyclical and coincidental, and thus directionless and random.

Amalek rejects belief in a future Tikun, because it does not believe in a past or a future; only a stagnantly cyclical vision of time in which nothing significant ever happened or ever will happen. When all events are random, there is no value in memory, and there are no soul-searching questions or positive commitments to be made based on past experiences. Amalek is committed only to empty memory, insignificance, non-commitment, futile questions and facile answers.

Amalek does not believe in the idea that Creation has purpose and is incrementally moving towards Tikun and Redemption; if there is no past there is no future. More deeply, Amalek does not believe in anything. It is only committed, resolutely and with Da'as, to noncommitment, doubt, chaos, relativity, and substance-less questions.

Torah asks us to act decisively: "Remember what Amalek did to you…You shall blot out the memory of Amalek from under Heaven" (Devarim, 25:17-19). However, this seems unclear. Blotting out the memory of Amalek means to utterly *forget* them, yet, the first passage says "*Remember* what Amalek did…" Which one is it? If we are remembering them we cannot at the same time blot out their memory. And if we blot out their memory to forget about them, we cannot remember them. The answer to this seeming paradox is that we must blot out Amalek precisely by remembering Amalek.

Remembering and contemplating our past, seeing the trajectory of history and learning from it, is the antithesis of Amalek. (The letters of the name עמלק stands for קהת ,לוי, ,משה ,עמרם. This means, Moshe's father was Amram, his grandfather was Kehos, and his great grandfather was Levi. In this way, Amalek's name alludes to Moshe's history, a remembering of his past. And Moshe is the first person to be told to battle Amalek.) Cultivating memory and using its meaningful lessons to move forward into a more fulfilled destiny allows us to eradicate Amalek and what Amalek represents. Therefore, the very act of recording our sacred history is a powerful weapon in the war against, and eradication of, Amalek. This is the reason Esther asked that the story of Haman, the Amalek of her generation, be written down and canonized in Tanach / Torah, "Write me for future generations."

Esther knew that to truly eradicate Amalek and its embodiment in Haman required memorializing the past as a guide for our future. Thus, the story of Purim became the third time in Tanach where Amalek is remembered and blotted out. ("Esther sent to the Sages: Write me the story of Purim for future generations and canonize the book of Esther into the Tanach. They sent her an argument: "It is written, 'Have I not already written for you three times?'" (Mishlei, 22:20) Meaning that the story of Amalek is already mentioned three times in Tanach: Shemos, Devarim and Shemuel 1. See, it says three times, and not four times! The Sages did not accede to Esther's request until they found a verse written in the Torah: כתב זאת זכרון בספר ושים באזני יהושע / "Write this for a memorial in the Book, and rehearse it in the ears of Yehoshua, that I will utterly blot out the remembrance of Amalek from under the Heavens" (Shemos, 17:14). "Write this," the Sages realized, refers to that which is written in the Torah here, in Shemos. And in Devarim, the phrase "a memorial" refers to that which is written in the Prophets. "In the book" then, refers to that which is written in the Megilah. Thus, the Megilah is in fact the required third mention of Amalek, and not an extraneous fourth!" (Megilah, 7a).)

Purim needs to be remembered not only as an oral memory; an oral memory can be altered through transmission and the passage of time. Esther ensured that the story of Purim will be permanently remembered by means of a written text. The blotting out of Amalek must be done through reading aloud certain passages in the Torah. (Torah law demands that we remember Amalek by reading the Parsha of Amalek from an actual Sefer Torah (*HaEshkol*, Hilchos Chanukah v'Purim, 10. *Bach*, Orach Chayim, 685. *Mishnah Berurah*, ibid, 7:14). Although the Minchas Chinuch argues that "reading" Parshas Zachor is only a Mitzvah m'deRabanan / from the Sages (*Minchas Chinuch*, Mitzvah 603).) What Esther intuitively knew, and the sages of that generation revealed, is that blotting out the power of Amalek requires both telling the story, and also writing the story down, but it would not be enough to write it in a mere book of history. It had to be written as an indelible part of scripture. In order for the memory of Amalek to be recorded for all eternity, in fact, it needed to be written within all three types of the books of Tanach: the *Torah* / Five Books of Moses, the *Nevi'im* / Prophets, and the *Kesuvim* / Writings. In the Torah, the story of Amalek is recorded in Shemos, and its repetition in Devarim. In the books of the Nevi'im, the story of the descendants of Amalek is recorded in the Book of Shemuel. And now it is also inscribed in the books of Kesuvim, in Megilas Esther (*Yerushalmi, Megilah*, 1:5). This way, we are guaranteed to remember and thus blot out Amalek.

In another fascinating statement of the *Yerushalmi*, the reason why there is a particular *Maseches* / tractate in the Mishnah and Talmud for Purim called *Maseches Megilah*, is that it will help us to *not* forget Amalek: "And the memory of them shall never perish among their descendants" (Megilas Esther, 9:28). "From this verse our sages understood to establish a Meseches" (*Yerushalmi*, 2:4). In other words, not only does Amalek need to be recorded in all three types of the books of Tanach, but it even needs to be written in the oral aspect of Torah, Mishnah and Gemara.

This then is the meaning of כתב זאת זכרון בספר ושים באזני יהושע / "Write this as a 'remembrance' in the Book, and place it in the ears of Yehoshua" (*Shemos*, 17:14). To blot out Amalek, "Write this;" the story needs to be remembered and written down in all forms of Torah, all books of Tanach and even a full volume of Talmud. Furthermore, "and place it in the ears," means that it needs to be frequently read and re-read, "in the ears," in the living tradition of Klal Yisrael. It needs to be written down, repeatedly recited, heard and deeply listened to, as a living, relevant memory. And by this threefold act of *remembering*, Amalek and everything that Amalek represents will be "erased."

AMALEK & WAR

This understanding, that erasing Amalek requires a good sense of history, helps explain a puzzling event that occured the next time Klal Yisrael waged battle with Amalek, in the days of King Shaul.

In the Book of Shemuel we read how King Shaul was told by Shemuel *haNavi* / the Prophet to wage war with the Amalekites and destroy them. Shaul did go to battle and was victorious, yet, he kept the king of Amalek, Agag, alive. Following the battle, Shemuel rebuked Shaul for keeping Agag alive and then the Pasuk says that Shemuel said to Agag, "As your sword bereaved women, so will your mother be bereaved among women" (Shemuel 1, 15:33), and then Shemuel slew him.

The obvious question is, why does Shemuel justify his slaying of Agag with the fact that Agag was a murderer, when Agag was part of Amalek and there is a Mitzvah to eradicate Amalek?

The Brisker Rav brings down in the name of his father, Reb Chayim (*Reshimas Talmidim*, Nach, Shemuel 1), that the eradication of Amalek has to be done specifically during battle, as alluded to in the verse that says מלחמה לה' בעמלק / A war for Hashem against Amalek (*Shemos*, 17:16). For this reason, Shemuel was not able to slay Agag just because he was from Amalek; that battle had ended. As such, Shemuel killed him because he was a murderer, and not because of the Mitzvah to erase Amalek.

If the issue is to eradicate Amalek, why must Amalek be eradicated exclusively in a battle? If an enemy is intending to kill you, it is permissible to preempt them and kill them first, whether by assassination or battle. What is the difference?

Amalek, we understand, is more than a physical enemy of Klal Yisrael that needs to be erased, Amalek is a people with an ideology that is the diametrical antithesis to the overarching purpose and revelation of Klal Yisrael and the Torah. (Amalek is more than a people, it is also an ideology. According to the Rambam, a person born an Amalekite can throw off his beliefs and accept the universal Torah laws for all mankind, and no longer be considered 'from Amalek' (Rambam, *Hilchos Melachim U'Milchamos*, 6:4, as the *Kesef Mishneh*, explains).) Therefore to truly erase Amalek we need more than simply to 'kill them off,' we need to erase the entire ideology of Amalek. To accomplish this requires that we do so in 'battle.'

The difference between battle and assassination, for example, is that battle is waged in the open and there are *Halachos* / laws of war. The Halachos of battle ensure that a war is methodically defined, organized, and delineated; and that it occurs out in the open, which allows it to be properly recorded and monitored. The Torah tells us about a "book of the wars for Hashem": על-כן יאמר בספר מלחמת ה' / "Concerning this it is told in the Book of the Wars of Hashem..." (Bamidbar, 21:14). The Even Ezra (ibid), writes that there was such a book which described all the wars Hashem fought on behalf of those who fear Him, and it is possible that this book already existed in the time of Avraham. As the Rambam (ibid) explains, throughout all times wise people wrote down and recorded the details of all the great wars.

This is precisely the reason that Amalek needs to be erased in a field of battle, out in the open, in a public battle between known armies. The story of Amalek must be recorded and written down in "The Book of Wars." In this way, their erasure is doubly enforced. They are physically countered, and their story is also written into history. This then erases the mindset and ideology of Amalek, proving its futility.

HAMAN / AMALEK: HAPPENSTANCE

Without a sense of history, destiny and purpose, life is random and ultimately meaningless. Describing the first time Amalek breached and attacked Klal Yisrael, the Torah says, "Remember what Amalek did to you on your journey, after you left Egypt. אשר קרך בדרך / *He chanced upon you on the way*, when you were famished and weary, and cut down all the stragglers in your rear..." (Devarim, 25:17-18). The word קרך / chanced upon, denotes happenstance, a sense of randomness. The Rambam writes that we should not, observing what is occurring in our life, simply say, נקרה נקרית / "this was merely happenstance" (*Hilchos Ta'anis*, 1:3). This is the way of Amalek, and is, as the Rambam adds, a "cruel" way to look at life. We are to avoid the types of thinking and beliefs which assert that things just 'happen,' that nothing is holy, intentional or purposeful, without destiny, and that we are just circling through time on a proverbial merry-go-round, with no progress or Redemption.

For this reason, every time Klal Yisrael is about to build a Mikdash / physical structure dedicated to serving haKadosh Baruch Hu, Amalek comes and attacks, and tries, *Rachmana Litzlan* / may the Compassionate One save us, to destroy Klal Yisrael. A Mikdash is an intentional, purposeful, 'dedicated' place of holiness; establishing one is therefore the greatest affront to Amalek's cruel ideology of happenstance.

Amalek thus attacked when we were about to build the Mishkan in the Desert, as we read just before the Torah portion of Terumah, prior to the laws of building the Mishkan. Amalek attacked again in the times of King Shaul, before the building of the First Beis haMikdash. Haman, the descendent of Amalek, attacked during the Purim story, before the building (or the completion of the building) of the Second Beis haMikdash. The same pattern is unfortunately manifest in our days before the building of the Third Beis haMikdash (may it be built immediately) with the horrors of the 20th Century Amalek, the Nazis, *Yimach Shemom* / may their names be erased.

Amalek sees the world as a *Mikrah* / just a chance happening. Appropriately, this is the exact same words Haman uses when he tells his wife and family כל-אשר קרהו / "everything that happened to him" (Megilas Esther, 6:13). He was a descendent and embodiment of the quality of Amalek and thus viewed everything as mere happenstance.

Adar can also be split into two parts: the letter Aleph and the word *Dar*. This forms a sentence meaning, '*Aleph* / the One, is *Dar* / dwelling therein' — in Adar it was revealed that the One, Hashem, dwells even within our mundane lives (*Me'or Einayim*, Terumah). It was thus revealed that there are no accidents or happenstances; everything is meaningful and everything comes from Hashem (*Sefas Emes*, Tetzaveh, 631).

Realizing that nothing is ultimately chance or happenstance is one level of spiritual insight. A deeper level of insight involves realizing the holy side of 'happenstance.' Just as there can be positive, holy doubt that opens your mind to possibilities and opportunities which you could not have fathomed previously, there is a positive expression of happenstance and surprise. The ultimate *veNahafoch-Hu* / reversal in the pattern of the great turn-around of the Purim story, is the reversal and transformation of that very darkness into light.

A transformation of doubt into certainty is not an actual reversal within the same phenomenon, but rather a replacement with its opposite. *VeNahafoch Hu* / complete reversal, in terms of doubt, means turning negative doubt into positive doubt. The same is possible with the phenomenon of *Karcha* / happenstance. The name of Purim is itself a testament to this; a lottery, a process of happenstance and absence of intention, revealed the 'unexpected' deeper intention of the Creator. Even in 'happenstance,' Hashem is there, waiting to be acknowledged.

When you are expecting something, say a raise in pay, there can be a lack of excitement and maybe even a lack of delight when it is received. Yet, when we are open to being surprised by the blessings in life, to receiving spontaneous benefit from any direction and at any moment, you constantly have a sense of freshness and animation; everything is a blessing.

Just as 'positive doubt' catapults us to be more engaged in discerning our purpose, a positive sense of 'happenstance' allows us to be more excitedly appreciative of all life; to see every Mitzvah, every encounter, every opportunity to do good or give thanks, with a sense of freshness, surprise and preciousness. Therefore, when the Megilah speaks of the final turning around of events, and how salvation came to Klal Yisrael, it employs a similar word. At the end of the Megilah story it says, "For the Jews it was a time of light, happiness, joy and יקר / *Yekar* / glory" (Megilas Esther, 8:16). The climax of the Purim story is their attainment of *Yekar*, a holy, constructive, life-affirming, positive sense of surprise, in which every aspect of life becomes glorious. This comes about precisely through their sense of the unexpected, and their understanding that everything which arises is infinitely *Yakar* / precious.

OPEN TO QUESTIONS

On Purim we are asked to reach a state of joy beyond *Da'as* / knowledge: עד דלא ידע / *Ad d'Lo Yada* / "until you do not know" (*Megilah*, 7b). Da'as is certainty, and we must in general make proper choices in life via Da'as. However, when we arise to the level of *Lo Yada*, and tap into *Radla* / not knowing, we can make truly free choices from a place of *Etzem* / Essence, free from all coercion and conditionality — free from self-imposed limitations on our open-ended possibilities in life.

If one is confined to a space of Da'as, one can be full of answers and not open to questions. In a negative lack of Da'as, *Safek* / doubt, everything comes into question, and one is only left with empty, unanswerable questions; feeling crippled with passivity, without enthusiasm or stamina.

On Purim, we reach a positive, holy 'lack' of Da'as, the Essence-consciousness of *Lo Yada*, above and beyond Da'as, in which we can reveal our point of indestructible faith in boundless possibility through our unity with the Source of All. Here, answers are fluid and open-ended; they open us up to deeper questions, to higher states of wonder, and in turn to ever deeper answers. This enlivening play of questions and answers is itself a perpetual *Nahafoch Hu*, and a victory over Haman.

Merely turning negative *Safek* / doubt into ודאי / *Vadai* / certainty misses the full transformation available on Purim. The "Nahafoch Hu" occurs when we allow even disempowering, crippling or cynical questions, questions of the void, to become deep questions — healthy, inner probing, that opens us up to what is beyond what we currently know. For this reason, the word *Purim* in numerical value is 336 (Pei / 80, Vav / 6, Reish / 200, Yud / 10, Mem / 40=336), the same numerical value as *Sha'alah* / question (Shin / 300, Aleph / 1, Lamed / 30, Hei 5=336).

For example, say you have a passionate urge to build something holy, a skill or a public offering that will bring some benefit to others. Perhaps you sense a little bit of self-doubt, thinking to yourself that despite the fact that you can help some people, you weren't formally trained in this field, and there are others who are more authoritative and skilled in it. But you have the courage and audacity to step forward, learn from others and launch your project. Now, imagine some presumed authority figure asks a couple questions that strike at your most vulnerable point, "Is this a joke? Who do you think you are, presenting yourself as a resource to others?"

The full *Nahafoch-Hu* in this situation is not to flip directly from *Safek* / self-doubt to *Vadai* / certainty, merely replacing the 'questions' with their opposites. Rather, it may be possible to hear the questions more literally or more deeply to find surprising answers that transform the effect of the questions themselves.

'Is this a joke?' Without striking back, honestly reflect on the possibility that you yourself subconsciously think it is a 'joke,' or perhaps you accurately sense that you're fooling yourself or acting irresponsibly in some way. Is it indeed a joke? If you find that it is not, then own the answer within yourself, 'No, I may be taking a risk, but I am seriously committed to learning something new and continuing to grow as I go along. Helping others, even in a small way, is no joke.' The cynical question has just become a holy question, perhaps taking you beyond your previous level of Da'as.

'Who do you think you are, presenting yourself as a resource to others?' Turning this question inward, do you indeed think that you are more qualified than you are, perhaps venturing into territory where you could erroneously harm instead of help? Are you willing to refer someone to a provider with more training, as soon as you meet an issue that is outside your scope of expertise? Are you willing to say 'I don't know,' when appropriate? And actually, who do you think you are? Does part of you think your an incapable or unlovable person? Do you realize that you're created with a purpose, and that 'perhaps' you have been placed in your particular circumstances in order to fulfil part of that purpose? Do you think and realize that your yearnings to do good are from Hashem? Do you acknowledge that you are ultimately one with Hashem, who is the Only Resource for all beings?'

How do you feel inside, having transformed negative questions into positive ones? Are you lighter, freer, and more fluid? Or perhaps more grounded, rooted and stable?

Purim lets us convert negative, stifling questions into wholesome not-knowing. 'I don't know, and therefore I can explore and learn so much more, and reach so much higher. I am open to be surprised by what tomorrow brings, open to a much deeper knowing, and open to what Hashem has in store for me, despite what I know today.'

INFINITE NOT-KNOWING AND KNOWING

When the Baal Shem Tov came to the Yeshivah looking for a husband for his profound and holy daughter Eidel (called Udel), he asked the head of the Yeshivah who was the brightest, most learned and pious student. Reb Yechiel Ashkenazi (called the *Deitchel* / the German) was the response. So, the Baal Shem Tov walked over to the young student and asked him, nu, tell me something you learned today? "I don't know," he responded. Ok, so then tell me something you learned in the past or something you know, "I don't know," was again the response. The Baal Shem Tov said, very well, this young lad will be my son-in-law.

If you recognize that you don't yet know, you are open to so much more that *can* be known. There is a saying that is repeated by *Chachmei Yisrael* / the wise among Israel: תכלית הידיעה שלא נדע / "The ultimate extent (or purpose) of knowing, is not to know," or 'The deepest knowing is not knowing.' (The original version in the Rishonim is תכלית הידיעה, שנדע שלא נדעך / The ultimate extent (or purpose) of knowing, is to know that we cannot know You" (*Bechinos Olam*, 13:4). Yet, the above version is the way Chassidic sources and later writings quote the statement.) This does not refer to the 'not knowing' of an ignoramus, or to an experience of deficiency in Da'as. Rather it is quite the opposite: it is a ידיעה, a 'knowing' that there is a reality beyond the current knowing, implying the possibility of Infinite knowing. We *know* that we do not know.

The unknown of yesterday becomes the known of today, but today there is a deeper unknown, a deeper hiddenness that we recognize to be lying beyond our present knowledge. Hashem is infinite, and to reach true knowledge of infinity is an infinite quest. Whatever we can know of the mystery of the Ein Sof is finite, and therefore there is always a deeper hiddenness beyond it. Purim reveals the reality of the Esther / *Hester* / Hidden dimension. 'Behind' all manifestations hides Hakadosh Baruch Hu, Himself. No matter what is being revealed or known, the Essence of Hashem eternally remains hidden. Purim connects us directly to that Infinite hiddenness which can never be revealed (see Alter Rebbe, *Torah*

Ohr, Megilas Esther, 90d). Again, this does not indicate a deficiency in our ability to know *Giluyim* / 'what is revealed' to Da'as; rather it simply indicates that the revealed dimension is by definition not Essence, manifestation is not the 'Manifester.' Letting go of our knowing, of our perception of what we know, allows us to be one with the infinite mystery of the Ultimate Unknowable.

Our sages tell us אהב את השמא / "love the maybe" (*Derech Eretz Zuta*, 1. *Kalah Rabsi*, 3), which can simply mean 'be careful' where you walk and what you do (*Sefer Chasidim*. See also *Peleh Yoetz*, 31), but can also simply mean 'be open.' Be lovingly open to infinite possibilities, and thus you will be open to the Infinite unknown of HaKadosh Baruch Hu.

VADAI & ULAI

On a simple level, Purim acquaints us with the positive aspect of *Lo Yada* / the not-knowing borne of 'true' questions, which leads to deeper answers, and in turn to more profound, authentic questions and answers, ad infinitum. True questions are not asked merely for the sake of creating uncertainty, nor challenging authority and the status quo. True questions are not even like those of a child trying to stump his parent by challenging them to answer why the sky is blue. True questions are clearly aimed at finding deeper truths beyond what is currently known, engaging a humbling, mind-opening dialectical process.

Normally, one would think that the antidote to doubt, to Amalek, to uncertainty, would be mustering up great *Vadai* / certainty.

And in fact, one of the Names of Hashem is called Vadai, as we say in the *Nusach haTefilah* / liturgy of prayer, *haVadai Shemo* / "His Name is certainty." Yet, Purim is named after the Pur which means a lottery, an uncertainty. And as just mentioned, the numerical value of *Purim* equals the value of *Sha'alah* / question. Purim teaches us that the answer to the unholy uncertainty and doubt of Amalek is not simply *Vadai*, but holy doubt, which is filled with as yet unrevealed potentials.

Paralleling Hashem's Name *Vadai*, one of the names of the Shechinah is אולי / *Ulai* / Maybe (*Tikunei Zohar*, Tikun 69. *Koheles Yaakov*, Erech Aleph). This is the Divine *Lo Yada*. Pointing to this, Mordechai tells Esther, *Mi Yodea* / 'Who knows! — are we so certain regarding what we think about this predicament? *Ulai*, maybe there is another way, maybe we need to be open to other possibilities. Who knows, maybe you are where you are in order to bring forth salvation for our People.'

Fascinatingly enough, the river that surrounded the ancient city of Shushan where the whole Purim story took place was called *Ulai* (Daniel, 8:2). The life-giving waters of holy 'not knowing' are a *Sovev* / surrounding and transcendent light that 'encircles' the stories of our own lives. The Purim story is an intricate weaving of revelations of 'Maybe.' Providing us glimpses of the perspectival fluidity we need in order to realize that Hashem is here, always, hiding within every event.

Purim is unique in the objective to reach a state of *Ulai* or *Lo Yada*. All other holidays stand in stark contrast to this. On the Yom Tov of Sukkos, for example, the principal Mitzvah involves Da'as.

"You shall live in Sukkos for seven days in order that future generations יֵדְעוּ / *may know* that I made the Israelite people live in booths when I brought them out of the land of Egypt" (Vayikra, 23:42-43). Da'as is so essential to Sukkos, that without knowing why you are sitting in the Sukkah, the Mitzvah has not been performed at all. (The Bach, based on the words of the *Tur, Orach Chayim*, 625. *Bekurei Yaakov*, 625:3. With all other Mitzvos (of the Torah) there is a big debate if Da'as and Kavanah are indispensable. *Berachos*, 13a. *Eiruvin*, 95b. *Pesachim*, 114b. *Rabbienu Yona*, Berachos 12a. *Tosefos*, Sukkah, 39a. *Tosefos*, Pesachim, 7b. *Shulchan Aruch*, Orach Chayim, 60, *Magen Avraham*, 3. *Beis Yoseph*, Orach Chayim, 489.)

On Purim we drink wine, literally and metaphorically, until we transcend the *Da'as* / discernment between a blessing and a curse. On Purim, rather than focussing on Da'as, we focus on entering the waters of *Ulai*, the mystery of *Reisha d'Lo Isyada* / the Divine Head that does not know, the source of true freedom, true knowledge and truly life-affirming choices.

A transformation from doubt to holy uncertainty to certainty, plays out in the events of the Megilah. What began as a great doubt in terms of the people's fate, as the decree of the king and Haman loomed over the entire community, was turned on its head. The decree was completely annulled and Haman was hanged on the same gallows that he had prepared for Mordechai, the leader of the Jewish people at the time. The experience of uncertainty regarding their fate ultimately brought out within them a positive kind of uncertainty. This opened them to a deeper commitment to their faith and a radical re-acceptance of the Torah. In this way, their uncertainty brought about an even deeper sense of possibility, conviction and commitment.

ADAR AS A CLOAK

Adar is connected to the word *Aderes,* which means a cloak, clothing or covering. Our garments give us a sense of certainty and identity. Even while they 'conceal' the body, they 'reveal' something about our self-definition. In the Purim story, the characters frequently change their clothing. Our celebration of Purim includes shedding the external clothes that we accumulated in the winter, and playfully altering our identity.

Dressing up in costumes on Purim involves letting go of inhibitions and projections that have concealed us, and donning garments that surprisingly reveal an aspect of who we really are. We become 'lighter' and more fluid with our garments and our self-definition. We become childlike, free of the form and accumulated conditioning that we have carried. In this sense, Purim is like Yom Kippur / *Yom ha-kiPurim,* when we release all our conditioning, negativity and self-limitation; enclothing ourselves in royal purity and standing in the presence of the King.

On Purim, we recognize that HaKadosh Baruch Hu is concealed within this physical world, just like we are concealed within a grand Purim costume. As Rebbe Pinchas of Kortiz taught: "'The whole earth is full of His glory' (Yeshayahu, 6:3) — *Kevodo* / 'His glory' should be understood in the sense of 'His garment,' i.e., that HaKadosh Baruch Hu is enclothed in the corporeal" (*Likutei Yekarim*).

Even deeper, HaKadosh Baruch Hu is literally 'one' with the physical world and our bodies. It is only from our human *Da'as* / perspective that we see corporality as 'different' than HaKadosh Baruch Hu, and in that way like a garment. However on Purim, we let go of human Da'as and reveal to ourselves that ultimate 'one-ness' of garment, body, and soul.

☾

꙳

SENSE

*C*ONVENTIONALLY, THERE ARE FIVE SENSES, YET, *Sefer Yetzirah* speaks of twelve *Chushin* / senses. In addition to the more commonly understood definition of what comprises our senses, the word *Chush* can also mean 'a sensitive level of perception, understanding, appreciation or skill' in relation to a particular psycho-spiritual process or function. For example, a 'sense of sleep' is a deep understanding and appreciation of sleep which includes both what sleep represents spiritually, as well as the practical skills and abilities that make one's experience of sleep both peaceful and beneficial.

These twelve *Chushim* are also the twelve activities that the Torah says the Creator performs in the process of maintaining the world (Pirush haRavad, *Sefer Yetzirah*). As we are created in the Divine image we also possess all twelve *Chushim*, at least in potential. Even if one is blind, for example, he always has the potential for sight — it's just that he is currently missing the *physical* vessels or capacities for it. However, the sense of sight is included in the person's Divine image, as it were. Obviously, a physically blind person could have immense vessels for *spiritual* sight. Every month gives us the ability and strength to expand our vessels and potentials for a particular *Chush*, along with its corresponding Divine Attributes. When we align and refine our consciousness via these *Chushim*, we can harness the qualities of each month in a most profound and meaningful way.

According to *Sefer Yetzirah*, the *Chush* / sense connected with Adar is *S'chok* / laughter and merriment. In general, laughter is a much more developed and evolved 'sense' among the other senses; laughing is a uniquely human activity. Most other senses, like eating, sleeping, walking, hearing, and seeing are also found throughout the animal kingdom, but a developed sense of humor is uniquely human (Gra, *Sefer Yetzirah*, 5:2). Only human beings have a sense of irony, non-slapstick humor and laughter (Ya'avetz, *Mitpachas Sefarim*, 8:8).

Humor is also very individual and idiosyncratic. People laugh at different things. You can tell what type of person someone is, or what kind of subculture they are from, by the jokes they tell or laugh at. "A person's true character is ascertained (by his behavior in three areas): his cup (his behavior when he drinks), his pocket (his conduct in his financial dealings with other people), and his anger. And some say, a person also reveals his real nature in his laughter" (*Eiruvin,* 65b). You can tell a lot about a person by his particular sense of humor.

As mentioned earlier, there are two main categories of laughter: laughter that is grounded in wellbeing or the sacredness of life, and laughter that is cynical and superficial, expressing a belief that nothing is sacred.

Cynical or superficial laughter not only expresses but reinforces the misperception that life is meaningless or fundamentally alienating. This is similar to how laughing when we are scared or embarrassed reinforces those reactions and perceptions. Cynical laughter and mockery ultimately fosters depression. Positive laughter, in contrast, expresses and reinforces a sense of release from the limited perception of form; it leads to a recognition that everything paradoxically makes sense, albeit often ironically. When we respond to life with positive laughter, we can joyfully release ourselves from narrow, superficial thinking. This is holy laughter, regarding which King David says, "I have laughed (or played) in front of Hashem" (Shemuel 2, 6:21).

We need to continually evaluate our laughter, especially in this month of laughter. Are we expanding and growing from our laughter, or does it reinforce in us a sense of meaninglessness, purposelessness and cynicism? After laughing, do we feel slightly depressed, or light and released? When you laugh does it shake you free and open you up to new possibilities, or does it create more uncertainties? Does it come from belittling a person, group or situation, or glimpsing unexpected brilliance? Does it pull us down, and leave us feeling empty, or does it uplift and empower us?

BETWEEN COMEDY AND TRAGEDY:
RELEASING OR SHATTERING PERCEPTION

A fine line sometimes differentiates between what we call comedy and what call tragedy. Sometimes they are linked and sometimes they are even simultaneous. What makes one person laugh can cause another person to cry. Often, people start crying from intense laughter, or begin laughing when experiencing deep upset or regret.

Our brain is designed to observe and make sense of our three-dimensional reality. Observing the world in sequence, one image after the next, one sound after the next, our brains are conditioned to process information linearly and rationally — one plus one equals two seems to be iron-clad wisdom. Because of this affinity for logic, sequence, and predictable causes and effects, we imagine that life will follow expected patterns. If you eat healthily you will be healthier, if you work hard you will make money, if you study more you will know more information.

When something outside of expected patterns abruptly arises, whether it seems to defy logic or proportion, the brain's capacity to process can be suspended. If a healthy person becomes sick, or a person who never worked closes an unheard-of financial deal, the brain's regular mode of functioning can temporarily 'melt down.' An outward expression of such a meltdown is often laughter or tears.

Tears of laughter and tears of tragedy both originate from *Mosros haMochin* / excess of mind, a place beyond what the mind can fathom, digest or tolerate. When the mind is suddenly surprised by a disproportionate or incongruous relationship between what is expected and what actually occurs, the effect can be either comedic or tragic, and tears may flow.

Incongruity between expectation and actuality is a trigger for both comedy and tragedy. Both are founded on this tension of expectation. We expect a young person to live, and when they do not, it is tragic. We expect a person to be held up by the chair he is sitting on, and when they are not, it is comic. Still, there is a sharp distinction between comedy and tragedy: tragedy *shatters* our perception of what should be, leading to a sense of being broken; while comedy *releases* us from rigid perception, more gently taking us beyond our frame of reference, leading to a sense of joy. Comedy gently tampers with our perceptions of life and allows us to transcend our rigid frame of mind. We then feel freed, opened and released through comedy and laughter, and not G-d forbid, broken or unhinged as through tragedy.

LAUGHTER: INFINITE LIGHT

In Hebrew the word for laughter is שחוק / *S'chok*. This word has a numerical value of 414, the same as the term, אור אין סוף / *Ohr Ein Sof* / Infinite Light (or twice the word אור / *Ohr*. Arizal, *Sha'ar haMitzvos*, Vayelech). Through positive and holy laughter we can rise above trivialities, shallow norms and seemingly 'opaque' forms of this world. All limiting or stifling conceptions and perceptions release joyously into the Infinite light of Hashem through holy laughter. By seeing the comedy in a situation, we can break the defensive mold of habitual awareness and sanctimonious etiquette, and come in contact with infinity.

Rabba, the great sage of the *Gemara* / Talmud would begin each teaching session with a light joke in order to open up the minds of his students (*Shabbos*, 30b). This is a good suggestion for all teachers (See Rambam, *Shemone Pirakim*, 5) and all those who wish to impart some wisdom or information to another person who is seeking guidance or a fresh perspective on a particular issue. A teacher of Torah needs to maintain a sense of authority and lack of frivolity when teaching (Rambam, *Hilchos Talmud Torah*, 4:5). However, a light joke, if not undermining the seriousness of the lesson, can shake people out of their intellectual complacency. There is a release of rigidity that comes only through laughter. Humor can help us see things differently.

When people are downcast or gloomy, or even overly serious about their studies, the element of earth, metaphorically, domi-nates their consciousness. The earth's pull of gravity is likened to the heaviness of depression. When the mind is too anchored, when there is too much 'earth' energy, there is no creativity or freedom of thought. According to the Chassidic Rebbes, we need the element of 'wind' in order to counter the weight of earth (e.g., *Bnei Yissaschar*, Sivan, Ma'amar 2:3). Sometimes, to open ourselves to learn something new, we need a strong gust of the free association and spontaneity that humor can create.

MOCKING OLAM HAZEH & BEING "COLD" TO THE SHALLOWNESS OF THIS WORLD

Cold cynicism and self-righteous mockery are negative aspects of laughter connected with Amalek. Amalek is called a scoffer,

"Beat the לץ / scoffer" (Mishlei, 19:25). Our sages say, this refers to Amalek (*Yalkut Shimoni,* Yisro, 258:5). Amalek uses mockery to 'cool us down' in our path and undercut our enthusiasm and spiritual drive. As above, a true *Nahafoch Hu* / transformation is to use the very form of negativity for positive purposes; not to merely replace darkness with light, but to see the light within the darkness itself. How can we harness mockery, coldness and a lack of enthusiasm for a positive purpose?

The Gemara makes a *Siman* / mnemonic from the word *Amalek* to help students learn certain legal cases, עמלק סימן / "*Amalek* is a Siman..." (*Baba Basra,* 46b). We are invited and commanded to eradicate the name of Amalek; why do our sages then use the name as a Siman? Rav Yaakov Emdin, in his notes on this Gemara, writes that Amalek is conjured up into the *Beis Medrash* / the house of Torah study, to help break the negative power and choke hold of Amalek and release the spark of Kedushah that lies within it.˙

---

* Thus, מבני בניו של המן למדו תורה בבני ברק / "from among the grandchildren of Haman, there were those who learned Torah in Bnei Brak" (*Sanhedrin,* 96b). This is the spark of Torah and Kedushah that was revealed from within Amalek and Haman. Although, principally, converts are not accepted from Amalek (*Mechilta,* end of Beshalach. *Tanchuma,* end of Ki Tetzei), the Rambam holds that even Amalek - not during war time – can convert (*Hilchos Melachim* 6:4. See also, *Hilchos Isurei Bi'ah,* 12:17). As well, there was a mixing of the nations. And when one of them came to convert, the *Beis Din* / court did not realize that they were descendants of Amalek (*Chazon Ish,* Yoreh De'ah, 157:5). This answer, on a deeper level, could mean that on the level of Da'as, conscious awareness and Avodah, it is impossible to elevate any sparks within Amalek. Thus, ובבזה לא שלחו את־ידם / "And they did not lay hands on the spoils" (*Esther,* 9:15), yet, on a level of *Lo Yadah* / not knowing, beyond knowing, beyond Avodah, sparks within Haman and Amalek can indeed be elevated.

Our sages tell us כל ליצנותא אסירא בר מליצנותא דעבודת כוכבים / "All mockery is prohibited except for mockery of *Avodah Zarah* / idol worship" (*Megilah*, 25b. Hashem will mock the wicked. *Avodah Zarah*, 3b). Avodah Zarah, as a general category, can include all types of idle worship, such as prostrating oneself to the ego, financial success and money, power, fame, to celebrities and politicians, and so forth. This we can mock. Certainly real evil, or the worshiping of evil, should be mocked. We should use the coldness of cynicism to mock, discredit and trivialize such foolish worship, and laugh at the evils of the world. This reduces their appeal to oneself and others. Harnessing the coldness of Amalek for the positive can thus help you grow in *Avodas Hashem* / service of Hashem.

We can also use the 'coldness' of Amalek to argue with ourselves (and sometimes with others) in a way that cools off any excitement over trivialities such as power, money or fame. When heatedly tempted to do an *Aveira* / sin (*Chalila* / G-d forbid), cool yourself down, and say to yourself, as Rebbe Simcha Bunim of Peshischa would say, "Why are you getting so excited? A 'horse' (physical form) is just a 'horse!'" When you see the disproportion of your anxiety, that there is really nothing to get so worked up about regarding the pleasures of this world, you might even laugh, 'Ha, what a joke!' Imagine a future in which you have already indulged in your desire. In that image, are you feeling good about yourself? Does grabbing for pleasure really make you feel more whole, complete, joyful? Clearly no sustainable well-being is produced, so you might as well skip the clown-like 'middleman' of indulgence and move directly toward a more stable state of wellbeing. Just laugh off your seeming attraction to such meaningless activities and focus on what truly matters.

In the Megilah we read that Haman the *Rasha* / wicked, the descendant and embodiment of Amalek, is feeling haughty and grandiose, as he has just been called for a private meal with the queen and king, "And Haman went out on that day, happy and with a cheerful heart." However, his true nature was revealed in his anger, "When Haman saw Mordechai in the king's gate, ולא־קם ולא־זע ממנו / "and he neither rose nor stirred because of him, Haman was filled with wrath against Mordechai" (Megilas Esther, 5:9). The whole of the Persian Empire trembled at the sight of Haman, they bowed in humility when he passed them on the street. Not only did Mordechai not bow, but ולא־זע ממנו / he did not move when he passed. He was cold and indifferent to Haman, unimpressed and unfazed. Mordechai showed Haman a cold shoulder and this drove Haman mad, puncturing his balloon of pride. This eventually lead to Haman's demise, and the victory of the Jewish people.

In Avodas Hashem we too need to learn to create a *Naha-foch-Hu*, using the coldness and indifference of Amalek to rise up in battle and overcome our inner enemies.*

---

* As mentioned, מבני בניו של המן למדו תורה בבני ברק...ומנו רב שמואל בר שילת / "from among the grandchildren of Haman, there were those who learned Torah in Bnei Brak...and who was this? Rav Shemuel the son of Shilat" (*Sanhedrin*, 96b). The great Torah sage Rav Shemuel was the son of, and was birthed by, Shilat. שילת is an acronym of the phrase שויתי ה לנגדי תמיד / I have placed You Hashem, in front of me at all times (Tehilim, 16:8). The word שויתי is an expression of the word השתוות / equanimity. This means, to live in a place where everything is equal, whether one is praised or denigrated, eating delicacies or the opposite, all is equal to him (*Tzava'as HaRivash*, 2). The positive 'Torah' that comes from within Amalek is Shilat, 'indifference.' It is a general sense of 'coldness' to all the trivialities of this world. Although, healthy השתוות / equanimity is not actually indifference, as explored in the book on The Month of Shevat.

♈

SIGN

ℰACH MONTH CONTAINS THE ZODIAC INFLUENCE OF A
particular constellation called *Mazal*. A constellation is
comprised of a perceivably patterned grouping of visible
stars. Today, we count 88 constellations in the night sky. Out of all
these, one constellation is predominantly visible on the horizon at
the beginning of each month.

Each constellation refracts the light of the cosmos differently,
alternately reflecting times that are more conducive to war, and
times that are more conducive for peace to flourish, for example
(*Yalkut Reuveini*, Bereishis, Os 56). The *Zohar* teaches that each sign can

manifest positively or negatively (*Zohar* 3, 282a). In other words, the constellations can have either a productive or destructive influence on one's life. However there are some important considerations to keep in mind. It is not that the created cluster of stars itself actually has any real influence over us, rather, the formation in the sky is an external expression of how the Creator is, *Kiviyachol* / so-to-speak, interacting with creation at that moment.

It is also important to keep in mind that whether our proclivities are innate or celestially influenced, we nevertheless possess the free choice of how to respond to situations that arise in our lives. In other words, we have the ability to choose how to reflect back what has been projected onto us, even from the stars. A person born under the influence of Mars may have a tendency to be involved with blood, for example, and that is part of their Tikun, but he or she also has the ability to employ this inherent tendency for either good or ill. Such a person could still choose whether to be a violent criminal or a life-saving surgeon.

Due to the popular belief that the stars exert a kind of fatalistic influence upon world history and human development, we need to repeatedly emphasize that anyone can rise above these influences altogether and be unaffected by them. Despite all the forces and influences in life — physical and psychological conditions, upbringing, education, environment, financial status, etc. — we always have the freedom to choose. We have the choice to live as the *effect* of our conditions (as passive receivers of what life serves us), or as the *cause* of what comes next, thereby becoming proactive co-creators of our lives. When we begin to live more proactively, the influences of our birth constellation and the *Mazalos* of each month function less as *influences*, and more as *tools* that help us climb ever higher into our freedom of being.

Adar has 'strong' Mazal; it is a time of בריא מזליה / *Bari Mazalei* (*Ta'anis*, 29b), a month of *Hatzlachah* / success, and *Tov* / goodness (*Aruch HaShulchan*, Orach Chayim, 686:6). The particular astrological influence of this month is *Dagim* / fish or Pisces (see also Rashi, *Baba Metziya*, 106b).

The Yom Tov of Purim reveals a simple connection between fish and Adar. What overtly distinguishes land animals from fish is that land animals are 'revealed' to us, while fish are 'hidden' from us. Such hiddenness alludes to the hidden miracle of Purim, a miracle that was concealed within the workings of history and nature. A mighty ruler was easily convinced by his evil minister to sign a death warrant for Klal Yisrael, and then later reversed his decree at the request of his newly married wife who was secretly a Jew. In the language of our sages, הרג אשתו בשביל אוהבו ואחר כך הרג אוהבו בשביל אשתו / "He (the king) killed his wife (Vashti) because of his friend (advisor, Haman, who advised him to kill her for disobedience), and then killed his friend (Haman) because of his wife (Esther)" (*Medrash Rabbah*, Esther. *Yalkut Shimoni*, Esther, 1045). This seems like a simple, straightforward story of intrigue and drama, without any 'revealed' supernatural miracles on display. However, Hashem's Presence was concealed within the workings of nature.

Numerically, אדר / *Adar* is 205 (Aleph / 1, Dalet / 4, Reish / 200 = 205), which is the value of the words בחסד מכוסה / *b'Chesed M'chuseh* / with hidden kindness. The kindness of Hashem was veiled within the Purim story, and this is the root of the custom to wear veils and masks on Purim. At the time, things seemed very uncertain and difficult. Only in retrospect could Hashem's kindness in these matters be perceived. Besides the reversal of the decree itself, there was also great kindness in the fact that the Jews' uncertainty brought them into a deeper dedication to HaKadosh Baruch Hu and the Torah.

The word *Dag* / fish also alludes to *Da'aga* / worry (*Tikunei Zohar*, 53, *Kaf Hachayim*, Orach Chayim, Siman 583:9). In fact, in Tanach the word *Dag* / fish is once spelled *Da'ag*: in Nechemyah where he is rebuking Klal Yisrael for desecrating Shabbos, he tells them והצרים ישבו בה מביאים דאג וכל־מכר ומכרים בשבת לבני יהודה ובירושלם / "And the Tyrians (who) sojourned there were bringing **fish** and all types of merchandise and selling on Shabbos to the people of Judea…" (13:16).

As Adar progresses, we can evolve toward overcoming and transcending any tendency to worry. (Interestingly, the body part of the month is *Techol* / spleen, and according to traditional Chinese medicine, the stomach, and more so the spleen are most affected by chronic worry and anxiety.) We worry when we have a lack of clarity, especially when we feel uncertain and doubtful about our future. At such times, it is very helpful simply to settle the mind in the present moment, which is the only true reality. It also helps to understand that when a future moment actually happens, you too will be different and will have new *Kelim* / vessels and resources, including the wisdom and strength to deal with whatever is then present. On a deeper level, we need to learn to leverage our sense of doubt for openness to mystery, and our sense of the unknown for transcendence of worry. Then these previously anxiety-inducing experiences will elevate and free us, much like good, healthy, productive humor does. When we do so we will be able to laugh and be joyous always.

This is the 'Nahafoch Hu' of Purim; a source of negative worry becomes a source of striving for infinite positive growth and dedication to serving the truly Infinite One (ישראל דדייגי במצות. *Shabbos*, 86b. *Nidah*, 34b).

PISCEANS & WORRY

Pisceans naturally worry, this is perhaps due to their being extremely sensitive to the suffering of others. This sensitivity is also the reason that Pisceans often become charismatic, powerful, and focused leaders. Moshe, the ultimate leader of Klal Yisrael, was born in Adar. On the flip side, Pisceans can be so open to others that they can develop weaknesses and be influenced by others' opinions, or they can even become 'dependent' on external substances and addictive behaviors. The *Tikun* / perfection for Pisceans generally involves overcoming worry through cultivating positive uncertainty, holy not-knowing, and self-liberating laughter.

LIGHTNESS OF THE BODY, LAUGHTER & JOY

Adar is associated with a lightness of being, wholesome humor and a sense of unbounded joy: "When Adar arrives we increase in joy." When people feel unhappy and lose their zest for life, they often attribute such malaise to some external or existential issue in their life. In truth, their state is sometimes merely a physiological issue. The mind needs to find a 'reason' to explain why one is feeling low, and, not being sensitive to the body, the mind most often finds a reason in some illusory or augmented emotional or interpersonal narrative. To counter this tendency, it helps to be sensitive to one's body, to tune into the physical needs and sensations manifesting in the present moment. Sometimes people believe that they are sad, but in truth they are simply fatigued or hungry, or even just lethargic after a heavy meal. The mind, trying to make sense of the raw data of experience, interprets these experiences as psychological feelings of melancholy.

In accord with this, to fully experience joy, we need to include an enhanced consciousness of the body. Haman wanted to annihilate the bodies of the Jewish People. This fact is in contrast to Chanukah, when the evil decrees were directed at disabling the spiritual and ritual practices of Torah (Shabbos, Rosh Chodesh, Bris, and so forth). Since Haman wished to annihilate our very physicality, we celebrate physically — with a festive meal and lots of drinking (*Levush*); whereas on Chanukah, we celebrate with light.

At Matan Torah when we initially received the Torah, "our souls departed our bodies" (*Shabbos*, 88b), and we went to sleep on the night before the giving of the Torah (*Medrash Rabbah*, Shir HaShirim, 1:12). We did this so that we could receive the Torah in a dream state (The Rebbe, *Likkutei Sichos*, 4, p. 1024-1027). In the story of Purim, however, we re-accepted the Torah when we were fully awake. As discussed, the miraculous overturning occurred on the night of great awakening: both the king below and the King above were unable to sleep. We thus received the Torah with our whole being, cognizant of and totally in tune with our bodies, as the Alter Rebbe explains (*Torah Ohr*, Hosofos, Megilas Esther, 118b).

Accordingly, *Purim* is connected to the word *Guf* / body. The root letters of *Purim* are Pei, Vav and Reish. In the At-Bash system, the first letter in the Aleph-Beis, Aleph, is exchanged for the last letter, Tav, and the second letter, Beis, is exchanged for the second to the last letter, Shin, and so forth. Using this methodology, the letters of *Pur* are exchanged with the letters Vav, Pei and Gimel, which spell גוף / *Guf.*

Purim and Adar teach us to include the body in our joy, and to ensure that the body is not a hindrance to true joy.

We need to make sure our bodies are supple and free-flowing, with an agile ease in our movements. The natural lightness and fluidity of *Dagim* / fish is expressed in the ease of their frictionless movement through water, as well as the fact that we do not need to *Shecht* / ritually slaughter them before preparing them as food. This lightness of being is connected to laughter and playfulness, as we find with the Leviasan, the great primordial fish: "There is Leviasan whom You have formed to laugh with" (Tehilim, 104:26). In fact, Chazal tell us that Hashem 'laughs' and 'plays' with this great fish every day (*Avodah Zarah*, 3b. *Baba Basra*, 74b. See also *Machshavos Charutz*, 13).

In comparison to the meat of kosher land-animals, fish are a 'lighter' protein, and eating fish is a *Birur Kal* / an easier form of digesting and elevating sparks. In terms of our own lives, we need to elevate ourselves and become lighter, perhaps a way to achieve this on a fundamental level is to eat lighter, to move more, and make sure we are properly hydrated. When our body is light and awake, it is easier to ensure that our physicality is not a blockage or hindrance to our joy and sense of wellbeing.

FISH, CHILDREN & LIGHTNESS

Fish have received a special Divine blessing to be fruitful and multiply (Bereishis, 48:16). As mentioned, the Mazal of Adar is fish, and this is also a month that is connected to the power of procreation and the blessing of children (*Rosh Hashanah*, 8a. *Resisei Layla*, 49). The word *Adar* is related to the word *Dor* / generation (*Beitzah*, 15b), as in generations of children.

This blessing of creating new life, literally and metaphorically, is intricately linked with the qualities of lightness, humor and positive laughter that we have previously spoken about. To open up to the possibility of the new, for a new life to be conceived, there needs a softening, a lightening, a releasing of tension and stiffness, which gives room for new life to emerge. We find this idea clearly illustrated in the birth of the first born Jew, Yitzchak, the son of Avraham and Sarah.

Avraham and Sarah were advanced in age, and Sarah was barren. Seemingly against all logic, they were told that they would have a child, and they both laughed: "And Avraham fell on his face, and he laughed, and he said in his heart, 'Can a one-hundred-year-old give birth?'" (Bereishis, 17:17). When Sarah heard the surprising news, "Sarah laughed in her heart, and she said, 'after I am worn out and my lord is old, will I now have this pleasure?'" (*Ibid*, 18:12). Whether their laughter was warranted or not, and whether it was a laughter of joy or of disbelief, it served to break a certain tension within themselves and within their marriage. The lightness of their laughter uplifted them, untangling and removing a persistent resistance and blockage. Only then, after they had a good laugh, were they open and ready for the birth of Yitzchak to miraculously occur.

Avraham and Sarah laughed at the unbelievable, seemingly impossible news that was being revealed to them. This broke down their sense of a fixed fate for their family, as explained. Additionally, their laughter was also an expression of the paradoxical nature of their promised child. How so? Avraham and Sarah are the archetypal embodiments of Chesed, the attribute of expansive giving, and they are told they will give birth to a child who will be the embodiment of Gevurah, introverted restriction. It was Sarah's laughter in particular which allowed the pregnancy to occur, and yet for both Sarah and Avraham, this unexpected paradox triggered laughter which opened them up, individually and as a unit, to become fit vessels to receive and birth such a Divine paradox. Thus, the name of their child is Yitzchak, from the root word S'chok / laughter. Sarah says צחק עשה לי ...יצחק־לי כל־השמע / "(Hashem) has brought me laughter; everyone who hears will laugh with me" (Bereishis, 21:6). As such, the essence of this child is יצחק / laughter. Born through laughter and named "Laughter," Yitzchak also causes others to laugh, as he embodies the seeming impossibility of *Gevurah* / restriction that is rooted in the ultimate *Chesed* / kindness, that of his parents.

Their positive, redemptive laughter was preceded by negative laughter: "...the mocking and cynical laughter of the ליצני הדור / scoffers of the generation, who laughed and said it is impossible for Avraham, such an old man, to have a child" (*Tanchuma*, Toldos, 1. Rashi, Bereishis, 25:19). This initial negativity was overturned through Avraham's and even Sarah's holy laughter. The dark laughter of the 'naysayers' of the world asserts negative impossibility. Avraham and Sarah's light laughter is an eruption of wonder and bewilderment at the positive, joyful 'impossibility' of the revelation.

A similar idea is found with regard to Dovid HaMelech / King David. The Zohar calls him "the King's jester" (*Zohar* 2, 107a). He is a person who is able to 'laugh' and take himself lightly even in Hashem's Presence. As the *Aron* / Ark was being returned from captivity, he was overwhelmed with holy joy and did not take into consideration his personal position of public power and began dancing ecstatically in full view of the people. His wife, Michal, who was the daughter of King Shaul, became upset. She thought it unbecoming for a king to act this way. "As the Aron of Hashem was entering the City of David, Michal the daughter of Shaul watched from a window. And when she saw King David leaping and dancing before Hashem, she despised him in her heart" (Shemuel 2, 6:16).

At the end of this episode, after the return of the Aron, the verse concludes, "And Michal daughter of Shaul, had no children to the day of her death." It thus appears as though her not having children is connected to her criticism of Dovid haMelech's behavior, and was perhaps a form of punishment. If so, why would such a harsh punishment be evoked? And why specifically this harsh punishment of not bearing children?

Perhaps she was barren all along, and she was not blessed with the miracle of children precisely because she lacked a childlike openness. She showed no receptivity to childlike behavior, even when it was rooted in complete holiness and nobility. Not only did she not appreciate David's dancing, she was unable to 'lower' herself enough to even begin to understand it. She was stuck in her defined narrative and was not light, open and fluid like a fish, who can switch or adapt their direction at a moment's notice. This is in sharp contrast to Avraham and Sarah who were able to laugh, lighten up and be vulnerable; they thus opened themselves to the blessing of childbirth.

MICRO AND MACRO BIRTH BEGINS IN LAUGHTER

When Avimelech sees Yitzchak "laughing" with Rivkah / Rebecca, he realizes she is Yitzchak's wife, not his sister (Bereishis, 26:8). Laughter, as the term is euphemistically used here, means marital intimacy, the potential creation of new life. Conception and the birth of children demands love, vulnerability, openness and fluidity. Meaningful laughter breaks tension and gives space for a new entity or new reality to come into being. This is a reflection of the macrocosmic creative process that gives birth to our universe.

The Infinite Light of Hashem is *Echad* / One and Unified. For the creation of an (apparently) finite reality to occur there must first be a process of *Tzimtzum* / constriction and self-restriction of the Infinite Light. By withholding His Infinite expression, Hashem allows for finitude to emerge. But what caused Hashem's initial cosmic desire to 'limit' Himself in order to create an 'other'? And even more perplexing, how can a movement of desire — which already implies something outside, something that is 'other' — even appear to arise from within the unity, stillness and omnipresent Oneness of Hashem?

In a highly original metaphor, the *Emek haMelech* (*Sha'ashu'ai haMelech*, Sha'ar 1. Chap 2), illustrates the phenomenon of cosmic desire, revealing what 'caused' it, and how it can appear within a unified boundless Infinity. The metaphor he offers is that of a person who, when greatly overjoyed, begins to chuckle to himself. Before the chuckle, the body is still. One's posture may be erect, and the body placid and 'smooth' like the surface of a restful pond, but when a person chuckles, a ripple moves through the belly and throughout the whole body. These ripples of laughter create crevices, indents or 'spaces' throughout the body (so to speak) as the muscles tighten and release with the vibration of the laughter. This physical phenomenon that we experience in our own bodies is a reflection of the One Above. There was a Divine 'chuckle' within the placid Infinite Unity of Hashem, which created a ripple-effect, manifesting the 'space' in which the desire to create was able to appear.

This is a stunning image, Hashem 'laughing into being' the space of the world. But why did Hashem burst into a chuckle? The Creator imagined the wonderful spiritual work that would eventually be done in the world by the *souls of the righteous*. We too, when startled by an awesome, new or paradoxical creative insight, may suddenly laugh out loud. This is because we, the microcosm below, mirror the Macrocosm Above. All of our creativity, birth and movement, begins with the opening of an inner space, a relaxing of rigidity. This is rooted in the power of *S'chok* / laughter and lightness of being. Thus, *S'chok* has the same numerical value (414) as מקור חיים / *Makor Chayim* / source of life.

In this month, the magnified 'sense' of laughter opens us to receive blessings for children, and other types of birth — a rebirth of self, a birth of new ideas and understandings, new opportunities and ventures, and new levels of spiritual service and aliveness.

LAUGHTER AND THE BIRTH OF SELF

As life evolves, we are in a constant state of becoming. Without a sense of lightness, fluidity and a continuous rebirthing of ourselves, we can become rigid and frozen in our identity. In this month of laughter and Mazal of fluidity, Purim gives us a chance to re-enter the flow. To facilitate this, many have the custom of dressing up, donning a mask, and humorously concealing or altering their normal identity. This playful fluidity of self-image allows a release of the superficial self that has been shaped by our past or is but a frozen image of our past which we project into the present and future unthinkingly. This way, in costume, one may tangibly sense the fact of being created anew, moment by moment.

Our *Avodah* / spiritual work in Adar and Purim — increasing in lightness, openness, freshness, holy laughter, holy doubt, and holy questions — draws us into our deeper authenticity, and allow us to tap into the sublime Infinite Light. Indeed, the word *S'chok* / laughter has the numerical value (414), the same as אור אין סוף / *Ohr Ein Sof* / Light of the Endless One.

MAZAL OF THE SECOND ADAR

As explored earlier, on a leap year there are two months of Adar, and the second Adar is the thirteenth month of the year. The numerical value of the word *Echad* / unity is 13. This demonstrates that the second month belongs to a world of unity, beyond Mazal, beyond the world of influence. On another level, the thirteenth month is connected to a "Mazal" that includes all preceding twelve Mazalos. This too represents unity; the unity of the many as one whole.

Sefer Yetzirah speaks about the idea of a תלי / *T'li*, which in more modern Hebrew means a suspensory hanger, used for instance to hang up your clothes, but in our mystical context also means a *curled one* or a *coiled serpent*. It is upon this *T'li*, writes the Gra, that all the twelve Mazalos are suspended and rotate. In this way, it is the *T'li* which includes them all. The *T'li* is the hidden, astrological element unknown to the wise men of the world, and is much like the heart within the body (*Sefer Yetzirah*, 6:1, Pirush haGra). As the heart and axle of all the Mazalos, the element that includes them all in one essence, the *T'li* corresponds to the thirteenth month of the year, the Echad within the months.

☾

♉

TRIBE

   EVERY MONTH OF THE YEAR IS CONNECTED WITH ONE OF the Twelve Tribes of Israel, the sons of Yaakov (*Sefer Ye-tzirah*; Medrash, *Osyos d'Rebbe Akiva*, Dalet). According to the Arizal, Naftali is the tribe associated with Adar. Yaakov blessed his son Naftali to be an *Ayalah Shelucha* / a swift deer (Bereishis, 49:21). Indeed, the tribe of Naftali inherited this trait of *Zerizus* / alacrity (Rashi, Ramban, ad loc). Worry and negative doubt can weigh you down physically, emotionally and mentally, but to be 'light on your feet' is to embody a sense of emotional and mental lightness or flexibility. These are the traits that allow us to laugh, relax and tolerate paradox, while dancing joyfully through the complexities of life.

Alacrity means to get things done quickly, in their right time and without procrastination. When we stop and hesitate, linger, think, rethink, and second-guess our decisions, we may allow Amalek, negative and crippling doubt, to enter into the equation. We can always find a hundred and one more reasons why not to do something than to do it, and such laziness has many guises. The quality of Naftali embodies swiftness and empowers us to act in the present moment, making sure we do not sink into paralyzing uncertainty. When doubts do arise, the alacrity of Naftali allows us to escape being crippled by them. Then we can focus on the 'not-knowing' quality of the doubt, and allow it to destabilize our rigid thinking rather than completely deconstructing our ability to decide and move in the moment. Then the doubt opens us to unimagined possibilities.

When one's body is tired and weighed down, perhaps after a heavy meal or a night of compromised sleep, one may easily mistake this feeling for depression or negative spiritual resistance; one way to break this Kelipah is to simply 'do something' and do it with alacrity. Like Naftali, one should move quickly; maybe even do some exercise or stretching. They will then notice the sadness lifting. The more we physically counter such physical heaviness (over-abundance of the element of earth) the lighter we feel (like the wind) and the more joyous we become.

Because of this mind-to-body and body-to-mind loop, it is also important to avoid ruminating too much about your life — where you are heading and what you have achieved — while fatigued, sick or lying tired in your bed. When you are fatigued and sleepy, everything can look bleak and miserable. Your lack of strength in those moments can cause you to get stuck in dwelling upon false impressions of the facts of your life and let negative doubts grab the steering wheel of your consciousness. It follows that a spiritual practice of *Cheshbon haNefesh* / self-evaluation should be performed at times when one has the strength to be compassionate, resilient, forgiving and relatively swift in judgment and execution.

ADAR AND YOSEPH

There is a debate regarding the correspondences of the tribes to the months of the year. The Arizal says that the twelve months follow the order in which the Twelve Tribes camped in the desert when they left Egypt. The formation of the encampment was like a square; in the center was the Mishkan, and the tribes were divided into four groups, one to the east, one to the west, one to the south and one to the north. Each group was comprised of three tribes. In this model, the Tribe of Levi is not counted and does not have a corresponding month, since the tribe of Levi did not camp with the other tribes, rather they had a separate encampment. In this formation, which does not count the Tribe of Levi, in order to bring the number of tribes to 12, the tribe of Yoseph is subdivided into two: the House of Ephrayim and the House of Menashe.

The order of the tribes and months, according to the Arizal, are as follows:

Month	Tribe	Location of Tribe, encamped around the Mishkan
Nisan	Yehudah	
Iyyar	Yissachar	East
Sivan	Zevulun	
Tamuz	Reuvein	
Av	Shimon	South
Elul	Gad	
Tishrei	Ephrayim	
Cheshvan	Menashe	West
Kislev	Binyamin	
Teves	Dan	
Shevat	Asher	North
Adar	Naftali	

This system of the holy Arizal is what is being followed in the course of these volumes, and as such, Adar corresponds with Naftali. However, there is another system, namely the *Shita* / opinion of the Ra'avad (*Pirush on Sefer Yetzirah*; see also *Yalkut Reuveini*, Vayeshev) and the *Ya'vatz* (*Siddur*). From this perspective, the order of the months follow the order of Yaakov's sons as recounted in the beginning of the Book of Shemos when it lists the names of the people who came down into Egypt. To quote, "These are the names of the sons of Yisrael who came to Egypt... Reuvein, Shimon, Levi, and Yehudah. Yissachar, Zevulun and Binyamin. Dan and Naftali, Gad and Asher... Yoseph was (already) in Egypt" (Shemos, 1:1-5). Yaakov had two wives and two maidservants. The first six months correspond to the six sons of Leah in order of their birth, from Reuvein to Zevulun, then the son of Rachel, Binyamin (Yoseph is mentioned last, as he was already in Egypt), then the two sons of Bil'ha and Zilpah. The last month, the month of Adar, then corresponds to Yoseph.

These are the correspondences between the months and the tribes, according to the perspective of the Ra'avad :

Month	Tribe
Nisan	Reuvein
Iyyar	Shimon
Sivan	Levi
Tamuz	Yehudah
Av	Yissachar
Elul	Zevulun
Tishrei	Binyamin
Cheshvan	Dan
Kislev	Naftali
Teves	Gad
Shevat	Asher
Adar	Yoseph

In this formation, the Tribe of Levi is counted and corresponds to the month of Sivan. Yoseph is not divided into two, rather Yoseph's own name appears and corresponds to the month of Adar. It is interesting to point out that the name Yoseph comes from the word *Asaf* / gathered, and the name *Adar* is related to the Aramaic Talmudic term אידרה / *Idra* / a meeting, or place of gathering.

ELUDING THE AYIN HARA

As explored earlier, *Dagim* / fish / Pisces is the Mazal of Adar, and Dagim are hidden away from human view, making them immune to the influence of how other people see them. Similarly, Yoseph is connected to fish and to this idea of being beyond the influence of an *Ayin haRa* / evil eye, the qualities potentially imposed on one by another person's negative view.

The letters of דג / fish, when reversed, spell גד / Gad. Gad also means 'good Mazal' or good fortune (Bereishis, 30:11. When Gad was born, his mother Leah said, *Ba Gad* / "Now good Mazal has come." Rashi on Bereishis, 30:11, quoting *Medrash Rabbah*, 71:9. See also the *Targum Yonason Ben Uziel*), and Adar is likewise a time of strong, good Mazal. Perhaps it is because of this Torah-based symbolism that many cultures use fish as a symbol for protection from the evil eye, and that Pisces are associated with good fortune.

Members of the tribe of Yoseph once complained to Yehoshua saying, "Why have you assigned as our portion a single allotment and a single district, seeing that we are a numerous people whom Hashem has blessed so greatly?" To which Yehoshua responded, "If you are a great people, you should go up to the forest..." (Yehoshua, 17:14-15). According to our sages (*Sotah*, 36b), Yehoshua is telling them, "Go and hide yourselves in the forests, so that the *Ayin haRa* / evil eye will not have dominion over you, as you are such a large number of people."

In response, the tribe of Yoseph says, "The evil eye does not have dominion over the offspring of Yoseph, as it is written: 'Yoseph is a fruitful vine, a fruitful vine by a fountain'" (Bereishis, 49:22). Do not read the verse as saying 'By a fountain (*Alei Ayin*)'; rather, read it as: 'Those who rise above the evil eye (*Olei* / rise above the *Ayin* / eye).' Teaching that Yoseph and his descendants are not susceptible to the evil eye.

An alternative source for the assertion that the evil eye holds no sway over Yoseph and his descendants is derived from when Yaakov blesses the sons of Yoseph and says to them, "And let them grow (וידגו — from the word דג / fish) into a multitude in the midst of the earth" (Bereishis, 48:16). Just as with regard to fish in the sea, waters cover them and the evil eye therefore has no dominion over them, so too, with regard to Yoseph's descendants, the evil eye has no dominion over them.

Our sages teach that a person should protect himself from an Ayin haRa (*Baba Basra*, 118a), and they advise: "If a man going into a town is afraid of the evil eye, let him take the thumb of his right hand in his left hand and the thumb of his left hand in his right hand, and say: 'I, so-and-so, am of the seed of Yoseph (which we all are, regardless of our genealogy; Tehilim, 80:2), over which the Ayin haRa has no power'" (*Berachos*, 55b). As a general principle, all of Klal Yisrael is *essentially beyond* the influence of Ayin haRa (*Pesikta Rabsi*, Parsha 20:2, Matan Torah).

All of these qualities are fully manifest in our lives during Adar, reflecting and refracting the light of the Mazal of Dagim, being 'hidden away from view.' We too, like Hashem in the story of Purim, are on some level concealed from view, yet still imminently present and pregnant with potential.

TRIBE OF THE SECOND ADAR

A question remains: on a year with two Adars, which tribe corresponds to the second Adar? According to the Ra'avad Adar is Yoseph, and Yoseph can be divided into two. Therefore, according to this opinion, Adar One is Ephrayim and Adar Two is Menasheh. When Yaakov gives a blessing to Ephrayim and Menasheh he says, "...And let them grow into a multitude in the midst of the earth." This blessing is reminiscent of the blessing that Hashem gave the fish in the beginning of the Torah; after the creation of fish Hashem says, "Be fertile and increase, fill the waters in the seas" (Bereishis, 1:22). Ephrayim and Menasheh, are thus both connected to the paradigm of fish and it is thus fitting that they correspond to Adar One and Adar Two.

According to the Arizal, however, the first Adar corresponds to Naftali, and the tribe of Yoseph is already divided into two; Ephrayim for the month of Tishrei and Menashe for the month of Cheshvan. Which tribe, then, corresponds with the second Adar from the Arizal's perspective?

There are sources which teach that the second Adar corresponds to all the Twelve Tribes together (*Pnei Menachem* in conversation with the Rebbe, *BeTzeil haChochmah*). This parallels the correspondences to the Mazalos, above: the second Adar is the thirteenth month of the year, and 13 is the numerical value of the word *Echad* / one; the inclusion of the previous 12 Mazalos or Tribes within a single unity. This extends to other coordinates as well, for example, the formation of Hashem's Name for the second Adar includes and unifies all twelve possible formations of The Name.

Extending the idea that Adar Two corresponds to all the Tribes, we can call it 'the month of *Klal Yisrael'* / the all-inclusive collective of Israel. Adar is "the source of the souls of Klal Yisrael" (*Yismach Moshe*, Tetzaveh, 1:5), as it contains the power of all of Klal Yisrael.

The second Adar can thus be viewed either as a month of very strong Mazal, as a combination of all Mazalos (all the Tribes together), or it can be viewed as a month (of Klal Yisrael) which is beyond all Mazal, because *Ein Mazal l'Yisrael* / "Klal Israel is beyond Mazal" (*Shabbos*, 156b).

The Tzemach Tzedek, on the other hand, teaches that the second Adar is connected to the tribe of Levi (as, according to the Arizal, Levi does not correspond to any of the twelve months, whereas according to the Ra'avad, Levi is the month of Sivan). This is similar to 'all of the tribes' being connected to Adar Two, for, "The entire progeny of Levi was set apart to do the work inside the sanctuary (on behalf of Klal Yisrael)" (Rambam, *Hilchos Kli haMikdash*, 3:1). In this way, the tribe of Levi is the representative of all Klal Yisrael. In another fashion, anyone and everyone of Klal Yisrael can be like Levi, and dedicate their life to a higher cause (and Hashem will provide sufficiently for his needs. Rambam. *Hilchos Shemitah v'Yovel*, 13:13). In this way, the Mazal of Levi is essentially similar to the Mazal of all Klal Yisrael.

Echad is comprised of three letters: Aleph (1), Ches (8) and Daled (4). The letter Ches (8) represents the eight tribes who are from the house of Rachel and Leah: Reuvein, Shimon, Yehudah, Yissachar, Zevulun, Menasheh, Ephrayim, and Binyamin. Dalet (4) represents the four tribes from the maidservants, Dan, Naftali, Gad and Asher. And Aleph (1) refers to the tribe of Levi, who unites all of Klal Yisrael into one unit, into *Echad* (13). This supports the idea that the second Adar is Echad, the quality of the whole of Klal Yisrael, beyond all Mazal; connected to the Infinite Source of all life, Hashem alone.

Adar in general, and more specifically the second Adar, creates the unity of all of Klal Yisrael, and the ultimate unity between all apparent opposites which we have been discussing: certainty and holy uncertainty, knowing and unknowing, anchored-ness and lightness, seriousness and laughter. Adar as *Echad* represents the Keser of all Kesarim, the Essence of Hashem, and the Unity of all Unities.

♉ BODY PART

ACH MONTH IS ASSOCIATED WITH THE GENERAL QUALITY, particular function, and conceptual themes of a specific body part. This pairing helps us to focus on the miraculous functioning of the physical body, and to refine its spiritual properties, as the year spirals around its Divine axis. The month of Adar is connected to the *T'chol* / spleen.

According to our Sages the spleen is connected with laughter: טחול שוחק / "The spleen laughs" (*Berachos*, 61b). The Zohar, on the other hand, tells us that the spleen is associated with *Atzvus* / depression (*Tikunei Zohar*, Tikun 48). The reconciliation of these, apparently opposite ideas, rests in the fact explored earlier: shallow, superficial or cynical laughter fosters a sense of meaningless and purposelessness, leading to eventual depression (*Pri Tzadik*, Rosh Chodesh Sivan. In a similar vein, our sages tell us that "Wine first brings (a shallow) joy and then leads to depression" (*Sanhedrin*, 70a). Coldness, deadness and depression are clearly linked. See also, *Sheim miShemuel*, Chanukah, 216).

Negative forms of laughter, mockery and comedy are in fact symptoms of an underlying stream of depression. A sense of nihilistic emptiness, numbness and purposelessness lurks below the surface of such humor. Laughing at it only reinforces those life-hollowing sentiments. Nevertheless, at certain moments, this kind of humor may help to relieve a person temporarily of his anxiety and sense of purposelessness; and in rare cases it can even be a tool of survival. Sometimes humor, even negative humor, can break through extreme nervous tension, or suddenly re-frame a sense of powerlessness in the face of social oppression. It may also serve as a distraction from fear and anxiety, allowing one to laugh rather than weep. Yet, sadly, in the end it still tends to make the person and those laughing along feel even worse. This only serves to reinforce the hopelessness and helplessness from which this kind of laughter had sprung.

Senseless mockery / ליצנות is an attempt to conceal inner futility and despair. It is not a coincidence that many professional comedians, who feed off cynical or ungrounded humor, suffer from depression. The more famous and admired they become, the more rewarded they are for reinforcing and spreading their spiritual despair, the more depressed they become.*

---

* The word לץ in numerical value is 120. This corresponds to the 120 letter combinations of the five letter Name of Hashem, the Divine Name of Judgment, Elokim (the five letters can be arranged into 120 possible formations). Through ליצנות a person draws upon himself the *Dinim* / judgments of the Name Elokim and does not allow for the Divine *Shefa* / flow to be revealed through the world below or into his own life, thus he feels lifeless and depressed; and even his physical sustenance suffers, as our sages tell us, "Anyone who scoffs, his sustenance is lessened."(*Avodah Zarah*, 18b).

When Klal Yisrael were finally redeemed from their deep existential and literal slavery in Mitzrayim, the *Pasuk* / verse says, "Now
when Pharaoh let the people go, Hashem did not lead them by way
of the land of the פלשתים / *P'lishtim*, although it was nearer. For
Hashem said, "The people may have a change of heart when they
see war, and will return to Egypt" (Shemos, 13:17). They have just
received their freed from the mightiest nation on the planet, the
greatest power of the ancient world, and now Hashem says there is
reason to fear the P'lishtim? Why? The P'lishtim represent the idea
of ליצנות / mockery and thus cynicism (See *Avodah Zarah*, 19a). Hashem did not allow Klal Yisrael to pass through the world of mockery
because mockery kills all enthusiasm, drive and ambition. Mockery
is the worst enemy of growth and movement. It pokes fun and
laughs at any desire for positive change. And when some changes
begin to take hold, ליצנות comes along and says, 'Is this a joke?'

Rebbe Mendel of Rimanov, a great Chassidic Rebbe, once
quipped that had Pharaoh known the power of ליצנות / mockery,
he would have used its power, and Klal Yisrael would have never
been able to be redeemed from Egypt (see *Imrei Yoseph* (Spinka), Beshalach). Imagine if Moshe would have come to Pharaoh and to Klal
Yisrael to tell them that Hashem is about to redeem Klal Yisrael
from Egypt, and instead of Pharaoh resisting and thus creating
more friction and pent-up energy, he would have simply laughed at
Moshe, saying, 'Ha, ridiculous! Stop speaking foolishness!' Arguably, this could have diffused the enthusiasm for Geulah because
the news would have spread, and then when Moshe went to tell
Klal Yisrael to bring a Korban Pesach, they'd have laughed at him
as well, possibly preventing the Geula from happening, at least at
that time or in that way.

POSITIVE LAUGHTER & YIRAS SHAMAYIM

A person lives with a sense of mockery and purposelessness because of a lack in their *Yiras Shamayim* / fear (awe) of Heaven; a lack of awareness of the precious gift of life, of its meaningfulness, and of the great importance of working toward a more positive human destiny. Yiras Shamayim is the recognition that there is a Higher Power, an involved Creator, and we are therefore created for a purpose in relation to this world. More than merely intellectual awareness, Yiras Shamayim is an almost visceral sensation of standing in the Presence of *Elokim Chayim* / the living G-d, infused with a sense of urgency, holy humility and grounded joy. Life has intrinsic meaning and therefore we can choose to engage a life of deep meaning. Superficial laughter is clearly the antithesis to this awareness.

Speaking of, a person wearing Tefilin, choosing to do a Mitzvah and trying to connect to the world of meaning and purpose, the Rambam writes, "The *Kedusha* / sanctity of Tefilin is a high degree of Kedusha, and שכל זמן שהתפלין בראשו של אדם ועל זרועו הוא ענו וירא שמים ואינו נמשך בשחוק / "as long as the Tefilin are on a person's head and arm, he is in a state of humility and Yiras Shamayim, and is not drawn into שחוק / frivolous mockery (laughter)" (Rambam, *Hilchos Tefilin uMezuzah*, 4:25). Yiras Shamayim directly negates negative laughter. Without real Yiras Shamayim, a person is drawn toward nihilistic emptiness and purposelessness.

In contrast, the positive *Chush* / sense of laughter — and the paradigm of the body part of Adar, *T'chol* / spleen, as well — is a holy, anchored, 'serious' laughter; one that is precisely linked to true

Yiras Shamayim. We need to keep in mind that 'seriousness' is not to be equated with melancholy. Taking your life seriously is being open to the meaningfulness of every moment, to what life serves you and to what Hashem wants from you.

We ought not get stuck in old narratives and perceptions. To be fully alive in the moment and not held hostage to our past, we need to live with a sense of *Yirah* / awe. And just because some aspect of *Avodah* / spiritual work was successful yesterday does not necessarily mean it will be the same today. Yirah is living with a sense of surprise, amazement and *Lo Yada* / not-knowing; a perpetual openness to observing and responding to Hashem's guidance. This type of awe can be expressed in laughter, which opens us even more to the miraculous present.

LAUGHTER & THE FUTURE

When we open our minds and hearts to the present moment, we also open our vision to what is in store for us in the future. As laughter breaks the monotony of the present, it creates space for a bright new reality to begin unfolding. In this way, holy laughter has a propulsive trajectory into the future. The Rema miPano (Rabbi Menachem Azariah of Fano, Italy) writes that a distinction should be made between joy and laughter. Whereas joy is pleasure in the immediate present; holy laughter is infused with knowing that a positive and joyful event is going to occur in the future. The anticipation of that joy is laughter (*Asara Ma'amaros*, Ma'amar Chikur Din, 1:2). There is a good source for this idea in the various episodes recorded in the Gemara regarding the laughter of the great sage Rabbi Akiva.

Rabbi Akiva is fond of laughing, in fact, we find him laughing at various counter-intuitive occasions. A common denominator between all the episodes of him laughing is that every time he laughs, he is laughing because he sees a future that is positive and brighter. He laughs at the wealthy Roman woman who tries to entice him, knowing that in the future she will convert and he will marry her (*Avodah Zarah*, 20). He laughs when he is walking near the site where the Holy Temple once stood as he saw a fox emerging from the Holy of Holies. His colleagues cry, but he laughs. To Rabbi Akiva this tragic sight was a confirmation that the prophecies of the Temple being in shambles had already been fulfilled, and for this reason, so too would the prophecies that it be rebuilt in the future (*Makos*, 24b). Rabbi Akiva laughs seeing his teacher on his death-bed in great pain, because he knows that very shortly he will pass on from this world, and all the rewards of his actions which had been treasured up for him in *Olam haBa* / the World to Come would soon be enjoyed (*Sanhedrin*, 101a).

LAUGHTER IN AND FROM OLAM HAZEH

Laughter connects us to the future, and the full extent of such holy laughter will only be experienced in the world-to-come — however, one whose present life is already merged with the life of Olam haBa can experience it even now.

Dovid haMelech / King David tells us in the Book of Tehilim / Psalms, אז ימלא שחוק פינו / "...*Then* our mouths will be filled with laughter" (126:2). Only then, in Olam haBa, will we be fully allowed and able to "fill" our mouths with laughter (*Berachos*, 31a).

This suggests that we will be in a perpetual state of laughter. Today, as long as we are in exile, we cannot authentically fill our mouths with laughter (Ramban, *Toras haAdam*, Sha'ar Aveilus. *Sefer haEshkol*, Hilchos Tefilah, p. 6. *Meriri*, Berachos, 31a. And that is the way the Tur rules, in exile, in this time, *Orach Chayim*, 560). As long as we are in *Olam haZeh* / this world (consciousness), whether in exile or not (as the simple language of the Gemara (*Talmidei Rabbeinu Yonah* ad loc) and the ruling of the *Shulchan Aruch*, Orach Chayim, 560:5. Taz, *ibid*, 7), we are not 'allowed' to *fill* ourselves with laughter.

Regarding this, the Gemara (*Niddah*, 23a) tells us that Rav Yirmeyah once tried to get Rav Zeira to laugh, ולא גחיך / "but he did not laugh." Says Rashi, this is because דאסור לאדם שימלא פיו שחוק ור' זירא מחמיר טפי / "It is prohibited to fill one's mouth with laughter in this world, and Rav Zeira was scrupulous with this law."

In other words, although there is a prohibition against filling one's mouth with laughter — meaning to laugh with full-out laughter — perhaps a little laughter is still allowed. Rav Zeira was so *Machmir* / careful with the observance of this Halacha that he would not even permit himself to begin laughing at all, and Rav Yirmeyah was trying to get him to relax a little bit and laugh (see also, *Berachos*, 30b, רבי ירמיה הוה יתיב קמיה דרבי זירא חזייה דהוה קא בדח טובא אמר ליה בכל עצב יהיה מותר כתיב).

In contrast to this strict and ascetic approach, we find that Rabbah, מקמי דפתח להו לרבנן אמר מילתא דבדיחותא ובדחו רבנן / "Before he began teaching the sages, he would say some humorous comment, and the Sages would be cheered" (*Shabbos*, 30b. *Pesachim*, 117a). Our version of the Gemara says רבה / Rabbah, yet the Alter Rebbe (in

Tanya, Chap. 7) cites this in the name of רבא / Rava. And indeed it is also Rava who says, חמרא וריחני פקחין / "Wine and good scents make me wise" (*Yuma*, 76b). In this way, Rava (meaning *large*; in a somewhat similar vein to Rabbah) seems to also be connected with a more *Harchavah* / expansive form of Avodas Hashem. For this reason, Rava, who embodies a more expansive modality of Avodah, upholds the principle that לא נתנה תורה למלאכי השרת / "The Torah was not given to the ministering angels" (*Berachos*, 25b). *Zeira* (meaning *small*) on the other hand, is connected to constriction (see *Likutei Sichos*, 31, p. 177). We may learn from this that there are two paths in Avodas Hashem: the *Derech* / path of Rav Zeira — refraining completely from laughter, and serving Hashem through restriction and discipline, and the Derech of Rabbah / Rava — serving Hashem through expansion, openness and joy (still, within limit; see *Berachos*, 30b, אביי הוה יתיב קמיה דרבה חזייה דהוה קא בדח טובא אמר וגילו ברעדה כתיב). Rav Zeira, who in this case exemplifies the consciousness of *this world*, never laughed; while Rabbah / Rava, who acted out of a prophetic connection with the world-to-come, used holy humor as a tool or skill in his service of Hashem.

Laughter itself, as explained, is triggered by an incongruity. Such as when we expect one result, and there is a reversal, and the unexpected emerges. The greater the reversal and the more unexpected the result, the greater the laughter. The ultimate laughter will be when we laugh at the Divine concealment often called *Olam haZeh* / this world. When all the evils and trivialities of the world will be revealed for what they truly are, nothing more than a grand and ridiculous joke. This level can only be achieved in *Olam haBa* / the World to Come. Or in the world of Torah and Mitzvos, which is a dimension of the World to Come (*Zohar* 3, 56b). Similarly, the Meor

Einayim teaches, a Tzadik (who lives with Olam haBa consciousness while still in this world, in complete D'veikus with HaKadosh
Baruch Hu) lives in a world of perfection that transcends Olam
haZeh — and he too can be filled with laughter (*Meor Einayim*, Yismach Lev, Berachos, p. 370).

There will come a time when ותשחק ליום אחרון / "She laughs at
the final day" (Mishlei, 31:25). This verse can mean either a liberating laughing at mortality and death, or laughing at all of Olam
haZeh which will come about in Olam haBa, with the ultimate
Nahafoch Hu / turning around of reality. All the pain and suffering,
all the hardships and concealments, will be flipped into joy and
redemption. All will be unexpectedly shown to be part of the process of revelation. The *Tzimtzum* / constriction itself will be *Ya'ir*
/ illuminated. Not only will there be a disclosure and revealing of
Hashem's light within the place of this world of Tzimtzum, but
the 'Tzimtzum's shine' itself will paradoxically reveal the Infinite
Presence of Hashem from within the apparent void.

As we are getting closer and closer to the footsteps of Moshiach
and the doorstep of the great future of Olam haBa, there seems to
be a lessening of this exile-prohibition of laughter in Olam haZeh
(as we find today the *Minhag Yisrael* / custom of Jews around the world on Purim
is to laugh, drink and be merry, although, the Taz (*ibid*) writes that it is not allowed.
See, Shu't, *Mishnah Sachir*, Orach Chayim, 2:2), along with a corresponding
increase in the sense of holy laughter; and joy too is increasingly
palpable among all of Klal Yisrael.

Perhaps, this began with the deeper revealing of the light of
Moshiach through the teachings of the Baal Shem Tov and the

Torah of Chassidus. Ever since then, the divide between Olam haZeh and Olam haBa has diminished and it is increasingly possible to taste Olam haBa — the perfection beyond Tzimtzum and the Essence of Hashem in Olam haZeh, as it were — and to sense Heaven in every moment and touch Infinity in the palm of your hand.

Indeed, as we approach a Moshiach world, not only does there seem to be a diminishing of the prohibition of full laughter, but it seems that there is at least the beginning of a positive movement toward real laughter (See *Toras Menachem* (Nun-Aleph) The Rebbe, Vol. 4, p. 210-211) and transcendent joy.

May we merit to experience the true ותשחק ליום אחרון / *laughter* on the *final day of exile*, with the coming of Moshiach and revealing of Olam haBa, now.

♈

ELEMENT

*T*HERE ARE FOUR PRIMARY ELEMENTS, FOUR FUNDAMENTAL building blocks of Creation: fire, air, water and earth. Each month is associated with one of these four elements. However, it is important to note that while manifesting physically, these elements are also meant to be understood in a much more metaphysical sense as well, as they represent numerous properties, qualities, and correspondences.*

---

* For a more in-depth exploration of these elements and their relationship to the calendar, please see the introductory volume of this series: *The Spiral of Time: Unraveling the Yearly Cycle.*

Adar is connected to the fluid element of water, as well as with the Mazal of *Dagim* / fish; it is thus a month that is 'grounded' yet fluid, surging with lightness, laughter and openness. It is for this reason that on Purim there is a Mitzvah to drink wine and become even a little more light-headed and flowing than usual; until we reach a point of *Lo Yada* / not-knowing beyond rigid knowing. From this place of not-knowing, we attain a more real and holy Da'as; we can choose freely to embrace Torah and Mitzvos, goodness and righteousness. This is perhaps the meaning in what our sages tell us, "Whoever is appeased by his wine (whoever becomes more relaxed, easy, less rigid, after drinking), has in him מדעת קונו / an element of דעת / Da'as, the real Da'as, of his Creator" (*Eiruvin*, 65a). In Adar, and especially on Purim, all are "appeased," more relaxed and freed up, and from this state of Lo Yada we gain true Da'as, which is aligned with the Da'as of our Creator.

Fire, air, water and earth are also viewed as the properties of hot (fire), moist (air), cold (water), and dry (earth) (R. Sadiah Gaon, *Emunas v'Deios*, Ma'amar 1:3). Water is the 'cold' property within Creation. On the Yom Tov of Purim, and throughout Adar, there is an emphasis on eradicating Amalek, the aspect of *Karcha* / coldness, and the force that tries to cool down our spiritual passion. In Adar, as in all times of the year, we need to counter this coldness with spiritual warmth and excitement. On a deeper level, we need to utilize the qualities of coldness itself in our Avodah, namely, to show coldness toward the Yetzer haRa and the nonsense of this world.

ᴦ

THE TORAH PORTIONS

O VER THE COURSE OF A GIVEN MONTH, FOUR WEEKLY
Torah portions are usually read (when there are double portions, there can be five or even six Parshios in one month). These
individual portions can be viewed together as a single unit based on
the particular month in which they are most commonly read. Indeed, one finds, when viewing the *Parshiyos* / portions through this
calendrical lens, that an astounding array of thematic elements is
revealed, consistent with the spiritual, mental and emotional qualities of the month.

Throughout Adar on a non-leap-year we read the portions of Terumah through Pikudei. These are the portions in the Torah that deal with the Mitzvah of building the *Mishkan* / Tabernacle in the desert. The Mishkan was a highly complex physical structure, a 'form' in which the Formless, Infinite Divine Presence, was able to be tangibly sensed.

One of Adar's overarching qualities is reflected in the dual nature of the Mishkan. The idea of 'structure' and physical building allude to the rootedness of Kayin and Kedushah, while its Divinely inspired transience alludes to the nomadic nature of Hevel. It is a month conducive to building and planting; Adar alludes to *Adir* / powerful roots. Yet, the Mishkan was portable and it moves from place to place as Klal Yisrael traverses the desert, and in this way it has the quality of lightness, agility and movement - alluding to Adar's characteristics of fish, water and laughter.

The Mishkan also has a quality of *not-knowing*, as in, not knowing where its next location will be. It is paradoxically anchored while temporary, solid while continuously in process, light and open as well as grounded and defined. The laughter of 'Lo Yada' allows us to appreciate the paradoxical unity of form and formlessness, structure and freedom from structure, earthly and spiritual — all reflected in the Mishkan, where the Ultimate Formless One chose to rest with the confines of form.

☾

♈

SEASONS OF THE YEAR

*T*HE SEASONAL QUALITIES OF EACH MONTH ARE INTRI-
CATELY related with the spiritual qualities of that time of
year. When daylight lasts for either longer or shorter times,
different kinds of spiritual light are being revealed on a subtle level.
The physical experiences of spring are external expressions of an
internal reality emanating during that time, such as the vital pulse
of new life and growth. All dark and dank months reflect a quality
of corresponding spiritual coldness, stimulating us to seek warmth.
People tend to keep to themselves when winter begins and are
more outgoing when summer starts. All of these psycho-physical
weather patterns reflect deeper spiritual truths, as the mind-body
complex is a reflection of the metaphysical qualities of the soul and
spiritual realms.

Adar comes at the very end of the winter as the first glimpses of the spring are beginning to be palpably felt. During the winter months people spend more time indoors, and many become more introverted or oriented toward more intimate relationships. We cover our bodies with many layers of clothing, and many tend to gain weight. This is why the shift toward extroversion in the beginning of the spring can bring a sense of self-doubt. When people come out of their hiding, there may be a sense of relief and joy, lightness and laughter; but there also can be a sense of self-conscious uncertainty, certainly with regards to identity: 'Who am I? How do I appear to others?' As discussed throughout this text, Purim and the entire month of Adar deal with all these above issues, and teach us in a healthy and wholesome way to navigate these sentiments, turning them into keys that unlock deeper levels of consciousness and commitment to Avodas Hashem.

☾

♈︎

THE HOLIDAY
OF THE MONTH

"FOR EVERYTHING THERE IS AN APPOINTED TIME" (Koheles, 3:1). In other words, everything happens according to Divine timing (Rebbe Rayatz, *Sefer haMa'amarim*, Tav / Shin / Aleph, p. 59). When we left Egypt, it was the appointed time for such liberation. Indeed, Nisan is the perfect month for exodus and redemption. King David in the Book of Psalms says, "Hashem מוציא אסירים בכושרות / sets free the imprisoned" (68:7). The word כושרות is related to the word כשר / *Kosher*. This means Hashem took us out of prison (Egypt) in a Kosher or 'appropriate' month. Hashem took us out, says Rabbi Akiva (*Medrash Rabbah*, Bamidbar, 3:6), in a month that is perfect to be taken out and to travel in the desert; a month that is not too hot nor too cold (see also Rashi, ad loc. Rashi, *Sotah*, 2a).

Therefore, not only did our redemption occur in an appropriate time in history, but also at the right time of year — the season best-suited for this type of redemption. This is the same principle behind every Yom Tov: the narrative and observance of each celebration or fast reflects and refracts the light of the natural world through a spiritual lens.

Furthermore, in the months that contain a *Yom Tov* / holiday, that Yom Tov embodies and encapsulates the energy of the entire month in condensed form. In a month that does not have a major holiday, that absence is also an expression of the unique quality of the month.

For many years, following the giving of the Torah, there was no revealed Yom Tov during the month of Adar; then along came Haman. Haman complained to the king that Klal Yisrael are an idle people, always celebrating, always feasting, and always saying, "Today is Shabbos" or "Today is Pesach" (*Megilah*, 13b). Then came the radical *Nahafoch Hu*, and because of Haman, and what he instigated, there was a dramatic re-acceptance of the Torah with love and joy. This in turn reconnected us to the Mitzvah of being joyous and feasting on all the appointed Yomim Tovim throughout the entire year (*Megilah*, 16b), and moreover, on the new Yom Tov that was introduced — Purim (although it is not a 'full' Yom Tov, meaning, with a prohibition of doing mundane work, *Megilah*, 5b).

Purim is the ultimate Nahafoch Hu. The numerical value of *Purim* is 336, which is equal to three times the Name Hashem (26) plus three times the Name Elokim (86) (3 x 26 = 78 3 x 86 = 258. 258 + 78 = 336). The Name Hashem is the root of compassion, expansion and revelation, while the Name Elokim is the root of harsh judgment, contraction and concealment. The amplified inter-inclusion of these two Names is an illustration of the fact that on Purim there is a major *Hamtakas haDin* / sweetening of harsh judgment. However, the sweetening brought by the Name Hashem does not merely remove the concealment brought by the Name Elokim, to simply annul the decree of Haman. Rather, it is a complete transformation of the concealment; the Concealment itself becomes a Revelation of Divine Presence. The seeming harsh judgment in the Purim story was actually a form of compassion, albeit in costume (so to speak :) so we too, when we give thanks for the hidden compassion in our life story, can sweeten our Din and create a *Nahafoch Hu* in *our world*.

Adar not only contains the Yom Tov of Purim, Adar is completely interlinked and unified with Purim. Purim's quality of Nahafoch Hu therefore infuses and transforms the entire month. According to the *Yerushalmi* (*Megilah*, 1:1), under certain circumstances, the unique Mitzvah of Purim, reading the Megilah, can be fulfilled anytime during Adar, not only on the day of Purim. Such is actually the ruling of Halachah (see *Shulchan Aruch*, Orach Chayim, 688:7). All of Adar is thus permeated with the *Chayus* / vitality and energy of Purim.

Reading the Megilah of Esther is the foundational Mitzvah of Purim from which all the other Purim Mitzvos flow. In fact, this reading is also the first holiday Mitzvah that we perform on the day of Purim. (With regards to Purim and Amalek there is a principle that we need to first 'remember' and then 'do' / להקדים זכירה לעשיה (*Megilah*, 30a). This principle can be extended to the sequence of first reading the Megilah (the remembrance) and then performing the Mitzvos (the actions) of the day (*Sefas Emes*, Tav / Reish / Lamed / Hei). Thus we read the Megilah in the morning, which is the 'main' Mitzvah of reading, and then we do the other Mitzvos of the day: giving gifts to the poor, sending prepared foods to friends, and feasting. On Purim, first we activate the inner, spiritual world, and then the physical, outer world.) The phrase *Megilas Esther* / the Scroll of Esther, alludes to the words *Giluy Hester* / revealing the hidden, revealing the potential. Through reading the Megilah we reveal the latent holy, spiritual, healthy and life-affirming qualities of the very traits of Haman (revealing the way these traits exist in their root in Radla): randomness, coldness, mockery, and frivolity. Through reading the Megilah we overcome negative doubt and laugh with holy uncertainty in the infinite joy and endless possibility of *not-knowing*.

Purim is named after the lottery. *Pur* means a 'lot.' As the Megilah itself tells us, "In the first month... a *Pur* / lot was cast before Haman concerning every day and every month (until it fell on) the Twelfth Month, that is, the month of Adar" (Megilas Esther, 3:7). Then at the end of the story the Megilah tells us, על־כן קראו לימים האלה פורים על־שם הפור / "Therefore, they called these days 'Purim' after the name Pur" (*Ibid*, 9:26). The name of a Yom Tov expresses most accurately the theme of that day and tells us most clearly what it is all about. For example, the name *Pesach* / Passover reminds us of the important event when Hashem "passed over" the Jewish homes and we were spared. The term *Shavuos* / Weeks recalls the seven weeks counted prior to the receiving of the Torah. The question is, how does the name *Purim* relate to the miracle or holiday of Purim?

Once again, Haman threw a 'Pur' which landed on the 13th of the twelfth month of the year, which is Adar, "therefore, they called these days Purim after the name Pur." Yet, it is very peculiar to name the Yom Tov for an apparently inconsequential detail in the story of Purim. Seemingly, the name 'Purim' does not express or capture the main event or the essence of the holiday. More troubling is that this name is connected with the very medium through which the negative plot to annihilate us was to be orchestrated, rather than with the eventual turn-around and salvation. Why sanctify the day using the name of the tool that Haman used to attempt to obliterate the Jewish People? Other holidays are named after the miracle that they commemorate and represent. Purim is named after the potential attempted-murder weapon.

However, this very issue brings the essence of this day into stark relief. Purim's primary theme and main point is precisely that of the Pur, which is precisely the ultimate theme and point of Purim. A Pur is an instrument of randomness. However, whereas randomness usually leads to unholy, crippling doubt and uncertainty, a place of *negative transcendence*, on Purim there is a Nahafoch Hu, a reversal of this dynamic. On the level of 'Divine indifference' as it were, darkness and light are the same and all is just *random*, but with the power of Purim we tap into the deeper inner world of Radla, the Keser of all Kesarim, the unknown and unknowing potential of all actuality. From that place of utter freedom, unaffectedness, and wonder-full unknowing, we choose, as Hakadosh Baruch Hu has chosen, the path of righteousness and goodness, Torah and life. Haman attempted to use a device of doubt and choicelessness to destroy us, and he was destroyed by the holy meta-root of that very device: Radla.

This is the most radical surprise, evoking holy hilarity and endless wonderment: we are invited to take hold of the weapon of deepest inhumanity, and to reverse all of the destruction inflicted throughout history by wielding it to bring life, true purpose, open-ended Da'as, utter goodness, redemptive holiness and lasting peace. And in so doing may we activate the prophecy of our glorious, imminent future:

וכתתו חרבותם לאתים וחניתותיהם למזמרות לא־ישא גוי אל־גוי חרב ולא־ילמדו עוד מלחמה

"...And they shall beat their swords into plowshares and their spears into pruning hooks: Nation shall no (longer) take up sword against nation; they shall never again know war!" (Yeshayah 2:4)

☾

ツ
SUMMARY OF ADAR

S THE WINTER SEASON BEGINS TO DEPART, ONE
may experience residual winter heaviness or melancholy. Adar (the **name** of the month meaning
Adir / strong) encourages us to awaken and strengthen ourselves
with a **sense** of laughter and lightness. The zodiac **sign** of the
month *Dag* / the Fish / Pisces contributes to a newfound feeling
of fluidity and flexibility, while the **Torah readings** of the month
(detailing the building of the Mishkan) connect us to the paradoxical openness and transience of that precisely measured, grounded
structure.

Similarly, the **letter** of the month, Kuf, increases our sense of
holy playfulness, like a *Kof* / monkey, while at the same time keeping us grounded, like the letter's strongly rooted left leg (ק). The

element of water relaxes us, too, as it alludes to 'drinking' and wine — yet with its quality of coldness, it gives us the strength to act 'coldly' towards our *Yetzer haRa* / evil inclination. The spleen, a **body part** characterized by both depression and laughter, reinforces our ability to laugh off the depressiveness and negativity of the Yetzer and of the winter as it is wrapping up.

The **tribe** of the month in a regular year (i.e. without two Adars), whether Naftali or Yoseph, ensures our victory over negativity with powerful positive Mazal. Also, in a leap year, when the 'tribe' of the second Adar is Klal Yisrael itself, our invincible essence beyond Mazal is revealed. The **letter sequence of Hashem's name** for this month (Hei-Hei-Yud-Vav) illustrates our ability to rise up from a state of near-total concealment and trigger an unprecedented revelation and redemption from on High. The **verse** of the month, from which these letters derive, shows us how to do so; alluding to the drinking of wine, the verse directs us to rise up to a state beyond Da'as, beyond the cynical definitions of life imposed upon us by the forces of negativity.

All of these *Kochos* / powers of this 'month of strength' reach a limitless expression on the **holiday** of Purim, the ecstatic overcoming and reversal of all evil. The **name** *Purim* / Lotteries refers to uncertainty, the tool that the evil Amalek tries to use to undermine our passion for goodness and holiness. On Purim we rise up and convert this tool into the unlimited power of holy uncertainty; we use this not only to wipe out the forces of Amalek, but to decisively bring Redemption to the world.

12 DIMENSIONS OF ADAR	
Sequence of Hashem's Name	Hei-Hei-Yud-Vav; the 'receiver' letters preceding the 'giver' letters
Torah Verse	*...Iryoh... V'lasoreikah B'ni Asono* / "(He shall tie to the vine) his donkey, and to the vine branch his donkey's foal."
Letter	Kuf ('monkey'; also a 'rooted' letter)
Month Name	Lotteries (seeming randomness, or not-knowing)
Sense	Laughter
Zodiac Sign	*Dag* / Fish / Pisces
Tribe	Naftali / Yoseph / Ephrayim and Menashe
Body Part	Spleen
Element	Water
Parshios / Torah Portions	Terumah through Pikudei; Building of the Mishkan
Season	End of winter, first glimpses of spring
Holiday	Purim ('lotteries'; rising above Da'as)

PRACTICE:
BEING JOYFUL

"WHEN ADAR ENTERS WE INCREASE IN JOY" (*Ta'anis*, 29a).*
'Increasing in joy' actually implies that the joy was already there, a constant presence throughout the year, yet during the month of Adar it is increased. What's more, the joy we activate and internalize during this month is the source of all the joy that will be unpacked throughout the entire year. The word *b'Simcha* / with joy is numerically 355, which is the same as the word *Shanah* / year. This tells us, say the Chassidic Rebbes (see *Ohev Yisrael*, Purim), that all the joy which will be articulated and revealed throughout the entire year is received in potential in this joy-filled month of Adar.

---

* Neither the Rambam nor the Shulchan Aruch discuss the theme or quote the idea, "When Adar enters we increase in joy." The Rambam does, however, mention the opposite quote, "When Av enters, we decrease in joy." The reason could be that being joyous is a 'non-doing' Mitzvah — it is a feeling in the heart, rather than a positive activity. In Av, the Mitzvah to 'decrease in joy' is active, since it involves actively refraining from certain activities and foods. See also, Shu't, *Chasam Sofer*, Orach Chayim, Siman 170. *Nimukei Orach Chayim*, Siman 686.

THE FIVE LEVELS / TYPES OF JOY

Generally speaking, there are five principal types of joy, corresponding to the five times that the Torah, Prophets and Sages ask us to rejoice above and beyond the basic Mitzvah of being happy and joyous at all times. There are also five times throughout the year that there is a Mitzvah to accentuate our joy: on Shabbos, Yom Tov, Sukkos, Simchas Beis haSho'eiva, and Adar / Purim. These in turn correspond to the five forms of joy: physical joy, emotional joy, mental joy, spiritual joy, existential joy.

Physical Joy is experienced with and within the body. An example of emotional joy is feeling loved or in love. Intellectual or mental joy comes in the form of a new understanding, a new awareness, or a new idea that one discovers. Spiritual joy comes with an expansion of consciousness and a sense of being connected to something greater, beyond oneself. Existential joy is joy in 'being-ness' itself; sensing one's authentic and true existence in the moment unlocks this limitless wellspring of deepest joy.

These five forms of joy also correspond to the four letters of the Name of Hashem (Yud-Hei-Vav-Hei) plus the tip or *Tag* / crown on the top of the letter Yud (י). These five inner dimensions correspond to the five levels of soul: Nefesh (functional consciousness), Ruach (emotional consciousness), Neshamah (mental consciousness), Chaya (spiritual consciousness), and Yechidah (essence or Unity-consciousness).

Days of Joy	Level of Joy	Letter of the Divine Name	Dimension of Soul
Shabbos	Physical Joy	Final Hei	Nefesh
Yom Tov	Emotional Joy	Vav	Ruach
Sukkos	Mental Joy	First Hei	Neshamah
Simchas Beis haSho'eivah	Spiritual Joy	Yud	Chayah
Purim & the Days of Adar	Existential Joy	Tip or 'Crown' of Yud	Yechidah

These five types of joy can and should be experienced daily, yet, there are particular days within the yearly cycle that embody these qualities in a more pronounced way, increasing their accessibility. Those special days are sources for their respective types of joy which irrigate our experience throughout the entire year in every day of our lives.

I: PHYSICAL JOY

Physical joy is experienced in the body, and a joy that is related to Shabbos. The Torah says, "On the days of Simcha, on your designated holidays…" (Bamidbar, 10:10), according to our sages (*Sifri*, 10:10) this refers to Shabbos. (The Bahag rules there is an obligation to be happy on Shabbos. (See also, Radbaz, *Metzudos David*, Mitzvah 91. *Manhig*, Tefilos Shabbos. *Shibolei haLeket*, 82. *Beis Yoseph*, Orach Chayim, 281. And see also *Ye'aros Devash*, 2, Derush 10. *Shu't Chasam Sofer*, Orach Chayim, 168.) We do not make the special Seudah of Purim on Shabbos (Yerushalmi, *Megilah*,1:4), as to not mix the Simcha of Purim with the Simcha of Shabbos (*Pri Chadash*, Orach Chayim, 688).) The joy of Shabbos is one in which the entire physical self is incorporated, resting from physical exertion and taking pleasure in the special meals of Shabbos, added intimacy, or even with an extra nap in the afternoon. Such physical joy is related to the resting of the, perhaps overworked, body; and is associated with the final, 'lower' Hei of Hashem's name. Hei can be a silent letter, and therefore it represents the idea of rest. Shabbos is a day of rest and tangible joy, in which the body itself is honored as the house of the soul.

2: EMOTIONAL JOY

Emotional joy corresponds to the inner experience of each Yom Tov throughout the year, and it is also connected to the Vav of Hashem's Name, and the level of Ruach, our emotional soul reality. The Torah tells us, "You shall rejoice on your festival (Yom Tov), and you shall be only joyous" (Devarim, 16:14-15). On Yom Tov, if we are sensitive, we can actually feel a heightened sense of HaKadosh Baruch Hu's love for us. For example on Pesach, when we celebrate Hashem taking us out of Egypt, we can feel the love of our Parent in Heaven helping us get out of our individual Egypts, our constrictions and limitations. Every Yom Tov celebrates the Divine revelation of affection to Klal Yisrael as manifest on that day. This awareness of being loved and precious in the eyes of Hashem creates an emotional joy, the joy of being loved by HaKadosh Baruch Hu.

3: INTELLECTUAL JOY

Intellectual joy corresponds in particular to the Yom Tov of Sukkos, the 'upper' Hei, which is the world of Neshamah, intellectual awareness. It is a joy that comes about through achieving a mental breakthrough, the deciphering of a perplexity or the resolution of doubt. (In the language of the Zohar, "The arousal of joy is from the left side."

Zohar 2, 169b.) "There is no joy like the resolution of doubt" (*Metzudos David,* Mishlei, 15:30. *Mishbtzos Zahav,* Siman 682:1); or as the Ramah quotes a wise man, "One has not tasted the taste of joy until he tastes the resolution of intellectual doubts" (*Toras haOlah,* 1:6). This is a type of intellectual joy of the mind.

Besides the Mitzvah of rejoicing on every Yom Tov, the Torah singles out Sukkos as a time of joy, asking us to be joyous on it three times (*Yalkut Shimoni,* Emor 247:654). These three times allude to the three levels of *Mochin* / mind, the intellectual capacities of *Chochmah* / intuitive wisdom, *Binah* / analytic understanding, and most importantly *Da'as* / internalized knowledge.

The Torah says, "You shall live in Sukkos for seven days, in order that future generations ידעו / may *know* that I made the Israelite people dwell in booths when I brought them out of the Land of Egypt" (Vayikra, 23:42-43). Da'as is essential to Sukkos, as without knowing what you are doing, the Mitzvah of dwelling in a Sukkah has not been performed at all (Bach, *Orach Chayim,* 625. *Bikurei Yaakov,* 625:3). With regards to other Mitzvos there is great debate whether proper intent is indispensable, and whether a person who performed a Mitzvah without intention has fulfilled their obligation or not. However, without Kavanah, the Mitzvah of sitting in the Sukkah has not been fulfilled. Sukkos is intimately connected with having Da'as, as much as Purim is connected with *Lo Yada* / transcending Da'as. On Sukkos we draw Divine Da'as and higher Mochin down into our lives and into the world in general.

The extra measure of joy that we aspire to experience on Sukkos should be therefore permeated with Da'as, a mindful awareness of the events that transpired as we left Egypt, especially Hashem's protecting us in the Clouds of Glory or securing us in the booths that we assembled. We should have the Da'as that HaKodash Baruch Hu is protecting and directing us in the same way every day of our lives. This Da'as brings a higher/deeper form of joy and security.

In the past 1,000 years (or perhaps much longer than that), a 'new' Yom Tov and way of celebrating was added to the last day of Sukkos: the celebration of Simchas Torah, 'the joy of completing the yearly cycle of Torah reading' (See *Zohar* 3, p. 256b. See also, *Siddur Rasag. Teshuvas Rabbi Hai Gaon* quoted in *Teshuvas haRashba*, Siman 260. Tosefos also mentions Simchas Torah: Tosefos, *Beitzah*, 30b). Simchas Torah is also founded on an 'intellectual joy' as it is the joy of finishing the yearly cycle of reading and learning the Torah. The joy of Simchas Torah is the joy of Torah, the meta-root of all Mochin and intelligence, and thus, in a way, the culmination of the joy of Sukkos.

4: SPIRITUAL JOY

Spiritual joy comes about with an awareness of one's being connected with something higher and beyond themselves. This type of joy is associated with the special celebration (full of singing, dancing, and even rabbinic acrobatics) that took place during the nights of *Chol haMo'ed* / the intermediate days of Sukkos, in the Beis ha-Mikdash. This celebration was called *Simchas Beis haSho'eivah* / Joy of the Water Drawing, and was enacted to accompany the ritual drawing of water in the evening for the Mitzvah of the libation on the Altar during the days of Sukkos. The joy of this event was so overwhelming that the sages of the time declared, "One who did not see the joy of Simchas Beis haSho'eivah did not see joy in his life" (*Sukkah*, 51a).

From this description it would appear that the joy of this time was connected with the drawing of the water. Yet, writing about this festive event, the Rambam begins (Hilchos *Shofar, Sukkah, Lulav,* 8:12) by writing, "Although we are required to rejoice on all festivals, there was special rejoicing in the Beis haMikdash during the Sukkos festival, as it is written, "You shall rejoice before Hashem your G-d (meaning, in the Beis haMikdash) seven days" (Vayikra, 23:40). It seems clear from the words of the Rambam that the celebration of Simchas Beis haSho'eivah may be derived and even seen as inseparable from the Mitzvah to be joyous on all the Yomim Tovim, and especially on Sukkos. In our context, this means that this celebration and its joy are rooted in Da'as, and even the higher Da'as of *prophetic insight*, as we will now explore.

From this perspective, it would seem that, beyond the ritual act of just drawing the water for libation, there is an emphasis on the state of one's cultivated consciousness in relation to the event. Tosefos (*Sukkah*, 50b) writes in the name of the *Yerushalmi*, that the word *Sho'eivah* / drawing, alludes to the fact that the participants who celebrated on these special nights would *draw* down Ruach haKadosh, Divine intuition and flow, as they ecstatically and rapturously danced through the night.

On these powerful nights the sages of old would tap into higher states of consciousness and holy inspiration. We as well need to do this, on our own level. The joy of Da'as opens us up to an even higher level of *Mochin* / consciousness, which is more profoundly joyful than anything which this world provides. This level of joy corresponds with the letter Yud of Hashem's Name, the letter connected with *Chochmah* / higher wisdom and intuition. It is also the inner level of *Chayah* / spiritual consciousness.

5: JOY OF EXISTING

This is the highest *and* most all-embracing joy possible. Existential joy is not just a joy of immanence, of the fullness of self and the physical body. It is not just emotional, intellectual or even transcendent joy, rather, it includes all of these simultaneously. Our Nefesh-Ruach-Neshamah is the fullness of our 'finite' self. Chayah is the transcendence of the finite self; it is our 'infinite' self, as it were. But Yechidah is deeper and higher than both our finite and infinite selves, and it also includes them as one. Yechidah is our very uniqueness, and yet it is utterly transcendent of any separation. Yechidah is our uniqueness, so to speak, as it is one with the *Yechidah Shel Olam* / The Unique One of the World. It is the essence of our being that is one with the Essence of All.

The crown atop the Yud is a small dot on the tip of that smallest, elevated letter (י) indicating an utterly transcendent level. On the other hand, it represents the point from which all letters and manifestations emerge. This is the paradoxical joy of Purim. It is *Lo Yada* / utterly transcending Da'as, yet, it is also the point from which all Da'as and joy emerge. This is why the state of Lo Yada is not the mere negation of knowing. This not-knowing is actually the fountain of holy knowledge and wise choice-making in life; it is both lightness and groundedness, holy doubt and holy certainty. It is a transcendent state, while also being simultaneously rooted in the tangible presence of the physical body.

The crown above the Yud is 'beyond' the four letters of Hashem's name, as it were. With regards to Yom Kippur, the Torah says ...*Lifnei Hashem Tit'haru* / "Before Hashem you shall be purified" (Vaykira, 16:30). The phrase *Lifnei Hashem* can be translated as, 'beyond Hashem.' On Yom Kippur we reach a pristine, transcendent level "beyond the Name Hashem" — beyond the 'expression' or revealed will of Hashem. This alludes to the Essence of HaKadosh Baruch Hu, which is 'beyond' the Name of Hashem, like the crown of the Yud. Purim is compared, in its essence, to Yom Kippur, the day of atonement, and in this way it too is 'beyond' all Names and masks of the Infinite One. (In the Torah Yom Kippur is called *Yom haKipurim*, thus *Ki-Purim*, 'like Purim' (*Tikunei Zohar*, Tikun 21). Tellingly, we feast on Purim to make up for our lack of food and drink on Yom Kippur, as the Gra on this passage writes. Similarly, Rav Yitzchak Chaver (from the school of the Gra) writes that before Purim there is a fast day to make up for the day before Yom Kippur when we feast.)

"The *Etzem* / essence of the day (Yom Kippur) brings acquittal..." (Vaykira, *ibid*). Say our sages, this is because Yom Kippur is connected to the Etzem (as it were) of HaKadosh Baruch Hu. Purim as well is connected to our Etzem (the Yechidah), and to the Etzem of Hashem. For this reason, the joy of Purim is beyond opposites (a property of *Radla*, the Keser of all Keserarim). Each of the other four kinds of joy can be described and defined in terms of their opposites. The joy of Purim cannot be limited by definitions or descriptions, not even the description *unlimited joy*.

It is paradoxically a joy that is beyond joy. However, even this description of 'beyond descriptions' fails, for the joy of Purim is the root of all the four types of joy, and thus it includes each of them even while transcending them.

Existential joy is reached through, עד דלא ידע / *Ad d'Lo Yada* /
until you do not know, transcending what is known as joy. On the
other hand, the first letters of the words עד דלא ידע / *Ad d'Lo Yada*
spell the word ידע / *Yada* / know, as the joy of Purim also includes
every kind of joy, its un-knowing also includes and iterates deeper
and higher forms of knowing.

WORLD OF ETZEM / ESSENCE VS. THE WORLD OF GILUYIM / REVELATIONS, MANIFESTATIONS

There is a world of *Giluyim* / revelation/manifestation, and a
world of *Etzem* / Essence/the core. Apart from Purim, all the other
Yomim Tovim / holidays contain Giluyim, in large measure. For
example, Hashem revealed awe inspiring miracles to Klal Yisrael
as they left Egypt, and even revealed the Divine Presence in the
miracle of the oil on Chanukah. On Purim there was little to no
Giluyim, as nothing 'extraordinary' or openly miraculous occurred.

Purim is all about the Etzem, the *Anochi* / I of Hashem that
is, for lack of a better word, 'revealed' within the workings of nature, and within the normal and seemingly coincidental sequence
of events in our lives. Purim is a 'revealing' (*Kiviyachol* / as it were)
of the Etzem of Hashem in nature, in history, and in the physically
embodied celebrations of Purim.

Our body, in comparison to our soul, is our Etzem, while the
soul is our *Giluy* / revealed connection to the *Ohr Ein Sof* / Infinite Light. For this reason (perhaps), the *Atzmus* / Divine Es-

sence chooses *Davka* / specifically the bodies of Klal Yisrael, as our bodies are our essence, and the Essence of HaKadosh Baruch Hu chooses our essence.

This is why our sages teach that in the Era of Moshiach, when there will be revelations of the highest Light, all the Yomim Tovim will be 'nullified' or rendered superfluous, except Purim (and Yom Kippur; *Medrash Rabbah*, Mishlei, 9:2). When there is a higher light that is being revealed, a brighter Giluy, all the less intense Giluyim become obsolete and unnoticeable, as a "candle trying to shine in daylight" (*Chulin*, 60b). Purim (and Yom Kippur) is Etzem, and Etzem is always and everywhere.

One of the leading *Poskim* / Halachic deciders of our generation, Rav Shlomo Zalman Auerbach, once gave an interesting Halachic ruling. He argued, that although Purim as a whole will burn eternally and never be obsolete, one aspect of Purim will indeed be abolished, and that is the obligation of drinking *Ad d'Lo Yada* / until we do not know.

There is a Halachic reason for this ruling, and there is also a deeper meaning. In the world that we live in today, the world of *Galus* / exile, hardship, headache and toil, we need 'Lo Yada'; we need to get *out of ourselves*, out of our minds, and depart from the way we normally think and interact with the world, in order to be truly joyful and access the realm of Keser. (Although the highest level of Keser, Radla, or in this context, Etzem, does include our normative reality, only we are not necessarily conscious of it or living accordingly.) In the Era of Moshiach, however, we will already be absolutely joyous in every situation, and we will naturally embody the realm of Divine paradox. We will include within ourselves the opposite states of inebriation and sobriety, Heavenly and earthly, simultaneously. We will not need to use drink or any other external means to experience this essential joy directly.

The quality of the month of Adar is the matrix, the context that gives rise to Purim and its inner content and story. The reverse is also true; the *Kedusha* / holiness and *Ko'ach* / power of Purim suffuses the entire month of Adar. Adar and Purim are so intertwined that every day of Adar sparkles with the light of Purim, and under certain circumstances the Mitzvah of reading the Megilah can be fulfilled on any day during Adar. Throughout the entire month of Adar we have a special Ko'ach to attain this essential happiness, and convert all pessimism, hopelessness and insecurity into existential lightness and joy.

SERVE HASHEM WITH JOY — ALL THE TIME

"When Adar enters we increase in joy." The term 'increase' implies that we need to be joyous the entire year, but even more so during the month of Adar. Divine Inspiration urges us to make joy a constant in life: "Serve Hashem with joy!" (Tehilim, 100:2).* We are asked to see every moment as another opportunity to be joyful in a way that serves Hashem. Certainly, when it comes to performing a specific Mitzvah we aspire to perform it out of joy (Rambam, *Hilchos Lulav*, 8:1). Mitzvos performed without joy can actually generate

---

* The Arizal merited to receive the deepest Torah because he served Hashem with joy (*Sefer Chareidim*, Hakdamah l'Mitzvos, 4. The Chidah, *Avodas Hakodesh*, Morah be'Etzbah, 10:327. *Lev David*, 4:3. *Torah Ohr*, Toldos, p. 20b. *Sefer haBris*, 2:12:4. *Toldos Yaakov Yoseph*, Re'eh. *Sheivet haMusar*, 20:8. *Mishnah Berurah*, Siman 669:11).

negative consequences (Devarim, 28:47, as the Arizal reads the verse. Shaloh haKodesh, *Hakdamah l'Mitzvos*, Asara Ma'amaros, Ma'amar 3:4). Appropriately, the Hebrew word for *joy*, שמחה / *Simcha*, can be viewed as an acronym for *Simchas Mitzvah Chiyuv Hu* / "Happiness while performing a Mitzvah is an obligation" (Chidah, *Avodas Hakodesh*, Tziparon Shamir, 11:161).

When we do a Mitzvah with joy, that joy enhances and completes the Mitzvah (*Sefer haIkkarim,* 3:33). But not only does joy actively complete or 'crown' a project or good deed, joy is the feeling one experiences when something is completed (Maharal, Introduction to *Ohr Chadash* 2. Thus *Sason* / joy is connected to circumcision (*Megilah,* 16b) the completion of the body).

We should aspire to be in a state of Simcha all the time (*Tanya,* 26), as we are always serving Hashem, moment-to-moment. Furthermore, being in a joyful disposition contributes to our mental and physical health (*Orchos Tzadikim,* Sha'ar haSimcha). The Baal Shem Tov considered joy to be a 'Mitzvah' in itself (*Keser Shem Tov,* Hosofos, 169), and his spiritual inheritors each developed this emphasis in their own ways. "It is a great Mitzvah to be joyful" (*Likutei Moharan,* 2:24). This does not mean that Simcha is counted as one of the 613 Commandments, but rather it is a *meta-Mitzvah*, as in the words of Rebbe Aaron of Karlin, "Although there is no positive Mitzvah to be joyful and there is no sin to be depressed, yet the heights joy can bring a person to, no Mitzvah can; and the lows of depression can cause one to sink to where no sin can."

SERVING HASHEM, SELF AND OTHERS BY BEING JOYFUL

In a deeper way, the command to "serve Hashem with joy" means that being joyous is itself serving Hashem (*Kedushas haYehudi*, Simcha). Moreover, when we are joyful we are also 'serving' ourselves in the best sense, as Simcha contributes to our mental, emotional and even physical health. Joy brings us great benefit, from nourishing our soul to healing our physical body. Being *b'Simcha* / joyful helps everyone around us, as well. Our states are contagious. When people walk around gloomy, annoyed, and with despondency as their face, not only is it not pleasant to be around them, but they pull down everyone else's state as well. When we are happy and wear joy on our face, we create a happier environment around us and we lift the spirits of everyone we come in contact with. In this way, when we are inwardly and outwardly joyous, we are serving Hashem, serving the good in ourselves, serving others, and even the physical world around us.

Because our state of mind affects those around us, the 'spiritual' obligation to serve Hashem with joy is also a 'moral' obligation. It is *Mentchlich* / noble and polite to say good morning or good evening to others in the street, but it is also a moral imperative that as we encounter people throughout the day we lift them up and not pull them down.

One should not think, 'If I am feeling sad or annoyed, who am I bothering? It is my internal issue.' The truth is, if you are expressing your bad mood you are actually disturbing others around you, in addition to yourself. And if you are harboring negativity inwardly, you are probably expressing it outwardly in some way, and influencing your environment. If considering your own well-being is not sufficient, think about your obligation towards other people.

We may not always have the *Ko'ach* / power, and mental or emotional stamina to 'think' ourselves out of a bad mood, but the core ability is always there. Reflectively, the word *b'Simcha* / with happiness / בשמחה has the same letters as the Hebrew word for thought, *Machshavah* / מחשבה (*Tiferes Shelomo*, Sha'ar haTefilah. p 10). We always have free choice as to how we think about our lives. It is always possible to simply choose to cease, in any given moment, bemoaning our experiences. At the very least we can choose to 'act' joyfully, even if we do not feel it, as our internal moods are known to follow our external actions.

If you find yourself depleted of joy, surround yourself with more joyful, upbeat and positive people. Surround yourself with sounds of joy. The Alter Rebbe even suggested to someone who was feeling down to hum joyful tunes to himself (*Ma'amarei Admur haZaken,* Inyanim, p. 403). Today, it is extremely easy to find and listen to recorded *Nigunim* / holy melodies and songs of praise that can stimulate your inner song. When listening to a joyful song, perhaps you can sing along, and maybe even clap or dance — notice how this changes your consciousness.

In short, we should do whatever we can to maintain a joyful posture. As mentioned, if you are not feeling joy, acting joyfully can stimulate the feelings, as "the heart follows actions" (*Sefer haChinuch*). Our emotions follow our physical actions; inner experiences are triggered by outer, physical activities. The mere act of choosing to smile can stimulate an inward response of joy.

JOY OF PURPOSE

There are various types of joy, as explored above, but what is joy, really? Sometimes by analyzing an opposite issue we can better understand the issue we wish to understand. The root of sadness is purposelessness and lack of direction. Many people who struggle with sadness do so because they lack a sense of cohesiveness and meaning in their lives; life feels like a collection of random or unrelated events. Joy, by contrast, stems from an acute awareness of purpose, mission, meaning and direction.

People who wake up every morning infused with passion for their mission and purpose, have a sense of inner drive, experience more joy in their day to day life. The nature of the human being is to work, to grow, to move, to evolve: "Man is born for toil" (Iyov, 5:7. See *Sanhedrin*, 99b). Therefore when we work hard, when we have something in life that we *want* to accomplish, that is often when we feel most human, most alive and most joyful.

The word שמח / *Samach* / happy is similar to the word צמח / *Tzamach* / plant (Shin and Tzadik are interchangeable, as צחק is also spelled ישחק Tehilim, 105:9.). To be happy means to grow, to sprout, to evolve. When we experience some payoff from our toil, there is joy. When we have exercised or cared for our body and feel stronger/healthier, or even when we have set financial goals and achieved them, a natural joy arises. When we learn a new skill or cover ground in *Limud haTorah* / learning, or when we realize we have grown emotionally and become more mature or wholesome, or when we have grown spiritually and are living with more D'veikus — all of this brings joy on its own level. Of course, the joy of working out pales in comparison to the joy of deep emotional healing, and certainly to that of D'veikus, but each level of joy is integrally important in its own realm.

In reference to the celestial spheres, we say in the Shabbos *Piyut* / liturgy, שמחים בצאתם וששים בבואם / "they experience *Simcha* when they go out and *Sason* (another form of joy, as there are ten expressions of joy, *Avos d'Rebbe Nason*, 43:9) when they return." Simcha is related to a 'going out' movement, growth and development, whereas Sason is a form of contentment (*Gra*, on Iyov, 3). When there is *Tz'michah* / growth there is Simcha.

Deeper forms of Simcha are revealed when we attain *Yishuv haDa'as* / settling of consciousness (*Sheim m'Shmuel*, Moadim 139). In this clarified state, we know our purpose, our mission, what we need to do in this world, and how we can go about it. Chasing the next high, the next momentary excitement or relief, does not bring us lasting Simcha. We need Yishuv haDa'as in order to rise out of that addictive cycle, to focus on what we need to accomplish in this world and how best to direct our energy and talents. The more we live with this settled, purposeful awareness, the more Simcha we experience in our lives. (Simcha is from something that is *constant* (*Malbim* on Tehilim, 96:11 and Mishlei, 23:24-25). The *Gra*, however, writes (Mishlei, 23:24) that Simcha comes from something *new*).

SENSING THE PURPOSE & UPWARD TRAJECTORY OF CREATION BRINGS JOY

Just as we experience joy when we are aware of our own personal purpose and mission, deep inner joy also arises when we become aware that everything in life has purpose. There are no accidents or randomness in our own lives, but also throughout creation and all of history (*Reishis Chochmah*, Sha'ar haAhava 10). This is one of the messages of Purim and Adar; whatever may appear to be a mere 'natural' event is actually Divinely orchestrated. Our collective history is delicately guided, and there is a grand plan for everything and everyone in creation. The entire cosmos is inching toward the World of Yichud.

As such, everything is constantly evolving toward its ultimate purpose, perfection and redemption. Yes, there are apparent sets backs, descents, and regressions, but history is not just a straight line. From a wider viewpoint, the universe is indeed marching forward and upward, with humanity at the forefront. The movement is gradual, and sometimes it feels much too gradual, but nothing cannot reach its ultimate purpose. Individual and cosmic culmination are actually unavoidable. Joy is experienced when we are able to sense this positive evolution of all beings and all things, together as one.

ETZEV: THE DISCONNECT BETWEEN ACTION & REACTION

The more we cultivate a project and see the fruit of our labor, work hard and earn money, eat well and feel healthy, learn Torah and feel we have grown in it, invest time in *Davening* / prayer and feel that we have deepened in it, and so forth — the more joy we experience. Similarly, the more we are able to see the underlying purpose of Creation being revealed and manifest — for this too is an *Avodah* / mode of spiritual work — the more joy we feel.

עצבות / *Atzvus* / depression comes from the root עצב / *Etzev*. The first time the Torah introduces the word *Etzev* is in the beginning of the Torah, after Adam and Chavah / Eve ate from the Tree of Knowledge of Good and Evil; leaving the Tree of Life reality and entering into a world of separation, sin and death. Only after erroneously identifying with the Tree of Knowledge does Etzev or Atzvus set in.

First Hashem addresses Chavah regarding her having eaten from the Tree of separation, "I shall surely increase עצבונך/ *Itzvone-ich* / your hardship (in) your pregnancy; בעצב / *b'Etzev* / in hardship you shall bear children" (Bereishis, 3:16). The term עצב refers to the hardship of childbirth (*Medrash Rabbah*, Bereishis, 20:6. Rashi, ad loc) and the hardship of raising children (*Eiruvin*, 100b. Rashi, ad loc). Next, Hashem addresses Adam, saying, because of what you did, "cursed be the ground for your sake; בעצבון / *b'Itzavon* / with hardship shall you eat of it all the days of your life" (3:17). Rashi comments (on 3:18) that *Etzev* means, "You will sow your fields with legumes or garden vegetables, yet, thorns and thistles will grow" (ibid.).

What is the connection between the hardship of childbirth and child-raising and the toil or despair of trying to grow vegetables and having thorns sprout instead? Essentially, what the Torah is describing as *Etzev* is a type of frustration that arises when there is a disconnect, a dissonance between our actions and their results. This is the real definition of hardship, the 'curse' that Adam and Chavah received after eating from the Tree of Knowledge. This hardship is not that human life is physically burdensome, or that it is very labor intensive to plant food or raise children. Rather, this is a psychological, existential anxiety that arises in us when an end product is disappointingly inconsistent with the anticipatory work we put into it.

A person plants seeds of legumes and expects legumes to sprout, but if thorns appear, there is a disconnect between their actions and their results. Or if a person puts all their *Ko'ach* / energy into raising their child with certain virtues, but the child takes another path in life, Etzev can arise. On a lighter note, if a parent *Schleps* their child around to music lessons for many years, and then the child gives up playing music as soon as they are more independent, this could also bring up the Etzev of raising children; not to see the fruit of one's labor.

Etzev arises when life feels disjointed, inconsistent, and not following a rational sequence. When there is a sense that the unfolding of one's life is random, and mere happenstance eclipses higher order, Amalek is ascendent. When we do not feel any cohesiveness in our body or world, an anguish or even *Atzvus* / despondency sets in.

Adam and Chavah were specifically cursed with Etzev as a result of eating from the Tree of Knowledge. Why? Because there was a disconnect between their actions and the results: both Adam and Chavah, when questioned about their choices, did not take responsibility.

When Hashem asks Adam about what happened, Adam responds, "The woman that You gave me, gave it to me" (Bereishis, 3:12). He is ultimately saying, 'True, I ate from the Tree of Knowledge, but it is not my fault; it is either her fault or it is Your fault for giving me this woman.' Then Hashem turns to Chavah and questions her, and she responds, "The Snake convinced me" (3:13). She too deflects responsibility. Their Etzev was thus a form of poetic justice, as it were. As they did not admit to the connection between their actions and their results, they denied the fact that every action has consequences and every cause has an effect. They were from then on plagued with the Etzev of seeing a disconnect between cause and effect in their childbirth and in their working of the land, i.e., in their creative life.

Life does not have to feel this way. We can create a *Tikun /* rectification, at least in our own lives, to the Etzev that resulted from our eating of the Tree of Knowledge. The more we see and take responsibility for our lives, and for the ways our every action affects others, the more we are stitching back together the causes and effects in our lives. And the more we accomplish, this in the microcosm of our own lives, the more we see it also in the macrocosm of Creation. The more that life 'makes sense' and the more we glimpse the gorgeously harmonious tapestry of life and its patterns, the more we see the Hand of Hashem, and the more we sense Hashem speaking through Creation and through us — the more we undo the curse of Etzev, and the more joy we experience and radiate.

In the story of Purim, the moment that the people assumed responsibility for their spiritual lives, certain events began to unfold showing them that nothing is mere happenstance or accident. They could suddenly appreciate that all of life is guided, intentionally and meticulously coordinated by Divine design. This is when ultimate joy ensued.

There is a type of 'taking responsibility' that is heavy and burdensome, bringing with it a sense of self-consciousness and self-blame; 'I did such and such, how could I?' Beating yourself up for what you have done, or telling yourself that you are not such a good or righteous person, can become a self-fulfilling prophecy, for it re-enforces your negative vision of yourself, and thus your negative behavior. This is *Charata* / regret without an openness for *Kabbalah* / acceptance of a new paradigm of living. But there is also a type of responsibility that is serious yet it brings about a corresponding lightness of being: 'Yes, I made a mistake, I take full responsibility for my actions and choices — and I am open to immediately move on and be different, to begin anew and make better choices.' This is the type of responsibility that comes with an Adar-like joy. (Indeed, the *Ikar* / main aspect of the Teshuvah on Purim is that of *Kabbalah*: "הדור קבלוה" *Shabbos*, 88a.)

After eating from the Tree, Adam and Chavah "knew that they were naked." They were suddenly self-conscious and ashamed. The *Makor* / source of Haman is the *Cheit Eitz haDa'as* / sin os eating from the Tree of Knowledge — and in the associated qualities of self-consciousness, self-doubt and crippling shame. Therefore our Tikun is to drink wine to the point of losing self-consciousness, like a child without inhibitions who only wants to do good, who doesn't compare himself to others or worry what others may be thinking. In this state we are free from any sense of blame or deflection of causality. We become authentically innocent and light, and we feel the magical joy coursing through all phenomena.

PRACTICE HUMOR & LIGHTNESS IN THE HOME

We ought to serve Hashem, ourselves and everyone around us, with seriousness and devotion, yet also with joy and lightness. It is worth integrating an Avodah of bringing some healthy, productive, anchored humor and lightness into our relationships and family life, our communities and all our contacts. Being serious about our physical, emotional, mental and spiritual lives allows us to grow in all areas, but this should not become a fixed heaviness or gloom.

Heaviness is due to weakness, and is a result of sin ("My strength fails because of my sin" (Tehilim, 31:11. *Gittin*, 70a).). Being overly serious can drag us down and deaden us. Following Adam and Chavah's eating from the Tree of Knowledge, when they were warned, "and the day you eat from it, you will die" (Bereishis, 2:17), Hashem tells them, "Dust (of the earth) you are and to dust you will return" (Bereishis, 3:19). Once they deviated from the world of unity and the Tree of Life, the element of earth within them became most dominant. Earth is 'heavy,' pulling us ever into its gravity; earth returns to earth.

When we do something that is against our deepest nature it makes us feel heavy. If we then shame, blame or depreciate ourselves, the sense of heaviness can increase to seemingly unbearable levels. This is simply adding insult to injury. We need to ensure that our hearts and our homes, the sacred spaces we create, are filled with real joy, a sense of purpose, values, holiness and positive objectives, and also a good dose of healthy humor. With a balanced sense of humor we can create a pleasant and happy place, and when life takes an unexpected turn, we can soothe the situation and rebound more easily. If you slip and fall, it does not help to lie there and beat yourself up about it. Perhaps instead you can see a little bit of humor in it, laugh it off, freely choose to get up, and then swiftly establish measures to prevent this mistake in the future.

As discussed previously, Hashem's 'laughter' so to speak is the meta-root of all finite creation, and each day Hashem 'spends time' playing and laughing with creation ("Hashem laughs, plays with His creations (Leviyason)"; yet Hashem does not laugh *at* His creations, only on that day — in the future — alone" (*Avodah Zarah*, 3b).). Perhaps because of this Divine laughter at the root of our very creation, the quality of playfulness is integral to our wellbeing. We need a little dose of humor with all of our seriousness, a little *Hevel* (lightness) with our *Kayin* (earthiness); and we need to cultivate G-dly (*Alef*) joy in our *Dar* / dwelling. In this way, in Adar / *Alef-Dar*, we will increase in joy.

Anger is tantamount to *Avodah Zarah* / serving idols (Rambam, *Hilchos Deos*, 2:3. Note, *Shabbos*, 105b. *Nedarim*, 22a. *Teshuvos haRashbash*, 370). Often, anger arises when our expectations about ourselves or other people, or life in general, do not materialize as expected. People who are more rigid in their self-image are prone to greater eruptions of anger. A healthy measure of self-laughter, taking oneself lightly, albeit seriously and acknowledging an openness to alternative possibilities, allows one to break out of constricted modes of being and tap into the Ein Sof of Holy Uncertainty. This is the deeper reason that we need humor when it comes to our own 'personal' Avodah Zarah — our ego, attachments and self-serving nature.

As parents, for example, we have certain preconceived notions regarding our children and our family, for better or worse. The same is true with children regarding their parents. But to have a happy, embracing, nurturing home we need to ensure that this sacred ground which we cultivate for ourselves and our loved ones, our spouse and children, is irrigated with healthy humor.

With just a touch of humor we can create a pleasant and joyful atmosphere, and then if something goes unexpectedly wrong, it will be an antidote to dispel the tension. This can make our children feel safer, more valued and loved, especially when tension arises between ourselves and our children. For example, if your child was careless and dropped an expensive plate, you may need to gently guide them to be more careful, but adding a touch of humor before you do so, can help your child stay connected to you and increase the likelihood of them actually accepting the guidance. Or, for example, you are trying to convey a message to a child, perhaps that they would benefit from doing more homework, if you use humor you will find that you can transmit the message without them feeling threatened or lectured.

This is also true if the tension is already palpable, for instance, your teenager is experiencing frustration and asserting a narrative of how everything you do is wrong. As long as your humor cannot be interpreted as demeaning them or 'claiming victory,' the frustration may even flip into *Kibud Av vaEim* / honor given to parents.

Humor is also very powerful between spouses and in other close relationships, but in particular in relation to oneself. Sometimes we need to use a little humor to shake ourselves out of the stupor of anger, self-loathing or spiritual coldness. Of course humor is a tool that we need to employ wisely. A careless or misplaced joke or jibe can cause irreparable damage to a loved one's psyche or their sense of security within the relationship.

Adar, the month of laughter, is when we draw down all the *She-fa* / flow for all the holy humor of the entire year. We also receive the *Seichel* / intelligence and *Da'as* / awareness necessary to use laughter in a balanced way, at the right time, and with positive and productive results. We gain the ability in this month to lovingly laugh at our own mistakes so that we can learn from them and grow as human beings without being overly hard on ourselves or inflicting guilt.

Make it a practice to bring a touch of healthy humor and joy into your home life.

☾

ϓ
KAVANAH:
MINDFUL INTENTION

*A*S EXPLORED ABOVE IN DEPTH, JOY COMES FROM A deep awareness of our purpose, the deeper purposes of everything in life, and by acknowledging the fact that there are no such things as accidents, coincidences or random happenstance. An awareness of *Hashgacha P'ratis* / Divine Providence helps us use every experience as an indirect reflection of the Divine 'hand' that guides us and orchestrates all things.

Begin this experiment in mindful intention by thinking about your life and taking notice of how one thing led to another. When certain events occurred perhaps they seemed inconsequential, but eventually, they accumulated and shaped *who, what, where,* and *why* you are today.

Bring to mind all the 'big things' that occurred in your life, or perhaps just in the past year. Notice that most times it was the 'small things' that created the possibility for the 'big things' to happen. For instance, perhaps you came late to a meeting and because of that you met your spouse; or you just so happened to linger at work and because of that you spoke with the boss and landed a better job.

Extend your contemplation to the more spiritual aspects of life, such as finding the right *Rav* / rabbi and teacher or 'chancing' upon the *Sefer* / holy book that inspired you and took you beyond your previous understandings. If you take the time to make a clear-headed observation of your life you will surely notice that many of the 'big things' you have in your life, such as your spouse, children, job, and friends, are specifically in your life *because* of the 'accidents,' seemingly unimportant decisions or impulses.

Adar and Purim teach us that there are no accidents and nothing is ever random. The more we realize this truth and live with it, the more happiness we will sense and the more happiness we can then share with those around us. As you continue to contemplate the 'Megilah' of your life-story, uncovering the hidden harmonies, small 'miracles' and 'unlikely' blessings, breathe in the joy of beholding a Divine revelation.

As the *Navi* / Prophet says, "You shall go out with joy" (Yeshayahu, 55:12). The deeper reading of this verse is that with the power of joy we will "go out" of all our exiles, transcend all our challenges, limitations and constrictions. Joy is the great *liberator!* May we merit in this month to be truly joyous, and to allow this joy to permeate the entire year with a lightness and humor that uplifts us until we are freed from all of our real or imagined limitations and concealments, until we are lifted out of this *Galus* / exile and brought to the Ultimate *Geulah* / Redemption, speedily in our days.

☾

ESSAY 1:
PURIM AND THE BODY

HAMAN'S SCHEME WAS THE FIRST AND MOST SIGNIF-
ICANT attempt in Tanach to physically annihilate
the entire Jewish People. It was not the spirituality,
intellectual power, or idealism of the Jews that he wanted to kill
off, nor was there any issue of gaining Jewish territory. He wanted
nothing more than to remove the body of the Jew from the world.

Esther was instrumental in helping to save the Jews from this
evil plot. She did so through an act of physical self-sacrifice before
the king — although she first removed her Da'as from her body to
the point that the experience of 'intimacy' with him was nothing to
her, her body becoming like *Karka Olam* / insentient earth (*Sanhe-*

drin, 74b). (The Zohar teaches that it was not Esther herself that was intimate with the king, rather, a 'daemonic' double (*Zohar 3, 276a. Tikunei Zohar, 58a. Kinas Hashem,* 96). She first removed her Da'as from her body to the point that the experience of 'intimacy' with him meant nothing to her, thus her body becoming like mere *Karka Olam* / insentient earth, a 'dead' husk of the self.)

Whereas the gallows were meant to hang the body of Mordechai, Chas veShalom, it hung the bodies of Haman and his sons. Whereas the decree was to allow citizens of the kingdom to massacre the Jews, the new decree allowed the Jews to defend themselves physically. The victory is celebrated with physical rejoicing: we feast, drink, dance, distribute gifts of food and money, and some dress up in costumes (Although *Al-Pi Halachah* / according to the letter of the law, one should wear Shabbos clothing on Purim).

BEYOND DA'AS

Like Esther, on Purim we 'hide' our Da'as, our faculty of distinction, separation, and we enter a place beyond knowing and beyond mind; we exist as raw physicality. Esther's Hebrew name is Hadasah, which has a numerical value of 74 (Hei / 5, Dalet / 4, Samach / 60, Hei / 5=74). This is the same numerical value as *Da* / know (Dalet / 4, Ayin / 70=74). Hadasah hides her Jewish name and identity from public knowledge, calling herself Esther, which comes from the word *hidden*. She hides her 'Ha-*Da'as*-ah,' her self-awareness and faculty of discernment, becoming a 'mere body.' This allows her to infiltrate the physical power center of Shushan and bring forth physical salvation.

Reversing the letters of *Da*, the word *Ad* / until, also has a value of 74. *Ad* has the same spelling as *Ayd* / witness, as in mindful conscious awareness. On Purim the Mitzvah is to open ourselves *Ad d'Lo Yada* / until we reach a level of *Lo Da* / not knowing. To know is to distinguish and separate, to zoom in on an object in order to discern its value. On Purim we open up beyond this type of knowing, this world of good versus bad, allowing ourselves to 'just be,' like un-self-conscious child. We stop over-thinking and engaging in self-centered narratives; we let go 'until' we are deeply free of self-concern.

THE BODY KNOWS

As we surrender our Da'as on Purim, a new ability rises up within: to choose Hashem from a place of 'gut instinct.' We no longer need our Da'as to choose what is right; our body itself tells us, like Avraham whose *K'layos* / kidneys guided him in the paths of Torah wisdom (מהיכן למד [אברהם אבינו] את התורה? אלא זימן לו הקדוש ברוך הוא שתי כליותיו כמין שני רבנים והיו נובעות ומלמדות אותו תורה וחכמה *Bereishis Rabbah*, 61).

On Mount Sinai our Da'as, free choice, was taken away by the experiential force of the revelation (Maharal, *Gur Aryeh*, Shemos, 19:17). We could not refuse the revelation of Torah. On Purim, however, we willingly choose to give up our *free choice*, and our body instinctively guides us to accept the revelation of Torah, as it says, "They re-accepted it in the days of Achashverosh... they confirmed what they had already taken upon themselves through coercion at Sinai" (*Shabbos*, 88a).

Klal Yisrael's faculty of Bechira is *in the body*. If, within the right context, we set the body free from the yoke of heavy thinking and remove its blinds of judgmental thinking, the body will freely, automatically and joyfully choose Hashem. We allow this to happen through the drinking and laughter of Purim. When allowed, our *Atzamos* / bones and essence naturally choose the *Atzmus* / Essential Self of Hashem — because Hashem has chosen our bodies, and the *Bechirah* / choice of Atzmus is specifically the body (בנו בחרת מכל עם ולשון הוא הגוף החומרי הנדמה בחומריותו לגופי אומות העולם. *Tanya*, chapter 49), thus our bodies respond in kind and choose HaKadosh Baruch Hu.

On Purim we willfully surrender our Da'as and choose HaKadosh Baruch Hu from the most essential place. We 'choose' to give up our 'free choice' and allow our essential bodily instincts to choose Hashem, the Essence of all goodness.

DRINKING WINE AND LIVING BEYOND DA'AS

Getting tipsy on wine allows "the elevation of the *Nitzutz* / spark that is trapped in Kelipah" (Arizal, *Shar haKavanos*, Purim, Derush 1). The sage Rava says, מיחייב איניש לבסומי בפוריא עד דלא ידע בין ארור המן לברוך מרדכי / "A person is obligated to become inebriated on Purim until he doesn't know the difference between 'blessed is Mordechai' and 'cursed is Haman'" (*Megilah*, 7b). He does not say, "...until one doesn't know the difference between cursed is Mordechai and blessed is Haman." In other words, we are not drinking in order to confuse good and bad, but to go beyond the whole paradigm of polarity. And even when we rise above Da'as and do not distinguish or articulate the difference, still, we naturally choose 'Blessed is Mordechai' over 'cursed is Haman.'

Thus, even when we are 'inebriated,' on Purim we trust that our deeper body-consciousness will instinctively choose the good. This is a place 'beyond' the free choice of Da'as. We do good because it is who we are; good is not something outside of us that needs to be 'chosen.' We do not need Da'as to dictate to us what is right.

Our drinking on Purim is a Tikun for the drinking of Achashverosh. Because of his drunkenness he became irrational and killed his wife. We, in contrast, drink to go beyond rationality and perform life-giving Mitzvos, intuitively expressing love to our spouse, friends and family — and to every living being.

'Not knowing' is to act more on instinct, on bodily impulse. This is *Tohu* / raw or even 'boundless' energy. We dress up, drink, and act silly; like a child without self-conscious boundaries. We lose our Da'as, our distinctions between people; we give charity without restraint, "to anyone who opens his or her hand."

Living beyond Da'as is like the fruit of the Tree of Life, it is meant to be imbibed at certain times and under specific conditions. During most of the year, people generally need mindful Da'as in order to make good choices and elevate themselves. For this reason, the sages of the generation of Purim were reluctant to put the Megilah in the category of *Kisvei haKodesh* / The Holy Writings, even after Esther asked them to do so (*Megilah*, 7a). Its intrinsic holiness was not immediately apparent to them, but then again, that is the 'whole Megilah,' the point of Purim.

When our sages encourage us to drink wine on Purim, they use the term *Besumei* from the word *Besamim* / botanical fragrances, alluding to the sense of smell (There is also a type of wine that is called יין מבשם /fragrant/cooked (Shulchan Aruch, *Choshen Mishpat*, 230:10) wine. (*Baba Basra*, 98a). Significantly, only the sense of smell was left undamaged by the *Cheit Eitz haDa'as* / sin of eating from the Tree of Knowledge; all the other four senses are mentioned in the account of the Cheit. "Fragrant" therefore alludes to a Gan Eden state of innocence. All this implies that on Purim we are meant to transcend all Eitz ha-Da'as dualities, to 'lose' our dualistic minds a bit, by *l'Besumei ad d'Lo Yada* / connecting to the fragrant Edenic realm beyond knowing. (Indeed, Mordechai and Esther, are connected to pleasurable fragrance (*Chulin*, 139b, regarding Mordechai. *Megilah*, 13a, regarding Esther/Hadasah). Whereas Haman is connected to foul scent (Arizal, see *Kesem Ofir*, Esther 3:1).)

In this state of innocence beyond the mind, correct choices flow naturally. Just as by instinct you would choose not to sit on a burning coal, in *Lo Yada* you spontaneously choose the good without the faculty of premeditation. In fact, you do not make such a choice with your mind; it is arguably more accurate to say the choice is made *for* you. It is a non-choice.

Ultimately, in *Lo Yada*, we choose to be in a state where the Divine is choosing with us or through us. When Klal Yisrael stood at Mount Sinai, *Kafa Aleihem Har* / "Hashem placed the Mountain above their heads," and told them to accept the Torah or the Mountain would be their grave. In this scenario, reception of the Torah was not their choice, rather it was Hashem's choice alone. However, prior to this apparent coercion, Klal Yisrael said *Na'aseh veNishmah* / 'We now choose to submit our Da'as and live according to the directives of the Torah, and only later will our minds understand

and accept it intellectually.' It was their choice to enter that state of choicelessness. Purim is an integration of these two scenarios of choice and choicelessness; therefore there are three levels:

Choice; *Na'aseh veNishmah*

Choicelessness; 'coerced' at Mount Sinai

Choiceless Choosing; the *Ad d'Lo Yada* of Purim

In the story of Purim the turning point comes when "The King was unable to sleep that night..." And the Megilah continues, "and they — the chronicles of the King — were read in front of him" (6:1). It does not say, 'and *they read* the chronicles' rather "they were read." The Zohar says that whenever in a Biblical text an event is described but it does not explicitly mention who is doing the act, it suggests that Hashem alone was doing it.

When we reach a place of *Lo Yada*, all our choices are overtly Divine choices. We are not speaking of reaching a place *below* Da'as, rather a place *beyond* Da'as. And then HaKadosh Baruch Hu, so to speak, chooses through you.

RECTIFYING THE TREE OF DA'AS

Da'as is what separates us from the 'raw' experience of the body, and when we surrender our Da'as, there is no separation, but a unified flow of experience. "If there is no Da'as, there can be no separation" (*Yerushalmi, Berachos,* 5:2). Imagine a child eating ice cream with no self-consciousness, free of discursive intellect, purely in a state of 'flow.' On Purim we need to be like that child — innocent and carefree, as if we are naked in the Garden of Eden, prior to eating from the Tree of Da'as. The only problem is, this temporary state can become a dangerous ideology if misapplied; if it is not authentic, it can justify harmful lifestyles as well. A person can always argue, 'I am being guided to act this way, I am doing this from a place of being, not mere calculative thinking.'

The origin of all sin and negativity in the world is eating from the Tree of Knowledge of Good and Evil. The *Zohar* writes (*Zohar Chadash*, Eicha, 91b) that when it says they ate *m'Piryo* / from the fruit (Bereishis, 3:6), the Satan grabbed the Mem of *m'Piryo* and because of that *Maves* / death came to the world.

What does this mean? The letter Mem as a prefix before a word means *from*; "*from* the fruit." Since they ate *m'* / from the tree — they took 'from' it — their eating brought about a sense of separation. This sense of *from*, a departure from the state of flow, was vulnerable to the Satanic force, allowing it to be converted into death, the ultimate separation. Purim is a Tikun for the Cheit of eating *from* the Tree of Knowledge. The Tikun for the Cheit thus comes about through a person whose name starts with a Mem, Mordechai. (Incidentally, the Geulah from Egypt was also initiated by a person whose name starts with Mem, Moshe; so is the Geulah in the Chanukah story, Mattisyahu; and so is the final Geulah, Moshiach.)

On Purim we don't approach life from a place of 'taking from' — there is no *m'* in our eating. On the contrary, we must give without calculating how much a person 'deserves' (אין מדקדקין במעות פורים אלא כל מי שפושט ידו ליטול נותנים לו. *Shulchan Aruch*, Orach Chayim, 694:3). We must give gifts of food and drinks to friends. We don't even drink wine for our own gratification, rather, to serve Hashem beyond the boundaries of Da'as, and as a part of giving joy and laughter to others.

Truly, we have no ability or vessel to contain the abundance of the *Shefa* / flow of Divine love that is bestowed upon us on Purim. All that we can do is open ourselves to receive it, enjoy it, and attempt to carry it forward by giving it to others.

ESSAY 2:
DRINKING WINE:
Sound, Silence & Pleasant Scent

*T*HE GEMARA SAYS (*KERISUS*, 6B), "JUST AS A VOICE IS *NOT GOOD* for wine (production), *Kol Yafah l'Bisamim* / a voice is *good* for the (processing of) incense spices." The making of the *Ketores* / incense was meant to be accompanied by the sound of a voice. Yet, when this process was finished and the Ketores was being used in the Beis haMikdash, the Avodah was done in silence in the Holy of Holies. This was the Avodah of the Kohen: silence.

Wine, on the other hand, is made in silence, "Voice is not good for wine." When the winemaking was finished and the wine was used in the Beis haMikdash for the Avodah of *Nisachim* / libations, the service was accompanied by *Shirah* / song. This was the Avodah of the Levi'im: sound.

These are opposites. The Besamim are processed with sound but used in silence. The nature of Besamim, therefore, is to move inward, getting quieter and quieter, ending in a silent and meditative Avodah. Wine is made in silence but is imbibed accompanied by sound; this is an outward movement ending in song. Wine breaks self-conscious quietness and introversion, taking a person out of their shell into self-expression.

The Purim story begins in the mode of 'wine': Esther begins in *silence*, not expressing her identity, and eventually she shows her identity loudly and powerfully. However, when the sages ask us to drink wine on Purim, they indicate the opposite mode, calling this kind of drinking *l'Besumei,* from root word *Besamim.* This drinking should have within it an aspect of Besamim, moving inward from sound into silence; and yet it is still *wine,* moving outward from silence to sound. On Purim we need to move outward while also going inward, generating sound and quieting down at the same time. This is called the 'silence of sound' — these simultaneous opposites are unified as one.

Similarly, in the revelation of Purim, "Even in the *He'lem* / concealment there is *Ohr* / light" (*Resisei Layla,* 53). The concealment remains a concealment, a darkness, even though it is shining as light.

What does this actually mean? What does it mean to have a silent sound or a recognition that darkness shines as light while still remaining dark?

The idea of a 'silent sound' is a poetic expression of our 'comfortable silence' with Hashem. Upon perceiving the miracles of Purim there was no need to talk. We knew Hashem was there with us, even though there were no prophets projecting His words, and no thunder or intense Shofar blast, as on Mount Sinai. Like the closest of friends, we can just trust each other's presence; there is no need for words, no need for an outward revelation. In such a space, we do not need to hear what the other is thinking, we already see what they mean.

FRAGRANCE

Haman corresponds to the pungent ingredient in the Ketores called *Chelbanah*, which was one of its eleven ingredients. The words *Haman* and *Chelbanah* are both numerically 95 (Arizal, see *Kesem Ofir*, Esther 3:1). "The Chelbanah has a foul odor..." (*Kerisus*, 6b. The eleven ingredients of the Ketores correspond to Haman and his ten sons). A person 'smells bad' when they live inauthentically, trying to impress or manipulate others. The Baal Shem Tov once made *Aliyas haNeshamah* / a soul-ascent and met the spirit of a person who had a foul odor. The Baal Shem asked him, "Why do you smell so bad?" "Because," he responded, "I did Mitzvos with *Peniyos* / ulterior purposes."

L'Bisumei implies the pleasant fragrance of incense spices. Only our sense of smell remains undistorted by the Cheit Eitz haDa'as, and in this way, it connects us to a purity 'prior' to the existence of sin and negativity. The Mitzvah to drink wine on Purim is not to become *Shikur* / drunk, rather it is to reach a point of *l'Bisumei* (as it is brought down in many Rishonim, see *Kol Bo*, Hilchos Purim, Siman 45. *Orchos Chayim*, Purim, Os 38. See also Shaloh, *Torah she-b'Ksav*, Shovavim Tat, Parshas Zachor. Chidah, *Moreh b'Etzbah*, Os 307. *Yesod Shoresh haAvodah*, Sha'ar

12:7). We are not to become like a drunk who "stinks" and is "loud" and boisterous, as Haman who was always jumping to the front (*Megilah*, 12b. ויאמר ממוכן... מכאן שההדיוט קופץ בראש). On the contrary, in our wine-drinking we must give out a pleasant fragrance; our speech and behavior must be pure, gentle and delightfully inspiring to all around us. Our outward-moving self-expression must be rooted in the inner silence of D'veikus, so that all those around us will be drawn to Hashem's Indwelling Presence, as to a Heavenly scent.

To drink like Haman is to give forth a foul odor and be 'loud.' However, to drink like a *Yehudi* / Jew, is to give forth the beautiful fragrance of Gan Eden. To spread Torah and Mitzvos with joy and excitement, wonderment and openness, and to reach out to others with beautiful sincerity. On Purim, our drinking is meant to bring us *inward*, into a state of deep quiet, like the Ketores in the Holy of Holies, in the intimate embrace of HaKadosh Baruch Hu.

☾

ESSAY 3:
THE HIGHEST YOM TOV

*I*N CONTRAST TO OTHER GREAT HOLY DAYS, ON PURIM WE ARE allowed to perform *Melachah* / work and mundane actions. Although Megilas Esther calls Purim a *Yom Tov* (9:19), and this suggests that Purim should be a day of rest from Melachah; that Halachic status however was not accepted by the People (*Megilah*, 5b).

Everything has an outer and an inner reason. The outer reason given for our not accepting the prohibition of Melachah is that Purim is 'merely' a Rabbinic holiday, and so its laws are less strict. On an inner level, however, the 'collective prophetic consciousness of Keneses Yisrael' was tapping into a deeper reason: Purim is actually so holy that it transcends the paradigm of holy versus mundane, strict versus lenient. Thus, Purim can 'include' mundane work without disturbing its status as a Yom Tov. This is the deepest of the deep for those who understand.

Similarly, Megilas Esther is so holy that the Name of Hashem, meaning the 'revelation and manifestation' of Hashem, does not appear in it at all. At first glance, one might mistakenly think this is therefore a 'mundane' book, perhaps even unfit to be part of Tanach. However, Megilas Esther is 'all Hashem'; there is no *need* for a specific revelation of Hashem's Name to appear in it. This is the highest of the high for those with eyes.

On the year that the original Purim occurred, the three-day fast instituted by Esther in the month of Nisan 'pushed aside' the celebration of Pesach (*Megilah*, 15a, Rashi). Thus Purim is rooted in a paradigm of temporarily 'pushing aside' normative fixed levels and observances of holiness for the sake of attaining something even higher (Rambam, *Hilchos Mamrim*, 2:4). Purim belongs to *leAsid* / the future of unsurpassable holiness.

Purim is a *Moshiach Holiday*, i.e., it will continue to be celebrated even in *leAsid Lavo* / the 'arriving future' of Redemption. On the one hand, Purim is the "end of all holidays," occurring in the last month of the year; and it is also the 'final miracle,' or in the language of the Gemara, "the end of the miracles" (*Yuma*, 21a). Yet, on the other hand, Purim is the "beginning of all the holidays of the future" (See *Likutei Moharan* 2:74).

Despite the fact that it is a Yom Tov, we are still allowed to do mundane work on Purim. We could say that this is because Purim is an 'Essence' holiday, one that transcends and includes the opposites of mundane work and holy rest, just as it transcends the opposites of 'blessed is Mordechai' and 'cursed is Haman.' Even the unholy Haman brought us untold blessings. Purim is a holiday that brings us to the highest state of holiness even within our so-called 'mundane lives.'

This is also the inner reason why we don't make Havdalah at the end of Purim. The outer reason, again, is because it is a Rabbinic holiday, and we were allowed to do *Melachah* / work throughout the day. However, the inner reason is that the holiness of Purim extends seamlessly into the future, into the rest of the year and the rest of history — it includes everything and so there is no *Havdalah* / separation from anything. Such will be *Yemos haMoshiach* / Messianic Times, when we will have "a day that is all Shabbos" — every day will be Shabbos, as there will be no *Havdalah* / separation between the weekdays and Shabbos, between the holy and mundane, all will be seen as truly One.

Rav Shlomo Elyashiv, the Leshem, writes (Leshem, *Shevo v'Achlama*, De'ah, 2, p.116) that in the future, every day of the week will be a Yom Tov. The Medrash tells us that in the times of Moshiach there will be no more Yomim Tovim except for Purim and Chanukah. Why? Because, says the Leshem, all days and all moments will be infused with the holiness of the Yomim Tovim, and there will thus be no more weekdays. Without weekdays, there is nothing with which a holiday could contrast. As such, every day will be a holiday. On the other hand, since each day of the week is still different from the others, the Yomim Tovim that we have today will each correspond to one of the weekdays according to the *Sefirah* / attribute of that day.

Sunday (*Chesed* / kindness) will have the holiness of Pesach, the holiday of Chesed. Every Sunday will be Pesach.

Monday (*Gevurah* / power) will be Rosh Hashanah, the *Yom haDin* / Day of Judgment (Gevurah). Every Monday will be Rosh Hashanah.

Tuesday (*Tiferes* / splendor, the third attribute which unifies the previous two) will be Shavuos (which is in the third month and is the 'third element' which unifies Heaven and earth). Every Tuesday will be Shavuos.

Wednesday (*Netzach* / victory) is the Fourth Day of Creation, when the sun and moon began to function. Thus, every Wednesday will be Rosh Chodesh, the renewal of the moon.

Thursday (*Hod* / thanksgiving or humbleness) will be Sukkos, when we humbly and gratefully rejoice in the ingathering of blessings for the coming year. Every Thursday will be Sukkos.

Friday (Yesod, the final Sefirah of ZA, which focuses the others) will be Shemini Atzeres / Simchas Torah, the final and culminating joy of all the holidays. Every Friday will be Simchas Torah.

Shabbos (Malchus) is always Shabbos.

We also learn that while all the Yomim Tovim will become "nullified," Purim will remain, even in the Seventh Millennium. Purim is even deeper than the paradigm of seven days, and the Seventh Millennium when every day is a Yom Tov. Purim represents the Eighth Millennium.

Like the number 50 as mentioned earlier in this volume, the paradigm of 'eight' is a step beyond 'seven,' yet it includes seven within it. While every day will be a Yom Tov, still Purim will exist as an additional ('eighth') day, and yet it will also include and be enfolded within each of the seven days of Yom Tov. Today, Purim is expressed in a mode of permitting Melachah. In the Seventh Millennium, Purim will be expressed in the full mode of Yom Tov, in which Melachah is not permitted. As Purim is *Etzem* / essence, it includes and transcends work and non-work.

The Seventh Millennium will still function in a world of distinctions, the paradigm of six days plus Shabbos. The paradigm of 'eight' however, unifies all distinctions into a greater whole; it includes and enfolds within it both the 'seven' and the 'six.' In the words of the Rashba, 'eight' is *Shomer haHekef* / a circumference (*Teshuvas haRashba*, 1:9. See also *Ohr haTorah*, Vayeshev, 278:1) which contains and yet transcends the 'seven.'

Still functioning in a world of distinctions and opposites, the Seventh Millennium nullifies the labor of the six weekdays in its Shabbos holiness. However, as the paradigm of 'eight' enfolds within it both the 'seven' and the 'six,' it is only in the paradigm of 'eight' that the true nature of Purim will be revealed as a full-on Yom Tov. As the 'day' of Essence, Purim is expressed as both Melachah ('six') and Menuchah ('seven') simultaneously.

On a spiritual level, Purim is both a day on which we need to perform specific Melachos and Mitzvos, actions of *Menuchah* / transcendence, meaning, the unique Mitzvos of Purim; and also to experience Lo Yadah, the letting go of awareness, going beyond Avodah and all forms of Melachah, even spiritual Melachah.

On the one hand, the Melachos and Mitzvos of Purim are simply all the regular Mitzvos but with an extra measure added. For instance, every day we need to love our fellow neighbors, but on Purim we need to send them food; every day we need to give Tzedakah, but on Purim we need to actively find poor people to give charity to. Yet, on the other hand, Purim comes at the "end" of the lunar year, Purim is the "last miracle recorded," and it is connected to the "end of time." Purim is altogether beyond the world of 'doing' and is connected to the future world of 'receiving rewards'; thus, on Purim, especially towards the end of Purim, we need to reach a point of Lo Yadah, beyond knowing, beyond conscious doing, to be in a place of pure being.

EIGHT MILLENNIUM:

The Seventh Millennium is a time of *Yom sheKulo Shabbos* / a day which is entirely Shabbos, and a time when, in a revealed way, every day is Yom Tov. 'Seven days' corresponds to the seven Sefiros of revealed Divine emotion. Yet, there are also higher Sefiros: Chochmah, Binah, and Da'as or Keser. Additionally, there is also a higher Eighth Millennium, a step beyond 'seven,' which will simultaneously include and transcend the Seventh — this can be called the *Yom sheKulo Purim.*

The highest level includes the lower levels, as even 'the workweek' and 'the body' are parts of this holiness, there is truly no sep-

---

* From another perspective, the Eighth Millennium will be *Yom sheKulo Yom Kippur*, and there will be a Ninth Millennium which can be called *Yom sheKulo Purim*. At last even a Tenth Millennium will be revealed, which cannot currently be described.

aration. There will be a body in *Olam haBa* / the ultimate reality, as the Ramban writes; it will just be the highest level of body.

Despite the commandment, on the first Friday of creation, to refrain from eating from the Tree of Knowledge, we would have actually been allowed to eat it once Shabbos had arrived, says the Arizal. Shabbos is the paradigm of the Tree of Life or 'Unity.' An allowance to eat from the fruit of the Tree of Knowledge of 'Separation' within the context of the Tree of Life, meaning on Shabbos, would mean to include both realities as one in integral wholeness. Again there are three levels:

'Sixth': the mundane days of labor	Working toward Shabbos	Refraining from eating of the Eitz haDa'as	Separation
'Seventh': the holy day of rest	Entering a state of Shabbos	Eating the fruit of the Eitz haChayim	Unity
'Eighth': the all-permeating day of inclusive transcendence	Entering a state of 'Purim'; including labor within rest and rest within labor	Eating the fruit of the Eitz haDa'as within the context of the Eitz haChayim	Separation and Unity included together as one wholeness

From another perspective, the paradigm of the Eighth Millennium is Yom Kippur. Like Purim, Yom Kippur is a 'revelation' of Essence, "The *essence* of the day brings acquittal." Indeed, "Just as the essence of the day of Yom Kippur brings atonement so long as the person knows that it is Yom Kippur, so too it is with Purim, the essence of the day brings about the erasure of Amalek, so long as the person knows that it is Purim" (*Pri Tzadik*, Purim, 1).

Yom Kippur is an essential inclusion of 'unification' and 'separation'; as we fast, we transcend all separation and individual existence, attaining a near-angelic state, and yet we are still alive and embodied as a human being. For a person to transcend 'being an individual' is a paradox of Essence (*Basi LeGani* 29, about saying the Name of Hashem, as on Yom Kippur one is Essence). Similarly on Purim, a person transcends personhood through pure joy, yet remains a real human being with a material body.

In a way, Purim is even deeper than Yom Kippur: the purity that can be reached through a long day of fasting on Yom Kippur can be spontaneously attained through joyful feasting and drinking on Purim. Purim is the highest day, beyond all negativity and also beyond even what we normally think of as holiness.

☾

Other Books by the Author

RECLAIMING THE SELF
The Way of Teshuvah

Teshuvah is one of the great gifts of life. It speaks of a hope for a better today and empowers us to choose a brighter tomorrow. But what exactly is Teshuvah? How does it work? How can we undo our past and how do we deal with guilt? And what is healthy regret without eroding our self-esteem? In this fascinating and empowering book, the path for genuine transformation and a way to include all of our past in the powerful moment of the now, is explored and demonstrated.

THE MYSTERY OF KADDISH
Understanding the Mourner's Kaddish

The Mystery of Kaddish is an in-depth exploration into the Mourner's Prayer. Throughout Jewish history, there have been many rites and rituals associated with loss and mourning, yet none have prevailed quite like the Mourner's Kaddish Prayer, which has become the definitive ritual of mourning. The book explores the source of this prayer and deconstructs the meaning to better understand the grieving process and how the Kaddish prayer supports and uplifts the bereaved through their own personal journey to healing.

UPSHERNISH: The First Haircut
Exploring the Laws, Customs & Meanings
of a Boy's First Haircut

What is the meaning of Upsherin, the traditional celebration of a boy's first haircut at the age of three? Why is a boy's hair allowed to grow freely for his first three years? What is the deeper import of hair in all its lengths and varieties? What is the meaning of hair coverings? Includes a guide to conducting an Upsherin ceremony.

A BOND FOR ETERNITY
Understanding the Bris Milah

What is the Bris Milah – the covenant of circumcision? What does it represent, symbolize and signify? This book provides an in depth and sensitive review of this fundamental Mitzvah. In this little masterpiece of wisdom – profound yet accessible —the deeper meaning of this essential rite of passage and its eternal link to the Jewish people, is revealed and explored.

REINCARNATION AND JUDAISM
The Journey of the Soul

A fascinating analysis of the concept of Gilgul / Reincarnation. Dipping into the fountain of ancient wisdom and modern understanding, this book addresses and answers such basic questions as: What is reincarnation? Why does it occur? And how does it affect us personally?

INNER RHYTHMS
The Kabbalah of MUSIC

Exploring the inner dimension of sound and music, and particularly, how music permeates all aspects of life. The topics range from Deveikus/Unity and Yichudim/Unifications, to the more personal issues, such as Simcha/Happiness and Marirus/ sadness.

MEDITATION AND JUDAISM
Exploring the Jewish Meditative Paths

A comprehensive work encompassing the entire spectrum of Jewish thought, from the sages of the Talmud and the early Kabbalists to the modern philosophers and Chassidic masters. This book is both a scholarly, in-depth study of meditative practices, and a practical, easy to follow guide for any person interested in meditating the Jewish way.

TOWARD THE INFINITE

A book focusing exclusively on the Chassidic approach to meditation known as Hisbonenus. Encompassing the entire meditative experience, it takes the reader on a comprehensive and engaging journey through this unique practice. The book explores the various states of consciousness that a person encounters in the course of the meditation, beginning at a level of extreme self-awareness and concluding with a state of total non-awareness.

THIRTY – TWO GATES OF WISDOM
into the Heart of Kabbalah & Chassidus

What is Kabbalah? And what are the differences between the theoretical, meditative, magical and personal Kabbalistic teachings? What are the four paths of interpreting the teachings of the ARIzal? What did Chassidus teach? These are some of the fundamental issues expanded upon in this text. And then, more specifically, why are there so many names of G-d and what do they represent? What are the key concepts of these deeper teachings?

The book explores the grand narrative of the great chain of reality, how there was and is a movement from the Infinite Oneness of Hashem to a world of (apparent) duality and multiplicity.

THE PURIM READER
The Holiday of Purim Explored

With a Persian name, a masquerade dress code and a woman as the heroine, Purim is certainly unusual amongst the Jewish holidays. Most people are very familiar with the costumes, Megilah and revelry, but are mystified by their significance. This book offers a glimpse into the hidden world of Purim, uncovering these mysteries and offering a deeper understanding of this unique holiday.

EIGHT LIGHTS
8 Meditations for Chanukah

What is the meaning and message of Chanukah? What is the spiritual significance of the Lights of the Menorah? What are the Lights telling us? What is the deeper dimension of the Dreidel? Rav Pinson, with his trademark deep learning and spiritual sensitivity guides us through eight meditations relating to the Lights of the Menorah, the eight days of Chanukah, and a fascinating exploration of the symbolism and structure of the Dreidel. Includes a detailed how-to guide for lighting the Chanukah Menorah.

THE IYYUN HAGADAH
An Introduction to the Haggadah

In this beautifully written introduction to Passover and the Haggadah, we are guided through the major themes of Passover and the Seder night. This slim text, addresses the important questions, such as: What is the big deal of Chametz? What are we trying to achieve through conducting a Seder? What's with all that stuff on the Seder Plate? And most importantly, how is this all related to freedom?

PASSPORT TO KABBALAH
A Journey of Inner Transformation

Life is a journey full of ups and downs, inside-outs, and unexpected detours. There are times when we think we know exactly where we want to be headed, and other times when we are so lost we don't even know where we are. This slim book provides readers with a passport of sorts to help them through any obstacles along their path of self-refinement, reflection, and self-transformation.

THE FOUR SPECIES
The Symbolism of the Lulav & Esrog

The Four Species have inspired countless commentaries and traditions and intrigued scholars and mystics alike. In this little masterpiece of wisdom both profound and practical - the deep symbolic roots and nature of the Four Species are explored. The Na'anuim, or ritual of the Lulav movement, is meticulously detailed and Kavanos,, are offered for use with the practice. Includes an illustrated guide to the Lulav Movements.

THE BOOK OF LIFE AFTER LIFE

What is a soul? What happens to us after we physically die?

What is consciousness, and can it survive without a physical brain?

Can we remember our past lives?

Do near-death experiences prove immortality?

What is Gan Eden? Resurrection?

Exploring the possibility of surviving death, the near-death experience and a glimpse into what awaits us after this life.

(This book is an updated and expanded version of the book; Jewish Wisdom of the Afterlife)

THE GARDEN OF PARADOX:
The Essence of Non - Dual Kabbalah

This book is a Primer on the Essential Philosophy of Kabbalah presented as a series of 3 conversations, revealing the mysteries of Creator, Creation and Consciousness. With three representational students, embodying respectively, the philosopher, the activist and the mystic, the book, tackles the larger questions of life. Who is G-d? Who am I? Why do I exist? What is my purpose in this life? Written in clear and concise prose, the text, gently guides the reader towards making sense of life's paradoxes and living meaningfully.

BREATHING & QUIETING THE MIND

Achieving a sense of self-mastery and inner freedom demands that we gain a measure of hegemony over our thoughts. We learn to choose out thoughts so that we are not at the mercy of whatever belches up to the mind. Through quieting the mind and conscious breathing we can slow the onrush of anxious, scattered thinking and come to a deeper awareness of the interconnectedness of all of life.

Source texts are included in translation, with how-to-guides for the various practices.

VISUALIZATION AND IMAGERY:
Harnessing the Power of our Mind's Eye

We assume that what we see with our eyes is absolute. Yet, beyond our ability to choose what we see, we have the ability to choose how we see. This directly translates into how we experience life. In a world saturated with visual imagery, our senses are continuously assaulted with Kelipa/empty/fantasy imagery that we would not necessarily choose. These images can negatively affect our relationship with ourselves, with the world around us, and with the Divine. This volume seeks to show us how we can alter that which we observe through harnessing the power of our mind's eye, the inner sanctum of our imagination. We thus create a new way to see and experience the world. This book teaches us how to utilize visualization and imagery as a way to develop our spiritual sensitivity and higher intuition, and ultimately achieve Deveikus/Unity with Hashem.

SOUND AND VIBRATION:
Tuning into the Echoes of Creation

Through our perception of sound and vibration we internalize the world around us. What we hear, and how we process that hearing, has a profound impact on how we experience life. What we hear can empower us or harm us. A defining human capacity is to harness the power sound -- through speech, dialogue, and song, and through listening to others. Hearing is primary dimension of our existence. In fact, as a fetus our ears were the first fully operating sensory organs to develop.

This book will guide you in methods of utilizing the power of sound and vibration to heal and maintain mental, emotional and spiritual health, to fine-tune your Midos and even to guide you into deeper levels of Deveikus / conscious unity with Hashem. The vibratory patterns of the Aleph-Beis are particularly useful portals into our deeper conscious selves. Through chanting and deep listening, we can use the letters and sounds to shift our very mindset, to induce us into a state of presence and spiritual elevation.

THE POWER OF CHOICE:
A Practical Guide to Conscious Living

It is the essential premise of this book that we hold the key to unlock many of the gates that seem closed to us and keep us from living our fullest life. That key we all hold is the power to choose. The Power of Choice is the primary tool that we have at our disposal to impact the world and effect change within our own lives. We often give up this power to outside forces such as the market, media, politicians or peer pressure; or to internal forces that often function beyond our conscious control such as ego, anger, lust, greed or jealousy. Making conscious, compassionate and creative decisions is the cornerstone of living a mature and meaningful life.

MYSTIC TALES FROM THE EMEK HAMELECH

Mystic Tales of the Emek HaMelech, is a wondrous and inspiring collection of stories culled from the Emek HaMelech. Emek HaMelech, from which these stories have been taken, (as well as its author) is a bit of a mystery. But like all good mysteries, it is one worth investigating. In this spirit the present volume is being offered to the general public in the merit and memory of its saintly author, as well as in the hopes of introducing a vital voice of deeper Torah teaching and tradition to a contemporary English speaking audience

---

INNER WORLDS OF JEWISH PRAYER
A Guide to Develop and Deepen the Prayer Experience

While much attention has been paid to the poetry, history, theology and contextual meaning of the prayers, the intention of this work is to provide a guide to finding meaning and effecting transformation through the prayer experience itself.

Explore: *What happens when we pray? *How do we enter the mind-state of prayer? *Learning to incorporate the body into the prayers. *Discover techniques to enhance and deepen prayer and make it a transformative experience.

This empowering and inspiring text, demonstrates how through proper mindset, preparation and dedication, the experience of prayer can be deeply transformative and ultimately, life-altering.

WRAPPED IN MAJESTY
Tefillin - Exploring the Mystery

Tefillin, the black boxes and leather straps that are worn during prayer, are curiously powerful and mysterious. Within the inky black boxes lie untold secrets. In this profound, passionate and thought-provoking text, the multi-dimensional perspectives of Tefillin are explored and revealed. Magically weaving together all levels of Torah including the Peshat (literal observation), to Remez (allegorical), to Derush, (homiletic), to Sod (hidden) into one beautiful tapestry. Inspirational and instructive, Wrapped in Majesty: Tefillin, will make putting on the Tefillin more meaningful and inspiring.

SECRETS OF THE MIKVAH:
Waters of Transformation

A Mikvah is a pool of water used for the purpose of ritual immersion; a place where one moves from a state of Tumah; impurity, blockage and death—to a place of Teharah; purity, fluidity and life.

In SECRETS OF THE MIKVAH, Rav Pinson delves into the transformative powers of the Mikvah with his trademark all-encompassing perspective that ranges from the literal, Pshat observation and Halachic implications of the texts, to the allegorical, the philosophical, and finally, to the deep secrets of the

Mikvah as revealed by Kabbalah and Chassidus.

This insightful and inspirational text demonstrates how immersion in a Mikvah can be a transformative and life-altering practice, and includes various Kavanos—deep intentions—for all people, through various stages of life, that empower and enrich the immersion experience.

THE SPIRAL OF TIME:
A 12 Part Series on the Months of the Year.
The following titles from the series are now available!

THE SPIRAL OF TIME:
Unraveling the Yearly Cycle

Many centuries ago, the Sages of Israel were the foremost authority in the fields of both astronomical calculation and astrological wisdom, including the deeper interpretations of the cycles and seasons. Over time, this wisdom became hidden within the esoteric teachings of the Torah, and as a result was known only to students and scholars of the deepest depths of the tradition. More recently, the great teachers, from R.Yitzchak Luria (the Arizal) to the Baal Shem Tov, taught that as the world approaches the Era of Redemption, it is a Mitzvah / spiritual obligation to broadly reveal this wisdom.

"The Spiral of Time" is volume 1 is a series of 12 books, and serves as an introductory book to the basic concepts and nature of the Hebrew calendar and explores the special day of Rosh Chodesh.

THE MONTH OF SHEVAT:
ELEVATING EATING
& The Holiday of Tu b'Shevat

Each month of the year radiates with a distinct Divine energy and thus unique opportunities for growth, *Tikkun* and illumination. According to the deeper teachings of the Torah, all of these distinct qualities, opportunities and natural phenomena correspond to a certain data set. That is, the nature of each month is elucidated by a specific letter of the Aleph Beis, a tribe, verse, human sense, and so forth. The month of Shevat is particularly connected to food and our relationship to bodily intake. During this month we celebrate Tu b'Shevat, the New Year of the Tree, and aspire to create a proper and physically/emotionally/spiritually healthy relationship with food.

THE MONTH OF IYYAR: EVOLVING THE SELF
& The Holiday of LAG B'OMER

The month of IYYAR is the second month of the spring, a month that connects the Redemption from Egypt in Nissan with the Revelation of Torah in Sivan. The Chai/ Eighteenth day of the Month is the day we celebrate the Rashbi (Rabbi Shimon Bar Yochai) and the revealing of the hidden aspects of the Torah. This is the 'Holiday' of Lag b'Omer. The book explores the unique quality of this special month, a month that has a Mitzvah of counting the Omer every day. In addition, the book explores the roots and significance of the mystical 'holiday' of Lag b'Omer. Including the customs & Practices of Lag b'Omer, such as, bonfires, bows & arrows, parades, Upsherin, and more.

THE MONTHS OF TAMUZ AND AV:
Embracing Brokenness –
17th of Tamuz, Tisha B'Av, & Tu B'Av

Each month and season of the year, radiates with distinct Divine qualities and unique opportunities for growth and Tikkun.

The summer month of Tamuz and Av contain the longest and hottest days of the year. The raised temperature is indicative of a corresponding spiritual heat, a time of harsher judgement and potential destruction, such as the destructions of the first and second Beis HaMikdash, which began on the 17th of Tamuz and culminated on the 9th and 10th of Av.

A few days later, on Tu b'Av, the darkness is transformed and reveals the greatest light and possibility for new life. During these summer months of Tamuz and Av we embrace our brokenness so that we can heal and transform darkness into light.

THE MONTH OF ELUL:
Days of Introspection and Transformation

Each month of the year radiates with a distinct quality and provides unique opportunities for growth and personal transformation. Elul, as the final month of the spring/summer season is connected to endings. Elul gives us the strength to be able to finish strong, to end well. Elul also serves as a month of preparation for the New Year/Rosh Hashanah.

We inhale our past year, ending with wisdom and then we also gain the wisdom to begin anew and exhale a positive year into being. The mental, emotional, and spiritual objective of this month is introspection and the reclaiming of our inner purity and wholeness.

THE MONTH OF CHESHVAN:
Navigating Transitions, Elevating the Fall

Directly on the heels of the inspiring and holiday-filled month of Tishrei, Cheshvan is a month that is quiet and devoid of holidays. In the month of Cheshvan we use the stored up energies of the previous months to self-generate our inspiration and creativity and provide ourselves with the strength to rise up after a fall. In Cheshvan we are entering into a stormier, wetter and colder season. It is a month of transition. The mental, emotional and spiritual objective of this month is to weather the transitions, learn to self-generate and stand tall. And if we do fall, we use the quality of this month to get back up and do so with more conviction, strength, wisdom and clarity.

———

THE MONTH OF TEVES:
Refining Relationships, Elevating the Body

The quality of Teves is generally harsh—much like its counterpart Tamuz in the summer, thus the tendency for many is to hunker down, retract, curl up and wait for the month to pass by, only to reemerge when the harshness has dissipated. Think for a moment about the 'easier' months of the year, which, like gentle waves in the ocean, carry us where we want to go. We can ride these energies easily and they can propel us forward effortlessly, we just need to go with the overall flow, so to speak. The harsher months, on the other hand, can be compared to the more powerful waves that emanate from the belly of the ocean, which come forcefully crashing down and can easily drown a person before they even realize what has happened. However, those who want to utilize the momentum of the powerful energy that is available during such times can, with caution and creativity, harness these intense waves and ride them higher and farther than other, more gentle circumstances may allow. However, harnessing the power of Tohu, the raw energy of the body, does in fact need to be approached with great care and attention.

———

www.ingramcontent.com/pod-product-compliance
Lightning Source LLC
Chambersburg PA
CBHW060755100426
42813CB00004B/830